SAVING
SAN FRANCISCO

Relief and Recovery after the 1906 Disaster

ANDREA REES DAVIES

TEMPLE UNIVERSITY PRESS PHILADELPHIA

TEMPLE UNIVERSITY PRESS
Philadelphia, Pennsylvania 19122
www.temple.edu/tempress

Library of Congress Cataloging-in-Publication Data

Davies, Andrea Rees 1966–
  Saving San Francisco : relief and recovery after the 1906 disaster / Andrea
Rees Davies.
    p. cm.
  Includes bibliographical references and index.
  ISBN 978-1-4399-0432-9 (cloth : alk. paper) — ISBN 978-1-4399-0433-6
(pbk. : alk. paper) — ISBN 978-1-4399-0434-3 (e-book)
    1. San Francisco Earthquake and Fire, Calif., 1906.   2. Disaster relief—
California—San Francisco—History—20th century.   3. Earthquakes—
California—San Francisco—History—20th century.   4. Fires—California—
San Francisco—History—20th century.   I. Title.

F869.S357D38 2012
979.4'61051—dc22

                                                              2011016210

♾ The paper used in this publication meets the requirements of the American
National Standard for Information Sciences—Permanence of Paper for Printed
Library Materials, ANSI Z39.48-1992

Printed in the United States of America

2 4 6 8 9 7 5 3 1

For my daughters,

Mercer and Remy

Contents

WITHDRAWN

Acknowledgments

It took a village to create this book. I thank my colleagues, friends, and family, all of whom are entwined in these pages. So many helped me to make sense of raw ideas, while a brave few read along as I forged, and sometimes forced, thoughts into sentences. It all started with my dissertation at Stanford University, guided by Estelle Freedman and shaped by my peers Cecilia Tsu and Malgorzata Fidelis. And it ended with the passionate support of family and friends. I thank Brynly Llyr, Laura Irvin, and Tiffany Baker, who believed in this book before it had become one.

This book grew out of the willingness of others to share my passion for the 1906 disaster. In my search for historical evidence, my conversations with archivists, local historians, and descendants of earthquake survivors generated new material and additional enthusiasm. Numerous archivists and curators— Theresa Salazar at the Bancroft Library, Margaret Kimball at the Stanford University Library, Susan Goldstein at the San Francisco Public Library, Julia Tung at the Stanford East Asian Library, Wei-Chi Poon at the Berkeley Ethic Studies Library, and Kris Tacsik at the Geography Map Library at California State University, Northridge—pointed me toward new sources. Gladys Hansen's devotion to the 1906 disaster deserves special recognition. Gladys and her son, Richard Hansen, shared their archival sources and boundless energy for all things related to 1906 San Francisco. Archivists from smaller institutions were invaluable resources as well: Sister Marilyn Gouailhardou at Sisters of Mercy Archives and Chris Catalano at Presentation Archives. I thank Patricia Hatfield, Colma Historical Society president, for sharing her family stories and Philip Choy for opening his private collection of San Francisco Chinatown materials. Stephanie Rozek, from the Geography Map

Library at California State University, Northridge, helped me not only with the Sanborn Fire Insurance Maps but also by creating new U.S. Census data maps. I am grateful for research support from California State University, Northridge, which allowed me to complete U.S. Census research, and for support from the Clayman Institute for Gender Research at Stanford University during the early manuscript-writing stages. I am indebted to my colleagues at the Clayman Institute for their feedback, friendship, and flexibility: Shelley Correll, Lori Nishiura Mackenzie, Ann Enthoven, and Denise Curti. I am also thankful for help provided by research assistants Manwai C. Ku, Richard Harding, and Hannah Lynch. I am especially grateful to Manwai C. Ku for creating the Appendix tables. And a heartfelt thank-you goes to visual artist Stefanie Atkinson, who finalized the book's images. I am very grateful for the expert direction from my editor, Janet Francendese, and perceptive copy editor, Jan McInroy. I thank Cecelia Cancellaro and Heather Blonkenfeld for showing me clarity in writing.

While I came to be particularly adept at unearthing new historical sources, making sense of them was another matter. This book benefits from feedback from many historians. Richard White guided me through my dissertation and helped me to think more clearly about San Francisco as a place. I owe a special thank-you to Laurel Thatcher Ulrich, who encouraged me to pursue the family stories captured by disaster artifacts. I am indebted to Judy Yung for helping me to locate and think through sources on San Francisco's Chinese community. Gray Brechin, San Francisco's eloquent expert, gave insightful feedback and warm support during the project's early stages. I am grateful for my conversations with Bill Issel, Sherry Katz, Jill Lepore, Margaret O'Mara, and Josh Sides, all of which pushed me to explore new themes. And I offer a deep thank-you to the historians who critiqued manuscript drafts: Barbara Berglund, Brenda Frink, Mary Ann Irwin, and Kim Warren. Since I discover what I think through talking, I give thanks and sympathy to the family and friends who listened over the years: Francesca Applegarth, Anna Christina Büchmann, Jennifer Chu, Meli Cook, Lori Dang, Janet Diagojo, Mary Edwards, Cathy Greve, Nannette Griswold, Gillian Harkins, Lisa Henderson, Kristen Kennedy, Cindy Koehn, Mark Kress, Richard Lyman, Lance Martin, Jim McCullough, Meave O'Marah, Gina Marie Pitti, Tricia Porter, Susan Regis, Lisa Roth, Aubyn Severson, Polly Shulman, Maureen Sullivan, Alissa Van Nort, Chantel Walker, Tracee Whitley, Beverly Yates, Sandy Zaragoza, and Sue Zemel.

This book of survivor stories is dedicated to my daughters, Mercer and Remy.

Introduction

Before I was a historian, I was a firefighter in San Francisco. I learned to climb hundred-foot aerial ladders, slice holes through burning roofs with a chain saw, rescue panicked swimmers from the surf, and provide basic life support to unconscious victims. The fire academy instilled confidence that I could handle any emergency scenario. But I was unprepared for the emotional impact of the crises I encountered. Each real-life emergency told a story greater than the immediate effects of physical trauma. Fires and medical emergencies catch victims off guard. They interrupt routine and, for a moment in time, stop daily life—often for just a few hours but occasionally forever.

As a firefighter responding to 911 dispatches, I regularly found myself at the center of people's private lives. Emergencies of any size or sort exposed victims to unexpected examination. I walked into the lives that people really lived, not the versions that they put on display for relatives, friends, or neighbors. After all, there is no time to tidy up after dialing 911. I learned some of the intimate details that made up victims' daily experiences, often by seeing the condition of their homes or observing the emotions of close friends and family. I also witnessed how victims and their families struggled to make sense of their loss as they reimagined their future. While fires or medical emergencies unhinged their daily lives, their options for recovery (both real and imagined) remained firmly attached to their current social circumstances, especially their socioeconomic status and education, family, and cultural background. I was struck by how individual emergencies exposed social relationships and realities that many of us either ignore or take for granted, and I wondered what a large-scale disaster would disclose about the people and places where it occurred.

With this in mind, I found new meaning in San Francisco's 1906 disaster when I later was studying history at Stanford. From a historical perspective, catastrophes such as earthquakes and fires present an excellent vantage point for understanding the past because they interrupt both time and space. As historian Steven Biel explains, catastrophes render the "'normal' workings of culture, society, and politics" visible.[1] These disruptions are complicated, especially for the historian who relies on physical evidence. The 1906 fires in San Francisco, for example, wiped out City Hall records as well as personal papers and cherished photographs stored in thousands of homes. But even as this catastrophe destroyed vast quantities of physical evidence, it also produced a tremendous amount of new data. Need made this so. Newspaper accounts, relief reports, political debate, photographs, and personal letters to family and friends constitute a sizable body of evidence on turn-of-the-century San Francisco. Urban catastrophes also spur the imagination. San Francisco's earthquake and fires forced communities and individuals to define their losses and, perhaps more important, envision their place in the rebuilt city. Relying on the various records compiled in the wake of the disaster, my study of 1906 San Francisco offers both a snapshot of the turn-of-the-century urban environment and an expansive view of how survivors understood the world in which they lived.

San Francisco's well-known earthquake and fires stripped the ninth-largest American city bare. The 7.8-magnitude earthquake awakened city residents just before dawn. For most San Franciscans, Wednesday, April 18, 1906, started at 5:12 A.M. with sixty-five terrifying seconds of violent shaking and ended with an unknown number of dead family members and neighbors, as well as hundreds of thousands of people trapped in a city surrounded by water. Three days of relentless, raging fires defied the possibility of a coherent emergency response. By the following Sunday, 98 percent of the city's structures in the most populated 521 blocks lay in ruins, from the landmark mansions on Nob Hill to Chinatown to the working-class flats south of Market Street.

At first glance, the calamity appeared to affect all segments of the population equally because it transformed all of the city's survivors—the wealthy and poor, the Chinese and native-born—into refugees. It is likely that most San Franciscans stood in the long food-relief lines at one time or another, seeming to confirm the newfound belief in post-disaster social equality. As the *San Francisco Newsletter* described the disaster, "It did not discriminate between tavern and tabernacle, bank and brothel."[2] But the egalitarianism of disaster relief existed largely in the imagination of the press. Rosalie Stern, a prominent San Franciscan married to the president of Levi Strauss and Company and one of the few limousine owners in the city at the time, reminds us of how social status endured despite disaster. When Rosalie arrived with countless other survivors at San Francisco's Presidio to find supplies and shelter, she was given special recognition. As she stepped out of her car, a relief worker called to her by name, ushering her in ahead of the masses of refugees waiting in long lines for assistance.[3] As fires burned the city, Rosalie, like other high-profile San Franciscans, left the disaster zone with her social status intact. Instead of breaking down social barriers, the disaster and subsequent relief efforts put new emphasis on preexisting social differences, an outcome that would have long-term consequences for San Franciscans.

While 250,000 residents fled the city by ferry, train, car, and foot, at least 100,000 remained. Thousands huddled together in parks, in vacant lots, and on beachfronts. The disaster in general, and relief policy in particular, made San Francisco's tragedy a national event. American National Red Cross policy experts soon arrived on the scene to offer the latest theories for rapid recovery. Basing relief housing and funding criteria on traditional social hierarchies, policy makers reinforced pre-disaster social status by advantaging property owners over non-property owners, failing to support Chinese survivors, and evaluating poor and working-class refugees by middle-class standards.

The powerful influence of the disaster relief stemmed from the fact that the earthquake and fires destroyed *both* public and private property. The calamity left the public/private boundary—so important to contemporary understandings of social order—in shambles. This disruption of the private realm pushed domestic life into public space. Policy makers gained access to the private lives of relief recipients because so many San Franciscans lived in public parks or tended their makeshift kitchen stoves on city streets. Moreover, widespread fears of social disorder empowered civic leaders and relief agencies to redefine and rebuild the urban landscape. Despite its reinforcement of familiar social hierarchies, disaster relief was not a one-sided, "top-down" affair that served only elite interests. The temporary loss of a clear public/private boundary gave rise to a much more complex disaster story.

The brief break in the public/private boundary offered the city's peripheral social groups unprecedented opportunities to gain access to the public realm. Thousands of San Franciscans required immediate aid, and those who responded to this need, such as the middle-class white women and Chinatown business leaders who volunteered their services, gained new political leverage. As in the aftermath of the 1900 Galveston Flood, when relief work acted as a catalyst for middle-class women's civic activism, in 1906 women's work extended far beyond the confines of the home as middle-class women volunteers took on new responsibilities that led to their continued involvement in the political realm.[4] Poor and working-class women created new opportunities as well, as they took to the streets in protest to demand changes in relief policy. Meanwhile, Chinatown leaders gained economic and political influence by turning to their own national and international networks to oppose politicians and policies that threatened to excise Chinatown from the rebuilt city. These groups and contested spaces figure prominently in the account of the catastrophe presented here.

CONSTRUCTING DISASTERS

Most books on the 1906 disaster simply recount the city's annihilation and the residents' terror. San Francisco's first "instant histories" provided graphic details of the event to readers far from the American West. In fact, the disaster generated such public interest that at least eighty-two books were printed before the end of 1906.[5] Such immediate disaster histories were not a new phenomenon; in fact, similar publications trailed the 1871 Great Chicago Fire.[6] But the accounts of San Francisco's misfortune benefited from technological innovations, which allowed publishers to include spectacular photographic images that made most of the text seem more like extended photograph captions than historical accounts.[7] Kevin Rozario's study of American disasters from the seventeenth century to the present points out that, as a result of its growing appetite for sensational disaster stories, the American public devoured this material.[8]

San Francisco's instant histories presented the classic story of the fall of a great city and the rise of an even better one. As early as 1906, authors ended their thrilling tales of catastrophe with predictions of resounding urban recovery. "Will San Francisco rise again? Most certainly it will," reassured author Charles Morris in 1906.[9] These initial publications set the tone for future historical accounts of San Francisco's dance with death. The fifty-year disaster anniversary prompted a new round of publications that recapitulated the original instant histories.[10] While the more recent centennial anniversary brought to the surface deeper questions about the calamity's social impact, the original fall-and-rise narrative remains tethered to this disaster story.[11]

Like the newspapers of the time, instant disaster histories sold human-interest and sensationalistic stories to a seemingly insatiable public. But they also forged a disaster narrative—a story, whether published or oral, that makes sense of a calamity—that followed a prescribed pattern of development and conclusion. San Francisco's fire narrative was based on a "seismic denial," as Ted Steinberg phrases it.[12] By denying the seismic aspect of the disaster, politicians and business leaders rendered San Francisco no more vulnerable than any other city and touted its rebuilding as a sound investment. Urban fires were ubiquitous in the United States during the nineteenth century. Many established businessmen could remember Chicago's remarkable rebound after Mrs. O'Leary's infamous cow kicked over a lantern in 1871. And more recent proof of urban resurgence was offered by Baltimore's rapid recovery from fire in 1904.[13] In San Francisco, the "fire only" version quickly became the city's prevailing disaster story.[14] The May 5, 1906, edition of *Harper's Weekly* is but one example of the often repeated disaster narrative. "There seems to be no doubt," the magazine reassured its national audience, "that, in the case of San Francisco, most of the devastation was immediately caused by conflagration rather than by earthquake."[15]

The seismic denial narrative, in effect, dismissed other perspectives on the disaster. This simplified tale of ashes-to-resurrection overshadows the collective and individual survivor stories from San Francisco's varied neighborhoods and families, stories that shift our perspective to significant undercurrents of the catastrophe. In this book, I shine a steady light on disaster survivors in an attempt to connect their personal experiences to the prevailing disaster narrative and broader public debates over disaster relief. These stories reveal not only how those in positions of power can manipulate a catastrophic event to push political agendas but also, more importantly, how multiple voices helped forge the social and political landscape of the post-disaster city.[16]

I turn to new historical evidence to tell the story of disaster relief. For years, most historians have relied on the 1913 *San Francisco Relief Survey*.[17] This published volume is the only comprehensive source of relief documents; the American National Red Cross accumulated a voluminous trove of San Francisco records, which included refugee registration, relief applications, and administrative memorandums, but subsequently lost track of it. In addition, relief casework files disappeared when San Francisco's Associated Charities destroyed its records in 1916. But an influential relief administrator and a relief camp commander carefully preserved many of these documents— including relief committee meeting minutes, camp reports, and correspondence with refugees—records that, before this study, no historian or writer had ever examined. I use these documents to better understand the complex debates about nascent relief policy and, perhaps more important, how that policy was put into practice. The interactions among relief policy makers, providers, and recipients reveal the underlying social dynamics in San Francisco and expose some key themes of the national debates about aid and welfare for suffering Americans in general.

Eyewitness accounts, either self-published or reported by local newspapers, provide another familiar source of information about the 1906 calamity.[18] But interpreting the diverse experiences of disaster survivors through such accounts can be tricky. On the surface, they present a universal disaster experience; read more critically, however, they reveal key differences among neighborhoods and social groups. For example, few but the wealthier survivors were afforded the privilege of self-publishing eyewitness accounts, and the selection of personal stories printed in San Francisco's newspapers might have been influenced by the political leanings of publishers.[19] In my reconstruction of the disaster, I connect these accounts to the geographic locations of the city's diverse neighborhoods in order to tease out the social expectations and experiences of residents before and after the disaster. I also move beyond these written words to consider disaster artifacts and find the personal and communal stories embedded in the treasured objects that some victims managed to rescue from the fires. In addition, I turn to the Sanborn Maps and U.S. Census data (1900, 1910, and 1920) to make sense of post-disaster demographic changes. These data, when broken down by neighborhood, class, race, and family status, illuminate how the disaster intensified social differences among the city's vibrant neighborhoods. Together, these materials tell the story of how diverse responses to disaster helped define San Francisco after 1906.

Disaster history has a history of its own, beginning in the early twentieth century with the study of a 1917 munitions ship explosion in Halifax, Canada.[20] One scholar used the disaster to test "normal" social processes in Halifax because the ship explosion that destroyed the city originated "outside" the built environment. This seminal work established the view that natural disasters (fire, earthquake, flood, hurricane, and so on) occur outside the bounds of society. Since then, many scholars have turned to this natural disaster/society binary to understand the social consequences of calamity. But Mike Davis is among others who argue for an alternative point of view in the investigation of the social construction of "natural" disasters,[21] the view that disasters are both physical and social events.[22] Following this alternative approach, this book challenges the natural disaster/society binary by envisioning the disaster as simultaneously seismic and social: First, earthquake damage exposed social differences preserved by the built environment. Second, responses to the disaster—fire suppression, relief, and rebuilding—remained firmly attached to contemporary notions of social order.

When the 1906 earthquake struck, it interrupted a critical moment in the Progressive Era. Numerous scholars have written about the many social and political reforms that occurred between 1890 and 1920, but they have been unable to agree on precise definitions of the terms "Progressive Era" and "Progressivism."[23] One reason is that there was no single identifiable "Progressive movement." At most, there was a shared popular sentiment that *some* type of reform was needed in modern America, but there was no broad agreement as to what form it should take. Indeed, the Progressive Era included both democratic and undemocratic initiatives advocated by reformers who were either egalitarian or elitist.

Despite their differing approaches and goals, Progressives did share one attribute: a commitment to fixing the myriad problems that stemmed from industrialization. Progressives tackled the deplorable working and living conditions generated by unregulated factories and overcrowded tenements (to name just two pressing issues of the time) by means of new social science theories and bureaucratic structures. San Francisco's 1906 calamity created a moment of unity for local and national Progressive reformers, who sprang into action after April 18. The disaster zone opened up new space for Progressives in San Francisco and, at the same time, invited a wider audience to debate the efficacy of their proposed reforms.

This book also shows the 1906 disaster as a test case for the emerging field of professional social work, particularly for the approach known as "positive environmentalism." The disaster drew Edward T. Devine, one of the nation's leading social work experts, to San Francisco to put his theories into practice. As Devine developed new relief protocols, he worked closely with local Associated Charities leader Katharine Felton. Devine and Felton were Progressives who shared the perspective of positive environmentalists. As historian Paul Boyer explains, positive environmentalists believed that poverty was linked to an environment shaped by economic conditions rather than by hereditary factors.[24] This approach moved away from moral evaluations and toward professional expertise and training in the quest to improve the lives of the poor. Proponents of scientific social work relied on bureaucratic organization to implement what they considered to be objective criteria for the evaluation of need.

A close examination of 1906 disaster relief contributes to our historical understanding of Progressive Era reform by revealing the uneven transition from nineteenth-century approaches to charity to twentieth-century social work methodologies. In the translation from policy to practice, the objective, bureaucratic standards of twentieth-century scientific social work blended with nineteenth-century notions of charity that included moral assessment and personal involvement. In other words, despite Devine's and Felton's avowal of positive environmentalism, moral evaluations of those in need—based on nineteenth-century definitions of the "deserving" poor—crept back into twentieth-century disaster relief. Historian Linda Gordon notes that the long-standing fear that aid fostered pauperism was difficult for many reformers to overcome and that this belief, in turn, influenced the notion that "welfare called for supervision of a personal nature."[25] For all of the scientific progress made by new relief policy, it also reinforced a subjective, value-laden approach toward poverty.

Yet new relief policy did not grant officials unmitigated social control over disaster victims. Following the work of Michael Katz, Thomas Krainz, and Linda Gordon, I shift the focus away from the rhetoric of leaders to spotlight the everyday experiences of those on the receiving end of reform.[26] An investigation of records left by a young camp commander, for example, shows how refugee women adapted new relief policy regulations to serve their own needs, openly defying policy class and gender biases. Refugees in San Francisco used the agencies of social control to their own ends.

This examination of 1906 relief also highlights the contribution of women reformers to the professionalization of social work. Katharine Felton's approach to disaster victims in San Francisco adds to the rich body of literature on women social work leaders. After the disaster, Felton softened relief policy's new scientific and bureaucratic methods with her ambivalence about an entirely professional system that overlooked the idiosyncrasies of the poor. Felton taught Associated Charities caseworkers that "efficiency in charity work" depended on their "knowing the languages spoken by the poor of the city and thoroughly understanding how to deal with people in trouble."[27] Importantly, Felton did not stand alone in such views. Robyn Muncy's work on women reformers shows how some brought their old-fashioned, charity-based reform impulses to their new positions of authority in social work professions.[28] These women Progressives, among others, walked a tightrope between tradition and modernity, where the fervor for twentieth-century scientific experimentation and documentation was balanced with an attachment to nineteenth-century charity ideals.[29]

Disasters make messy subjects. To make sense of San Francisco in 1906, I use a model conceived by sociologists Robert W. Kates and David Pijawka to divide the city's post-disaster experience into four periods: emergency, restoration, replacement reconstruction, and commemorative reconstruction.[30] Although these phases can overlap and vary in duration and intensity, they provide a useful framework for understanding such a chaotic time and place.[31]

The emergency period started with the initial responses to the disaster, lasting from April to July 1906. Search and rescue, emergency food and housing, and debris removal all fell under this umbrella. The emergency phase ended once the San Francisco Relief and Red Cross Funds took charge of long-term relief policies. The subsequent restoration phase reestablished basic utility, housing, and commercial structures. During this time, thousands of refugees lived in relief camps, and their experiences reveal a more complex social dynamic at play. Rebuilding policies laid the groundwork for the third period, replacement reconstruction. Marking the return of San Francisco's social and economic activities to pre-disaster levels, replacement reconstruction was supported by local politicians, business leaders, and laborers alike. They moved quickly, and San Francisco's population returned to pre-disaster levels within three years of the first seismic tremors. The final period, commemorative reconstruction, symbolized the city's exultant recovery from disaster. City leaders sponsored two commemorative events. The first public celebration, the 1909 Portolá Festival, marked the end of replacement reconstruction. And a few years later, the more important 1915 Panama Pacific International Exposition showcased the rebuilt city to an international audience. Although most exposition structures were not built to endure, they provided tangible proof of San Francisco's disaster narrative that described a phoenix-like rise of the modern city from the ashes of a major fire.

ORGANIZATION OF THE BOOK

Chapter 1 begins with the geography of San Francisco, outlining how the urban landscape carved out social meaning for local residents. It then takes a closer look at emergency responses to the fires as they raged through the city's five densely populated residential neighborhoods. From this viewpoint, the earthquake and fires stripped away urban edifices but not social identity. Emergency responders and relief leaders turned to popular conceptions of gender, race, class, and ethnicity to salvage the turn-of-the-century city. Moreover, San Francisco politics raged alongside the inferno as the mayor took command of firefighting strategy and used the emergency to bolster his political power.[32] Equally important was the residents' response to the trauma. For purposes of survival, they clung to family bonds and community ties, keeping these social networks alive as their homes were destroyed.

Chapter 2 explores the historical origins and political implications of disaster relief. Seizing the opportunity for reform, Progressives rushed to the disaster zone in the hope of influencing San Francisco's recovery. Progressive relief experts evaluated both the disaster zone and the refugees, writing new relief policy aimed at reestablishing social order. The calamity gave

Progressives the opportunity (urban disarray and human need) and the means ($9.5 million in relief donations) to press for civic reform.

Chapter 3 describes "unofficial" relief work, using new evidence to show how the disaster intensified solidarity among San Francisco's peripheral social groups. Sheer need meant new opportunities for several groups and prominent individuals who created various forms of relief before Progressive policy assumed control. Disaster relief served a wide range of interests—from those of Catholic nuns and middle-class women to those of Chinatown leaders, working-class refugees, and philanthropic millionaires. Some of these unofficial relief efforts presented viable alternatives (and one a direct challenge) to Progressive relief policy. Refugee protesters, for example, publicly debated the efficacy of a policy that was administered by experts rather than by disaster victims themselves. All of these efforts stood in stark contrast to Progressive relief and, as a result, revealed how the policies that were intended to aid disaster victims further marginalized non-elite survivors.

Chapter 4 takes San Francisco's disaster relief camps as a case study to explore how relief policies politicized the language of race and domesticity. The official camps' "public home" facilitated social order by temporarily organizing refugees according to race, gender, and class criteria. On their most basic level, the camps redrew social boundaries by allocating space outside the disaster zone to contain poor and working-class refugees. By reaching beyond emergency food, shelter, and clothing, relief policy thus influenced private life, painting a new social landscape of order and progress. But relief camp documents show that even as Progressive policy scripted social order, many white women and Chinatown refugees openly defied the class, gender, and racial biases of policy.

Chapter 5 outlines the heated political and social battles during the reconstruction period. Reconstruction shared, and ultimately realized, many disaster relief goals. Both relief and rebuilding accelerated the development of several pre-catastrophe trends. Progressive reformers, for example, continued to take advantage of San Francisco's predicament as they thrust themselves into the rebuilding debate to put forth their ambitious plans for urban redesign. Although they did not rebuild the city in accordance with their standards, they successfully battled municipal government corruption and succeeded in replacing the mayor and his political allies shortly after the catastrophe. In another important Progressive victory, women—specifically white, middle-class women who were active in disaster relief—made significant advancements in the political realm.

Rebuilding solidified the boundaries among San Francisco's socially segregated neighborhoods. As William Issel and Robert Cherny establish, "patterns of residence, work, ethnicity, and family not only continued but also in some instances intensified" in post-disaster San Francisco.[33] I examine U.S. Census data to clarify the class, gender, and racial divisions in both old and new San Francisco neighborhoods and show how the disaster spurred urban decentralization and suburbanization. Ignoring these significant demographic changes, most civic leaders focused instead on San Francisco's public image by planning the Panama Pacific International Exposition in 1915 to launch the new San Francisco. While the visually stunning international affair symbolized the city's glorious recovery from disaster, the event also highlighted social differences that had reportedly been destroyed by the catastrophe.

The Epilogue takes on yet another disaster question: What do catastrophes mean to those who survive them? It is difficult, of course, to measure the personal meanings attached to life-altering events, especially when the primary disaster narrative, or the public story that defines a catastrophe's core meaning, masks alternative points of view. This book gives voice to those marginalized by the dominant narrative by finding their stories in disaster artifacts. For those hit hardest by the catastrophe, the bits and pieces of property they salvaged reasserted their identities and rewove family bonds. Moreover, these objects point to a symbiotic relationship between geography and identity. As Robert Self argues, "We cannot separate historical actors from their spatial relationships. Class and race are lived through the fabric of urban life and space," and I would add that so, too, is gender.[34] The stories of these artifacts illustrate the multiple meanings that a single catastrophe generated for survivors and that continued to resonate long after urban recovery.

The earthquake and fires created a messy moment of opportunity because such unprecedented need required a new kind of participation in the civic body. Who had what place in the devastated city was a critical question. At first, earthquake damage and emergency responses exacerbated preexisting social differences among San Francisco's neighborhoods. Reconstruction continued on the course set in motion by the first seismic tremors as new commercial buildings and homes spurred decentralization and solidified the pre-disaster tendency toward socially stratified neighborhoods. Thus, the 1906 disaster acted as a social accelerant that propelled some preexisting social groups and political agendas forward. Relief policy bridged the gap between material loss and rebuilding by reinforcing contemporary class, gender, and racial social hierarchies. Not surprisingly, relief became the nexus for political power and empowered those charged with its distribution to determine who belonged in the rebuilt city. But urban devastation and the widespread need of hundreds of thousands of San Franciscans also created many opportunities, enabling some marginalized groups and individuals to find a voice in the public realm. In the end, however, the 1906 disaster exposed preexisting social fissures that, in turn, guided relief and reconstruction in ways that would ultimately cement social differences in San Francisco.

CHAPTER 1

Points of Origin

Crises across the City

No one could fully realize what was in store when a 7.8-magnitude earthquake pulsed through San Francisco at a little past five in the morning on April 18, 1906. Some San Franciscans, seasoned by past tremors, dismissed the event. Roland Roche, a letter carrier for the U.S. Postal Service who lived with his family outside what would soon become the disaster zone, stayed snuggled in bed when the earthquake hit. "We were not ordinarily frightened by earthquakes, so the thing was in full blast when she [his wife] awakened me."[1] After the earthquake struck, the fires needed just wood and wind to take the city by storm. From San Francisco's landmark mansions on Nob Hill to the working-class flats south of Market Street, the fires traveled neighborhood by neighborhood, devouring everything in their path. By April 21, just three days after the quake, San Franciscans barely recognized their own city. As one survivor wrote, "Think of this enormous city with not a single hotel, every factory and wholesale and retail shop destroyed, all the markets gone, every office building and business block, nine hospitals, every theatre and half or more of the homes destroyed."[2] A reporter described the earthquake this way: "It did not discriminate between tavern and tabernacle, bank and brothel."[3]

The calamity appeared to be a social equalizer. After all, it claimed the homes of rich and poor, native-born and immigrant. But the disaster was actually not fair. Although all of San Francisco's residents may have felt the earthquake, they did not all suffer equally.

In 1906, San Francisco was a city of foreigners. At the turn of the century, three out of four San Franciscans had parents born outside the United States, and more than one-third were foreign-born themselves. Ethnic and racial groups clung together and, whether it was Ireland, Italy, or China, the country of origin was the heart and soul of a neighborhood. These resilient ethnic and racial ties controlled access to almost everything, especially jobs and housing.[4] San Francisco's landscape, with its rocky hills and sand dunes, compressed urban development and created physical barriers between neighborhoods. Russian Hill and Telegraph Hill cordoned the Italians living in North Beach, while the wealthiest San Franciscans perched high above the fray on Nob Hill. Urban construction added to these divisions. Market Street cut a wide swath from the bayside Ferry Building to the distant hills of Twin Peaks, which made for an easy dividing line between rich and poor. New technologies led the city's middle class to settle north of Market Street and west of downtown because cable cars and streetcars could easily bring men home from high-rise offices and women downtown for some of the best shopping on the West Coast.[5] Thus urban development and topography carved a sense of order in San Francisco's diverse population by creating divergent neighborhoods where everything, and everyone, appeared to have its place.

Earthquake damage intensified the differences between socially stratified neighborhoods—already separated by race, gender, ethnicity, and class—because some neighborhoods stood on solid rock while others rested on land-fill.[6] The fires ignited social discrimination when firefighters, for example, pooled water and resources to save the homes of the wealthy and left China-town unattended. But the conflagration destroyed evidence of the social discrimination that transpired while the fires burned. When the smoke cleared, it was difficult to perceive the inequity cultivated by the disaster because the physical boundaries that separated several neighborhoods had vanished. The barren urban landscape, memorialized in published photographs of the post-disaster city, validated the popular "disaster as social equalizer" viewpoint. In hindsight, San Francisco's fires disclose more than they conceal. Unlike the earthquake, which began and ended at specific points in time, the fires burned—block by block, at different rates and times—through several residential neighborhoods. In the three-day course of destruction, the fires (and the city's responses to them) revealed San Francisco's social fissures.

The catastrophe interrupted and disrupted the patterns of everyday life. As a result, many San Franciscans found themselves facing two kinds of danger. The first, and most obvious, immediately threatened life and property. The second threatened their social location, possibly changing their lives long after the flames died. When San Franciscans fled from their homes in the heart of the city as their physical world crumbled and burned around them, they became subject to an emergency response and, later, relief policy that redefined their place in the city.

EARLY SAN FRANCISCO

The magnitude of San Francisco's loss was half a century in the making. The renowned beauty of twenty-first-century San Francisco obscures the fact that the city was founded on a precarious site. Bound by a sizable bay (four hundred square miles) and the Pacific Ocean, the seven-mile peninsula was, in the words of geographer James Vance, "an eccentric location and a rough site."[7] Fresh water, timber, and wildlife were of limited supply. The local Coastanoan and Ohlone Indians recognized this well before the eighteenth century and wisely lived on the coast south of the peninsula or inland.[8] But the peninsula held both symbolic and real value to the varied empires seeking a prime hub for international trade. As Mel Scott concludes, San Francisco "was not so much at the edge of a continent as it was at the edge of an immense ocean that was connected with all other great seas of the world."[9] As early as the eighteenth century, the future site of San Francisco generated intense competition among Spanish, Russian, Mexican, and American governments. The local Indian population became unwilling participants when the Spanish empire founded a mission in 1776, followed by a pueblo in 1834. The new city, called Yerba Buena, was an active port as the early Spanish empire gave way to the Mexican Republic in 1821. The United States was deeply invested in Yerba Buena's success because the port shipped cowhides, or "California bank notes," to eastern factories from Mexican rancheros.[10]

As the United States expanded, it showed a determination to reach the western edges of the continent. In 1835, President Andrew Jackson offered $3.5 million to the Mexican Republic for all lands north of the thirty-eighth parallel. A decade later, President James K. Polk set his sights on annexing the Pacific coastline. War with Mexico, preceded by a revolt staged by American settlers, brought the rocky peninsula under the American flag in 1848. The Americans changed the city's name to San Francisco and soon welcomed the gold rush. This illusive promise of instant wealth rapidly transformed the embryonic city.

There was no turning back after President Polk announced an "abundance of gold" in northern California on December 5, 1848.[11] An enormous nugget of California gold on display in Washington made more than one heart race with anticipation. Men from around the world left for California, but few (mostly from Mexico, Peru, and Chile) were experienced miners. Economic distress was a primary motivating factor. Ireland's 1846–1847 potato famine, China's Taiping rebellion, and Germany's unpredictable farm economy led many to California to try their hand at mining. In 1849 alone, 40,000 immigrants arrived by sea, and nearly 42,000 walked and rode the overland trails from the east. San Francisco's population exploded from 1,000 in 1848 to nearly 25,000 in 1850 and then doubled only five years later.[12] President Polk was undoubtedly elated by the fact that millions in California gold emerged from American soil.

Mining created a unique city. The gold rush sparked what Richard White classifies as a modern migration, one in which "migrants did not look on their destination as either a site for re-creating an existing way of life or establishing a new and better one."[13] Men traveled alone because they wanted to make money quickly and return home. This made early San Francisco a transient city, a place to transact the business of mining rather than build a permanent home. "Then the city was composed, almost entirely, of men," wrote an Episcopal bishop at the time. "There were no accommodations for the ladies, and the gentler sex would have been sadly out of place among the hardships which marked those days."[14] San Francisco's unusual geographic location, mining economy, population boom, and haphazard construction made it a place that was built by and for men.

Early San Francisco is best described by Gunther Barth, who calls it an "instant city" that defied normative patterns of urbanization.[15] Gold rush growth, for example, stalled the experience of Victorian family life so familiar to other U.S. cities. The predominantly single male population—men outnumbered women by five to one in 1853—meant that families were few and far between. "This is the Paradise of men," confirmed one of the few women settlers in 1851. "I wonder if a paradise for poor *Women* will ever be discovered."[16] Nonetheless, nineteenth-century domestic ideology, which portrayed women as moral guardians of the home, was alive and well in San Francisco. As Barbara Bergland suggests, ideologies of white womanhood were not only "in good working order"; they may also have "intensified under the strain" of a setting in which men outnumbered women.[17] Thus popular gendered expectations—by which men provided for their families and women sustained the moral vitality of the home—took on additional meaning for women. One example of the conflict between gender ideals and urban life is evident in how some women responded to prostitution. The Barbary Coast, San Francisco's well-known vice district, drew women arriving from China, Mexico, Peru, Chile, France, and eastern U.S. cities to work as prostitutes. While white women worked for wages in brothels, Chinese prostitutes were more often indentured or enslaved, exemplifying the harsh social dynamics of the instant city.[18] When white, middle-class, Protestant women created mission homes to protect Chinese women and girls, they did so as a defense of white domesticity.[19] As men continued to outnumber women by a four-to-three ratio at the end of the century, popular gender discourse gave women in San Francisco the additional task of civilizing the city at large.[20] "Every steamer brings out ladies and families, domestic ties are forming or renewing," recorded Reverend William Kip. "Here as elsewhere the softening and refining influence of female society is felt, and San Francisco is rapidly settling down to be like every other civilized city."[21]

Gold forged two distinct social classes in San Francisco: the fabulously wealthy and the workingman. An elite class of San Franciscans emerged as early as 1850.[22] As in New York, Boston, and Philadelphia, a few (5 percent of the male population) owned most (75 percent to 80 percent) of the city.[23] Wealth proved elusive for the great majority of fortune seekers. In early San Francisco, only a few industrial leaders moved up from their working-class origins; most men did not improve their social or economic standing.[24] Many of the men who had swarmed to the northern California mines eventually resorted to wage work in the city. By 1900, they had built the strongest labor organization in America and made San Francisco the only U.S. city where one-third of the workers paid union dues.[25] The promise of gold, which pulled both foreign and native-born men into San Francisco's orbit, helped forge this new working-class consciousness.

Worker solidarity, the foundation of San Francisco's strong labor presence, was built on racial hostility. As gold prospects wore thin in the foothills, Irish and Chinese men competed for work in San Francisco, and Chinese miners and laborers bore the brunt of increasing racial hostility. As Philip Ethington points out, the California Workingmen's Trade and Labor Union (formed in 1877) congealed by using racial explanations for class conflict and economic crisis.[26] In fact, California politics hardened social class differences; in addition to the labor movement, new interest-group lobbies (legalized by the California Constitution of 1879) manipulated class identity for political victories by encouraging working-class men to identify as such and funding political campaigns based on race and class issues.[27] By 1900, San Francisco's social classes were becoming rock solid.[28]

In early San Francisco, racial and class identities evolved in tandem. The gold rush spurred Chinese immigration, and San Francisco became the main port of entry. The 1882 Chinese Exclusion Act, largely intended to deny entry to laborers, played a critical role in shaping the experiences of Chinese immigrants before and after their arrival in San Francisco. As Erika Lee summarizes, Chinese exclusion was an "institution that produced and reinforced a system of racial hierarchy."[29] Even before immigrants touched U.S. soil, they were scrutinized by a law that, especially as practiced by immigration officials, revived stereotypes of the Chinese as degraded and dangerous. The legislation's race-based exclusion, which singled out Chinese and separated them from other immigrant groups, depended on the physical markers of race and other indicators of racial difference, such as language. Immigration officials paid close attention to these indicators and evaluated immigrant behavior as well, intertwining their observations with existing stereotypes of Chinese immigrants in San Francisco.[30] That Chinese immigrants as a group were regarded as "unable to assimilate into American life and citizenship" meant that they entered and lived in the city enshrouded in racial difference.[31]

The exclusion law divided families and created class criteria for entry, intimately connecting gender and class to racial identity. The law reinforced class (prohibiting laborers) and gender (few women were eligible to apply for entry) distinctions.[32] Chinese men accepted low wages and took the blame for job shortages, thus galvanizing white working-class identity, while Chinese women were associated with prostitution, representing a sexualized danger to white domesticity.[33] Moreover, these class- and gender-based assumptions were tied to the notion of racial inferiority.[34] The popular belief that Chinese immigrant women were prostitutes, for example, exemplified the perceived racial threat of Chinese immigration in general.[35] Not surprisingly, those who gained entry to San Francisco relied on their own networks of support by living in Chinatown. The well-defined neighborhood housed the majority of San Francisco's Chinese, who constituted just over 4 percent of the city's population in 1900.[36] While the neighborhood offered physical protection, the distinct geographical space became a place that reinforced a racialized identity.[37] Chinatown was depicted as a dangerous, polluted space that could contaminate the city with vice (opium dens and brothels) and disease (bubonic plague), as Nayan Shah demonstrates. The perceived danger brought the "concern that Chinese bodies and conduct undermined the norms of white American society."[38]

By the turn of the century, social meaning was deeply embedded in the urban landscape. Class, gender, race, and ethnic divisions were as obvious as the cable car lines that ran along the main thoroughfare of Market Street. The unusually wide Market Street, which ran from the Ferry Building toward the original eighteenth-century Spanish mission, provided a simple barometer by which many residents measured social status. The often-heard phrase "south of the slot" was slang for the working-class folk living south of Market Street's metal slots that housed its trolley cables. "Market Street divides the city diagonally in two," explained one citizen. "South of it were the residences of the poorer people and wholesale houses. . . . [North were] the great shops, importing houses."[39] As Sarah Deutsch describes it, "In an urban landscape, you know who you are by where you are. At the same time, you understand the nature of the terrain by who lives there."[40] By 1906, San Franciscans knew *who* they were by *where* they lived. This meant that individual and family social networks were intimately connected to the land on which the people lived. That ground would determine their fate during the 1906 disaster.

THE UNPREPARED CITY

San Francisco was no stranger to fire and earthquake. A spate of fires between 1848 and 1851 made urban rebuilding an annual event. Flammable features like elevated, wood-planked sidewalks near the waterfront made this a city built to burn. Fire was more widespread in San Francisco than in other U.S. cities because of high winds, low summer rainfall, wood construction, and hills that defied fire engines and their sturdy horses.[41] Early attempts to mitigate fire hazards inadvertently increased vulnerability to earthquakes. Developers "made ground" out of sand, rubble, and trash to eliminate the pockets of oxygen trapped beneath sidewalk planks after the 1851 fire. Made ground turned the city's sagging waterfront, small lakes, and tributaries into valuable real estate.[42] When it liquefied during the 1868 earthquake, developers unabashedly scraped up the earthquake rubble and used it as landfill. Geologists cautioned against the "assumed indifference to the dangers of earthquake calamities" following the 1868 quake.[43] But only after the 1906 earthquake was the undeniable danger of made ground common knowledge. The 1906 scientific investigative committee reported, "The most violent destruction of buildings, as everybody knows, was on the made ground. This ground seems to have behaved during the earthquake very much in the same way as jelly in a bowl, or as a semi-liquid material in a tank."[44]

As city buildings grew taller, politicians and builders boldly ignored the latest fireproof techniques used in other cities. It was widely known that reinforced concrete buildings, popular at the turn of the century, offered the best earthquake resistance for structures more than six stories high. But San Francisco's design remained unaltered because the International Union of Bricklayers and Allied Craftworkers voted against the use of reinforced concrete.[45] Unfortunately, ordinary brick buildings lacked elasticity and cracked and crumbled under the earthquake's assault. Fire limit building codes, a popular fire prevention measure during this time, protected downtown San Francisco from potential fires by restricting new wood-frame construction. City codes, however, grandfathered existing wooden buildings, leaving them to stand like a box of matches beneath the city's office buildings and towers. All of these factors—landfill, brick buildings, and wood-frame construction— meant that valuable downtown property had little hope of enduring either earthquake or fire. Thus the city's magnificent skyline outlining stylish hotels, shops, and skyscrapers masked an open invitation to disaster.

From 1866, San Francisco was one of a handful of American cities with a professional fire department. The city maintained forty-two fire engines, still pulled by horses, and staffed a dozen ladder companies. In 1905, the National Board of Fire Underwriters lauded the "vigilance of the fire department" in protecting the city, but this vigilance was questioned after the 1906 disaster.[46] According to rumors circulating before the quake, Fire Chief Dennis Sullivan had developed a citywide disaster plan. But if Chief Sullivan had a plan in mind, he failed to share it with anyone else before the earthquake struck. The earthquake killed the chief and wiped out the fire department's alarm system, leaving fire crews to work around the clock without clear direction from a central command.

Captain Arthur Welsh's crew did not need an alarm to tell them there was an earthquake because they were trapped inside their Mission District firehouse. Even after breaking through the firehouse doors, the crew was unable to communicate with other crews because the "fire alarm system was out of order, [and] consequently we had to use our own judgment as to the best way to proceed."[47] Even if the alarm system had survived, there was simply not enough water to quench the flames.[48] Only after the earthquake did the city engineer admit that city water pipes were not suited for extensive firefighting: "The pressure is too low and many of the distributing pipes are too small. . . . Many of the mains pass over ground liable to serious displacement from earthquake."[49] In fact, the deadly 1906 fires inspired the fire department to invent a new fire suppression system altogether. The city's future emergency water supply would be fed by three reservoirs holding 11.5 million gallons of water and two power stations capable of pumping 16,000 gallons of salt water from the bay each minute.[50] But on April 18, 1906, there simply were not enough firefighters (575 were on duty that day), water, hoses, or strategy to stop the fires before they raged out of control.[51]

The low water supply and lack of central command made a deadly combination. San Francisco mayor Eugene Schmitz took charge, even though he had neither firefighting nor military training. Thus it was not surprising that the mayor's efforts suffered from inexperience and isolation. Military commanders stationed at the Presidio marched troops downtown to fight fires and protect property, while naval ships pumped water to anxious sailors fighting fires along the waterfront. When residents were allowed to remain near their homes, they joined the desperate fight against the fires. Despite their best intentions, these groups (military, municipal, and private citizens) did not work in unison. "I had no instructions with regard to my position as far as preserving order," reported one naval officer, "but from rumors which had reached me I learned that the military was in control."[52] In the end, the decentralized firefighting made the disaster worse instead of better.

Firefighters helped nature take its course and were inadvertently responsible for the fires spreading from one neighborhood to another. They turned to dynamite as a last resort, and sometimes ignited black powder, in an attempt to create firebreaks. Dynamite did have a track record of success as a fire suppression technique, but not in San Francisco, where firefighters were untrained in its use. Battalion Chief J. J. Conlon was not the only officer to report, "My experience with dynamite did not prove entirely satisfactory, due to the fact that up to this time I had never been called upon to use high-grade explosives."[53] The combination of inexperience and zeal to stop the fire was lethal. The fire department's chief engineer later admitted that "great harm was done during the first days of the fire by the indiscriminate use of black powder[. I]t developed that when black powder was exploded it threw off a combustion that ignited all woodwork with which it came in contact, thus starting additional fires."[54] While the fires burned, the dynamite made the city sound like a war zone. Brigadier General Frederick Funston, the Presidio's acting commander, who marched troops into the burning city, described "times when the explosions were so continuous as to resemble bombardment."[55] Experts knew that dynamite could have saved San Francisco, but they were not on hand to help. The editors of the *Mining and Scientific Press* later wrote, "The use of high-grade explosives by people ignorant of their strength and proper application, was instrumental in destroying a vast amount of property without the desired result, and in many cases it actually spread the conflagration."[56]

The city was unprepared for the 1906 catastrophe, as later aerial photographs of the disaster zone made abundantly clear. Hundreds of city blocks and thousands of homes were gone. Even scavengers were hard-pressed to find anything of value in the ashes. But this bird's-eye view of the disaster zone masks another important story. What one cannot see from viewing the post-disaster photographs of urban obliteration or reading about the destructive force of earthquake and fire on the city in general are stark variations in the

View of Market Street, 1906. Men and women walking and riding toward the Ferry Building. (Courtesy of the San Francisco Virtual Museum.)

catastrophe. Rather than discussing the earthquake as one mega-disaster, we can better and more productively understand it as a series of neighborhood disasters, integrally tied to the social standing of each residential area. The following analysis, which traces the progress of the fires through and between the residential neighborhoods, reveals the social dimension of a natural disaster.

Neighborhood Disasters

The South of Market District

At the boardinghouse on Fourth Street, the landlady always rose before sunrise. It was good for business, with several dozen workingmen depending on her for breakfast. Biscuits, bacon, eggs—all baked in and fried over her seasoned stove. And hot coffee, lots of it. But this morning was different. This morning, waking up early saved her life. After the first seismic jolt knocked her to the floor, she grabbed the bedroom windowsill and crawled out. She watched from Fourth Street as the house burst into flames. "Out of the 40 people in the house, she was the only one saved," recounted her friend. "Her husband was killed, too."[57]

At the beginning of the twentieth century, working-class San Franciscans lived on borrowed time—and borrowed space. Whether they walked along the docks, knelt for mass, or sat to order a beer in their favorite saloon, the earth supporting them was nothing but landfill. Hotels and apartment buildings built over former lakes and inlets sunk into the earth when seismic tremors turned solid ground into watery quicksand. Residents drowned in their sleep after their rooms disappeared below street level. At least 3,000 died during those few days in San Francisco, a figure that took decades to calculate.[58] But no one will ever know the real number of nameless San Franciscans—poor and working-class people who struggled to make ends meet and could not afford to own a home—who disappeared. A deadly combination of history and landscape sealed their fate.

Almost one-fifth of San Franciscans lived in the South of Market District. Most paid union dues or lived with someone who did. These workers were new to America, making up a densely populated neighborhood of first- and second-generation single men and young families. A working-class consciousness unified the neighborhood, with union membership helping to bridge cultural differences among the Irish, Germans, and Scandinavians. Michael Kazin argues that by the twentieth century, working-class consciousness superseded ethnic alliances.[59] The collective hostility toward San Francisco's Chinese bridged ethnic differences as well. Ethnic white identities, as Barbara Berglund points out, united "whites across lines that in other contexts often served to divide them."[60]

Family status, on the other hand, created a neighborhood dividing line. Sailors and migratory workers packed the waterfront, where single men found cheap rooms and simple entertainment. Families settled just a few blocks inland in the ever popular and overpopulated two- and three-story wooden row houses. These were homes, to be sure, but of a much different sort than the waterfront's boardinghouses or Nob Hill's mansions. Nearly every house was overcrowded, with two families instead of one. At ten people per dwelling, South of Market was 56 percent denser in population than the city average. Irish families of five or more became even bigger when they took in boarders. On a typical residential block, saloons outnumbered row houses. One block of Tehama Street, a narrow residential alley near the waterfront, included thirty-two saloons, fourteen lodging houses, and seven restaurants. The Lesaudros were one of several families who lived on Tehama Street. The parents and four children shared their home with extended family (Mrs. Lesaudro's sister and her husband). Family members working to support the household (Mr. Lesaudro was a day laborer, and the two oldest Lesaudro girls, ages ten and twelve, worked as hatmakers) was a typical arrangement for South of Market families.[61]

South of Market was an insular neighborhood, with churches, schools, union halls, and work all found within walking distance. Just two blocks north on Mission Street stood the largest parish in the American West, St. Patrick's Church. South of Market was also home to several Jewish congregations and a German Methodist church. Work was nearby as well—not just on the docks and piers but in the factories, foundries, and warehouses that filled the neighborhood. Family men most often worked in these factories and foundries, while women completed piecework at home or crossed Market Street to earn money as laundresses or maids in wealthier households. With the exception of visiting those relatives who saved enough to buy a house outside South of Market or traveling to do domestic work elsewhere in the city, many residents had little reason to leave the neighborhood.

South of Market was one of the most dangerous places to live in San Francisco, but not because, as many of the city's elite believed, so many transient single men lived and worked there. Its lethal qualities derived from the fact that, in early San Francisco, the center of the neighborhood was water. It was called Yerba Buena Cove then, a quiet place to dock Spanish vessels or gain easy access to the first Spanish mission. South of Yerba Buena Cove, Mission Bay welcomed bulk cargoes and small coastal carriers to its docks.[62] It did not take long for urban expansion to shrink the bay. Little by little, the shore was filled with dirt and debris to make way for streets boasting new warehouses and businesses. By 1906, Mission Bay's Long Bridge turned into Fourth Street. It was hard for anyone but the old-timers to remember the bay and cove. The imposing Southern Pacific terminal at Third and Townsend Streets, for example, spread across thirty acres of formerly submerged land.[63] There was simply too much daily activity on surface streets for anyone to stop and consider what was happening beneath them. Overcrowding in cheap wood-frame construction, unstable ground, and winds blowing off the San Francisco Bay all made South of Market the section of the city most vulnerable to earthquake and fire.

On April 18, 1906, South of Market residents had only a few seconds to find safety. "My father looked down the front stairs and found that they had fallen in. Then he went to the rear stairs and they were all raised up, almost ready to fall in," recalled two sisters. "Well, my father got us down those stairs as fast as he could, helping each one so we wouldn't fall. There was no time to try to save anything."[64] Patrolman Harry F. Walsh, on duty that fateful morning, noted how "buildings were then crumbling and shedding cornices, and it was dangerous to pass even in the middle of the street."[65] The shoddy wood-frame construction was no match for the earthquake, and everything from small row houses to enormous residential hotels tumbled down in an instant. The State Earthquake Investigation Commission later found that "less than a third of the frame buildings in this tract [South of Market] remained in their vertical positions."[66] On Sixth Street, four residential hotels—Brunswick House, Ohio House, Nevada House, and the Lormor—collapsed into one another and wiped out nearly a thousand rooms. One of the few survivors of Brunswick House escaped from his third-floor room by climbing to the roof, which was leaning into Sixth Street.[67] The death toll was anyone's guess. On Montgomery Street, Officer E. J. Wiskotchill tried to rescue men crushed by a falling parapet. "We helped all we could to dig and drag from the ruins the dead and the injured that were littered about," recalled the officer. "Legs and arms were sticking out here and there to guide us."[68] Many of South of

Market's working families were unknown to anyone but relatives and neighbors, while even more workingmen lived anonymously in boardinghouses or hotel rooms along the waterfront. "The papers here state that the death list reaches about 400," wrote one city resident to a friend, "but everybody knows differently."[69]

The earthquake was just the beginning of the crisis. A few innocuous fires mushroomed into a firestorm that overtook the neighborhood. Water mains and gas pipes running through landfill snapped in two, and the city water system ground to a halt. The chief engineer for Spring Valley Water Company discovered hundreds of ruptures, "especially where the streets crossed filled ground and, particularly, where such filled ground covered former deep swamps."[70] San Francisco Gas and Electric Company's chief engineer documented the "successive explosions in the feeding mains" on both sides of Market Street.[71] Flames bursting from broken gas lines torched nearby buildings while firefighters rushed from hydrant to hydrant in search of water. Once the collapsed row houses and hotels burned, the conflagration devoured wood from the abundant lumberyards and warehouses. Winds carried the flames to the ostensibly unlimited supply of wood nearby. A small fire from a waterfront hotel, for example, ignited the Sperry Flour Company's block-long warehouse. After decimating the flour warehouse, the burning

San Francisco's disaster zone. Produced by the Southern Pacific Railroad in 1906, this map minimizes the size of the disaster zone by showing the entire city. In fact, 45 percent of San Franciscans lived inside the disaster zone. (Courtesy of the Bancroft Library, University of California, Berkeley.)

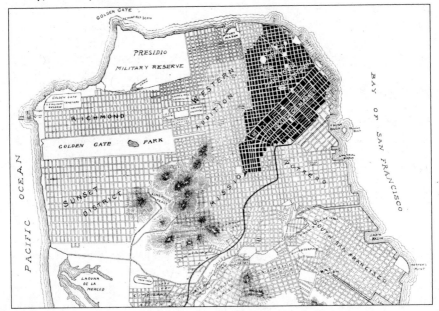

raged on to nearby lumberyards.[72] Before long, the South of Market fires spread to more valuable property when a row house fire left Fourth Street for the Grand Opera House, where legendary tenor Enrico Caruso had sung the night before. By nine thirty that morning the opera house was gone and the flames had moved on to Market Street, heading toward the landmark Call Building.

Outsiders feared South of Market's roaring flames and fleeing refugees. General Funston sent 1,700 troops into the disaster zone to guard federal buildings and protect upper-class homes. "San Francisco had its class of people, no doubt, who would have taken advantage of any opportunity to plunder the banks and rich jewelry and other stores of the city," wrote Funston, "but the presence of square-jawed silent men with magazine rifles, fixed bayonets, and with belts full of cartridges restrained them."[73] Soldiers worked overtime to control more than the South of Market fires, suppressing people as well as flames. Naval officer Frederick Freeman wrote, "During all of that day the men in my command were not only fighting fire, but also policing the territory in which they worked." A few South of Market residents played into working-class stereotypes by spending the morning walking from saloon to saloon, drinking heartily until all available liquor was gone. Police sergeant William M. Ross found the saloon at Mission and First Street packed with men at 10:00 A.M., "all drinking as hard as they could, I suppose to console themselves for the disaster that was going on all around them, and was then certain to destroy the saloon as well as every other building in the vicinity."[74] Officer Freeman reported "constant trouble" from intoxicated residents, who "rushed saloon after saloon and looted the stocks." According to Freeman, drinking was also a cause of death: "In my opinion great loss of life resulted from men and women becoming stupefied by liquor and being too tired and exhausted to get out of the way of the fire."[75] Meanwhile, fire suppression focused on commercial buildings rather than homes, and navy ships pumped water from the bay to spare the city's valuable waterfront. While South of Market's residential space vanished, soldiers saved nearby businesses like the Folgers warehouses, the Mutual Electric Light Company, and Southern Pacific's freight sheds.[76]

The only way to ensure safety was to get out of the neighborhood. Residents grabbed what possessions they could before fleeing the fires. "Then there was the endless trail of trunks that rattled and grated as they dragged along," noted police sergeant Maurice S. Behan. "There was a rope tied to the front handle of the South-of-Market trunk. The father or the mother hauled on this rope from the shoulder, while the wife or one of the children followed pushing the trunk with a pole—usually a broomstick."[77] Some fled west, walking to the city limits or stopping at the nearby Mission District. Others fought the crowds at the ferry docks, taking free rides east to Oakland or north to Marin County. A class-based social stigma clung to many working-class refugees who stayed in San Francisco. Colonel Thornwell Mullally, assistant to the president of United Railroads, helped frantic residents driven

Firestorm in San Francisco. The intensity surprised residents in the South of Market and Downtown Districts. This photograph was taken circa April 18, 1906. (Courtesy of the San Francisco Virtual Museum.)

from their homes when he opened up the company car barn for those wandering about "not knowing where to go." But as beleaguered South of Market refugees took shelter in the company building, the colonel observed that they "seemed to permeate like rats."[78]

For South of Market residents, one of the safest options was seeking shelter with local family and friends. One young family turned to nearby relatives after watching their flat burn: "It was an awful sight for our poor mother to see all her belongings, that she had accumulated since her marriage, go up in smoke. . . . My mother decided that the only place we could go for shelter was to her sister's home." Their aunt's undamaged house on Potrero Hill, just south of the fires, became a safe haven for any relation in danger. Despite the needs of her immediate family, their aunt "managed to make room for everyone as they were relatives." Neighbors supported these family networks. In this case, Potrero Hill neighbors brought clothes and supplies. "It seemed the word went around like wild-fire," recalled the young fire victim, "because soon after everyone was bringing us clothes and shoes and other things."[79]

South of Market refugees also fled west toward Golden Gate Park. Thomas A. Burns opened his home near the park to friends and strangers alike. "Our house, though it had been shaken from its foundations by the quake, was full of guests," said Burns, "some that we knew before and some that we did not know from Adam. All were refugees from the fire."[80] The recollections of John Conlon, son of an Irish fire department officer, also highlight the importance of family connections: "Everyone, like our family, offered shelter to relatives and friends." Friday, April 20, was remembered as "the night of deluge" at their home near Golden Gate Park as relatives "started to arrive . . . with only the clothes on their backs." After the disaster, thirty-five relatives carved out additional living space in the basement, "which was immediately partitioned by one of the men." The Conlons home extended into the public street, as homes soon would in other neighborhoods, and John's mother began preparing meals in front of her house on a lean-to stove built from salvaged bricks and sheet iron.[81]

By lunchtime on April 18, South of Market was an inferno; by midnight the entire district was gone. Nothing was left from Market to Townsend Streets. "I clambered my way over piles of brick and rubbish with fires smouldering on either side," wrote one South of Market observer on April 20, "and not a building as far as I could [see]."[82]

Chinatown

> "No time to pack anything," Mr. Shum called out to his family. He knew his family must leave everything behind in their Chinatown apartment. The large building tucked safely inside the fifteen-block neighborhood could no longer shelter his wife and daughter. He carried his wife down to the street while his neighbor helped Mr. Shum's young daughter, Bessie. Now their only protection was each other.[83]

Chinatown did not burn by natural causes. Dynamite, mixed with strategic decisions to save the city's elite, leveled the largest Chinese settlement on the West Coast. The fire department grabbed dynamite to stop the fires once the flames ate their way through downtown and began nibbling at the base of Nob Hill. The fires spread with no one there to stop them. Military firefighters, who spent the morning fighting blazes along the waterfront and downtown, stopped to eat breakfast, and without them, Chinatown firefighting was left in the hands of a civilian. Instead of quenching the flames, his use of explosives to create firebreaks abetted the conflagration that consumed the vibrant fifteen-block neighborhood.

To outsiders, Chinatown was defined by its difference from the rest of San Francisco. But the truth was that Chinatown had always been an integral part of the city's identity. As early as 1851, nearly 3,000 Chinese referred to San Francisco as "Dai Fow" (first city).[84] Almost everyone who stepped on a boat in China sailed through San Francisco's golden gate and, by 1890, nearly 30 percent of the Chinese in California called San Francisco home.[85] According to Chinatown insiders, the neighborhood housed at least 25,000 residents in 1906. But because of anti-Chinese legislation, residents avoided census workers. Thus only about half (just over 13,000) of Chinatown's estimated population was accounted for in the 1900 Census.[86] The 1882 Chinese

Exclusion Act stopped the regular flow of Chinese workers who mined for gold and laid tracks for the ever-expanding railroad. The immigration policy left Chinatown predominantly male because it prevented the migration of families by limiting admission to merchants, Chinese officials, students, and teachers. In response, Chinatown's merchant class rose to power by forming the Chinese Consolidated Benevolent Association (CCBA) to protect the political, economic, and social needs of their community.[87] Chinatown remained a double-edged sword for its residents. While many found safety in the insular neighborhood, its distinct spatial boundaries perpetuated a negative, racialized identity in relation to the rest of San Francisco.[88]

Racialized views of Chinatown made a difference during the disaster. As the few surviving records suggest, the men responsible for firefighting were not concerned with saving this neighborhood. Navy crews made diligent firefighters, but they were allowed to stop working once "the waterfront was apparently safe." As the seamen left the city to rest and eat, their officer watched the fires "sweeping through Chinatown" unattended.[89] Dynamite took its toll on the neighborhood as well. Fire officials hoped that exploding a drugstore and a rooming house on the corner of Clay and Kearny Streets would stop the downtown fires. Instead, a poorly set explosion sent a flaming mattress from a lodging house bedroom across Kearny Street and into Chinatown.[90] Things went from bad to worse when the mayor appointed a civilian, John Bermingham, to lead the Chinatown fire attack. Lawyer Abraham Ruef, political confidant of Mayor Schmitz and supporter of a post-disaster plan

Soldiers standing on Grant Avenue as Chinatown burned, 1906. (Courtesy of the San Francisco Virtual Museum.)

to remove Chinatown from downtown San Francisco, was responsible for supplying Bermingham with tools and city firefighters. According to one fire department captain, Ruef ordered a hose wagon and two firefighters "to the Lombard St. wharf to report to John Bermingham."[91] City leaders most likely trusted Bermingham because he was president of California Powderworks. Tragically, Bermingham's use of explosives coupled with his inexperience in firefighting started more fires than it stopped. After the disaster, John Bermingham was accused of igniting more than sixty fires in Chinatown while under the influence of alcohol.[92]

When fire threatened other neighborhoods, it was often the case that residents banded together to fight the flames. This was not true in Chinatown because civic and military authorities forced immediate residential evacuation. As one eyewitness near Chinatown recalled, "The authorities drove them [Chinese residents] up the hill and out of the range of the fire."[93] Police captain Stephen V. Bunner, interviewed shortly after the disaster, "was with a squad in Chinatown persuading or compelling reluctant Chinese to leave houses that were threatened by the oncoming conflagration." He explained that "some of these people were very unwilling to leave their homes and abandon their household goods, stocks, and other treasures."[94] In the end, almost all of Chinatown's landmarks were destroyed, from the famous Chinese Theater on Jackson Street to the first Chinese place of worship, Kong Chow Temple. As one sightseer from Oakland wrote on April 21, "I looked around in the ashes of one of the Chinese Bazaars for something to take home for a souvenir or relic and did not find one."[95]

The loss of Chinatown created two disasters for the Chinese: individuals lost their homes and businesses as well as their friends and family, and they also lost their safe haven in a racially hostile city. After their neighborhood vanished, Chinese refugees stood in place of the old Chinatown and became symbols of racial difference. As one eyewitness described Chinatown residents, they were "in the streets, gesticulating, crying, running around and acting like a lot of monkeys."[96] Not surprisingly, Chinatown refugees did not turn to strangers for help.

Out of necessity, disaster survivors clustered in informal groups of family, friends, and neighbors. Two-parent families remained intact throughout the catastrophe, often expanding to include the single men who were their neighbors and employees.[97] Leland Chin remembered how his family left their home on California Street to meet "the whole family, and our employees and neighbors in our building" at his father's shop on Taylor Street. They walked together as a group and later spent the night in a park near Chinatown.[98] Edwar Lee, also living with his family in Chinatown, joined tenants from a nearby building before traveling as a group to the East Bay. Alice Sue Fun's family, whose father lost his boardinghouse to the earthquake, spent three nights during the disaster sleeping on the lawn of a nearby park. "I had my younger brother by the hand and my mother was pregnant," recalled Fun. "Oh, it was hard then."[99] Thousands of Chinese found food and shelter by trekking down to the shrimp camps near Potrero Hill (just south of the South of Market District). They joined the Chinese enclave and obtained food from a nearby business. The general manager of the local slaughterhouse gave meat to thousands of South of Market and Chinatown refugees. When soldiers threatened to confiscate the food surplus on Thursday, April 19, the manager argued that the "meat was being regularly and judiciously distributed, absolutely free, to every applicant."[100] Perhaps the sheer number of both Chinese and white working-class refugees being served convinced the army captain on duty to leave the provisions on Potrero Hill.

Chinatown refugees also survived the disaster by turning to their white employers for shelter. Edith Rosenshine's father, a San Francisco tobacco dealer, allowed Chinese cigar makers to stay in their basement. But Edith's family never met, or discussed, those refugees: "Every night from seven o'clock on, Dad would hear them returning—one by one. He never knew where they were during the day, nor did he know how many Chinese were actually sleeping in the basement. . . . None of them ever came upstairs, and Dad never told anyone in the house that there were Chinese in the basement."[101] In another example, a Chinese cook asked his employer to shelter his friends. The employer first locked his house and then "opened the side gate for them, so that they could go into the laundry [shed], where the poor things were glad to huddle." After giving his cook's friends shelter, the employer returned to his front gate to watch the "throngs of Chinese [who] were now pouring out of Chinatown, like beetles from a burning log, and passing in procession" in front of his home.[102] The disaster destroyed neighborhood barriers and prompted new interactions among San Franciscans. But for many white San Franciscans, the chaotic reordering of their city did not alter their racialized worldview.

The fires initiated a new crisis for two Christian mission homes for Chinese women and girls. Peggy Pascoe's work shows how white middle-class Protestant women, acting on the notion that women were the proper moral guardians of the home, established rescue homes to save Chinese women from the abuse of men. They took the Christian home as a model for their work because the home, or private sphere, was so clearly delineated as the locus of women's moral influence. For mission home leaders, Chinese prostitution in San Francisco presented a visible threat to white female purity; thus the rescue and protection of Chinese women and girls safeguarded white middle-class ideals.[103] Indeed, Donaldina Cameron, the Presbyterian Chinese Mission Home's well-known leader, worked tirelessly to protect her charges from Chinatown's sex trade.[104] She moved quickly on April 18 because she believed that "our Chinese girls on the streets among these crowds after nightfall was a danger too great to risk."[105] With more than sixty residents to protect, Cameron found the odds stacked against her. She turned to her church for sanctuary. The group walked west from Chinatown to the First Presbyterian Church on Van Ness Street. After that, Cameron secured a ferry ride north to Marin County, where they found shelter at the San Francisco Theological

Seminary. Cameron believed their journey was divine "deliverance" from an unbounded Chinatown.[106]

The Oriental Home for Chinese Women and Girls, a Methodist Episcopal Church effort, followed a similar trajectory.[107] The mission home leader, Carrie G. Davis, also temporarily re-created the boundaries of the Christian home outside the disaster zone. During the calamity, forty-eight women and children fled to a church member's home in San Francisco. After a brief rest, they took a circuitous route to avoid the fires—walking for seven hours—before boarding an East Bay ferry. Their journey ended in Berkeley, where they found asylum in the homes of mission board members. In the meantime, Carrie Davis "still manage[d] to cross the bay and meet incoming steamers to carry on the Home's chief mission—that of rescuing girls sent from China to be sold as slaves."[108] The actions of the two mission home leaders stand out because of their determination to re-create their Christian mission homes' domestic space in order to protect their residents from perceived racialized danger.

Despite their best intentions, the mission homes reinforced negative conceptions of Chinatown. Even though they were far away in the countryside, Cameron's group nonetheless revived images of Chinatown as a corrupt and dangerous place. The *Oakland Tribune*, for example, reported that "in order to protect these girls from the class of Mongolians who traffic in slaves, it has been necessary to maintain a guard constantly around their camp at the seminary. Otherwise . . . they would be stolen and returned to the slavery from which many of them have been rescued."[109] The danger seemed so acute that seminary professor Reverend Edward Wicher allowed his students to put down their books to guard "our Christian Chinese girls."[110] He praised his students for arresting "a villainous Chinese who was prowling about" the seminary. Did the Chinese visitor intend harm? Reverend Wicher never identified the prowler because it was easier for him to act on, rather than challenge, Chinatown's negative racial and gender stereotypes.[111] Perceptions of racialized danger, as Pascoe explains, were based on Victorian gender ideology that depicted men "in general as sexually aggressive creatures in need of female restraint."[112] Thus the vigilant protection of Chinese women after the disaster reinforced stereotypes of Chinese men as predators. Carrie Davis's Woman's Home Missionary Society also confirmed this view, stating that "the Chinese enslavers, though scattered, are still with us." The society hoped that "the destruction of San Francisco's worst blot, the old, vice-sodden Chinatown, will forever dissipate the organized crime rampant there."[113]

Thousands of Chinese lost more than their homes on April 18. Their community vanished and, with it, the safety of the neighborhood social networks that they relied on so heavily in their daily lives. Even the mission home leaders, who envisioned Chinatown as a dangerous place, recognized this loss. After Carrie Davis's group arrived safely in Berkeley, she was careful to keep the Chinese women and girls away from their new neighbors so that there was "no one to molest us or make us afraid, since we are far removed from any of the Chinese people."[114] Without the physical boundaries of Chinatown, which both protected Chinese residents and reinforced their racialized identity, refugees relied on pre-disaster social networks for support both in and outside the city. Their post-disaster migration would ultimately expand the Chinese presence in the Bay Area.

Nob Hill and the Western Addition

Ah Wing breathed a sigh of relief because the mansion was intact. "After the quake, I went all over upstairs, and found all the walls uninjured. All the statues and vases were on the floor, broken. The pictures hanging on the walls were unhurt." Maintaining the beautiful home was one of his many accomplishments in California. Leland Stanford counted on Wing's professional services for twenty-five years—a period of time during which Stanford completed the transcontinental railroad and founded Stanford University. It was Ah Wing who was there to put the pieces back together at the exquisite Nob Hill estate. But Wing couldn't stop the fires. He watched as "the wind blowing from Market Street drove the fire toward us like a tiger." He did not concede defeat until the estate next door caught fire. But his instinct for protecting the Stanfords' property continued to the end and he was mindful to lock the front door before he fled. With a note of sadness, Ah Wing "looked back and found that the Stanford House was in flame."[115]

When nothing was left to burn in South of Market, the fires blew into the better parts of town. High winds off the bay carried the flames up the waterfront near the Ferry Building, taking the conflagration to downtown. Westerly winds pushed the blazes toward the most prestigious neighborhood in the city, Nob Hill. The fires also crossed into the Western Addition, an up-and-coming neighborhood just one mile west of the Ferry Building. Losing their homes to fire came as a shock to these neighborhood residents. After all, their homes had withstood the earthquake. The earth did not open up and swallow entire buildings as it did in South of Market. Elite social status protected them as well. The mayor did everything in his power—diverting water supplies, blowing up buildings, and staging safety patrols—to save their homes. Although this effort did not save Nob Hill, it clearly stopped the fire's headway through the Western Addition.

For protection from earthquakes, Nob Hill was one of the safest places in San Francisco to live. Scientists later recorded that "on the rocky slopes and ridge tops, where, for the most part, the vibration communicated to buildings was that of the elastic underlying rocks, the destruction was at a minimum."[116] Although seismic protection was a benefit, the wealthiest San Franciscans first chose Nob Hill for its view, not its seismic-resistance qualities. The hill became fashionable in the 1870s, when new cable cars hoisted the city's elite to new heights. The railroad's Big Four—Leland Stanford, Charles Crocker, Collis Huntington, and Mark Hopkins—bejeweled the hill with their mansions. However, Nob Hill was more of an architectural statement than a neighborhood. The mansions, which one writer later described as "a mess of anachronisms," engulfed entire city blocks and left little real estate for single- or multifamily dwellings.[117] In 1906, Nob Hill claimed three valuable assets: panoramic views, high property values, and earthquake protection.

But the hill was not immune to fire. Once the blaze reached the base of Nob Hill, the winds took over. Mayor Schmitz supervised as the fire department's chief engineer drained water reserves to protect this valuable real estate. He was especially concerned with the Mark Hopkins Institute, saying he "was very desirous of saving" its "many very valuable paintings and sculptures."[118] The mayor found a cistern with forty thousand gallons of water and directed a fire engine to douse the Nob Hill wall facing Mason Street. But there was not enough water to quench the fire and Nob Hill succumbed to the flames. More so than in any other neighborhood, this loss was depicted as catastrophic for the city because the fires eliminated the most powerful representatives of San Francisco's visible landscape. As one journalist reported, "Nob Hill stands almost as bare as when it was primitive, rolling sand. The walls of the Flood building, a chimney of the Crocker home, alone remain to tell of the old landmarks."[119] Without the architectural evidence of San Francisco's instant progress, it seemed as though the disaster had pushed the city back in time.

Fire took the Western Addition by surprise as well. This had always been a safe neighborhood. From the stunning homes along Van Ness and on the hills of Pacific Heights to clusters of two- and three-story row houses, Western Addition real estate was more valuable than that of the South of Market or Mission Districts. The neighborhood claimed a wide swath of the city north of Market Street when it opened for residential construction in 1855. It stretched all the way from downtown to include the impressively broad Van Ness Avenue. The cable cars and electric streetcars made it easy, for the San Franciscans who could afford it, to live in a better neighborhood without losing access to downtown. By the time of the earthquake and fires, the Western Addition stood out as an upper-middle-class San Francisco neighborhood.[120]

Life was pleasant for many in the Western Addition before the calamity. Economic necessity did not force families to share their homes with relatives or rent-paying strangers. Not only could most families buy their own home; they could afford servants as well. Most of the men in the neighborhood were merchants or employed by merchants, and they left the neighborhood for work downtown each morning. Although downtown was just a streetcar ride away, women did not need to travel far in order to find good shopping. Polk Street, Western Addition's commercial center, was lined with small shops and stores. A high proportion of the neighborhood's residents were German, many of whom were Jewish. San Francisco's instant-city past meant that the Jewish elite in San Francisco did not compete for status with an older,

Gentile elite. "By virtue of their early arrival and economic success," Mary Ann Irwin explains, "German Jewish immigrants to San Francisco gained an almost instant certification as Americans."[121] German immigrants spread out when they arrived in San Francisco, choosing to settle by religion rather than nationality. German Catholics put down roots in the Mission District, surrounded by working-class Irish Catholic families. German Jews, on the other hand, moved to the north side of Market Street. The city's oldest and most successful Jewish families—the Gerstles, Slosses, and Lilienthals—built elegant homes along Van Ness Avenue.[122] Then fire crept into the Western Addition from almost every direction. The South of Market and Nob Hill fires moved in from the south and east, while several smaller fires started inside the neighborhood.

In an interesting turn of events, one fire, and one woman, took the blame for burning some of the most valuable buildings in the Western Addition. From its humble origins in a Hayes Valley home, a single fire spread to burn St. Ignatius Church, the civic auditorium called Mechanics' Pavilion (which had become a temporary medical evacuation center), and many homes along Van Ness Avenue. Reporters and residents alike called it the "Ham and Eggs Fire" because it was allegedly started by a woman cooking breakfast in her kitchen. The widely circulated tale accused the woman of foolishly cooking breakfast right after the earthquake struck (when gas lines were potentially damaged). Before long, the small kitchen fire engulfed nearby buildings, making the fire an urban legend of sorts. The often repeated story transformed over time, and eventually, cooking breakfast on that fateful morning became a criminal act. One resident recalled, "She disobeyed the law and went in and started cooking on her stove, and that area started blazing."[123] There was indeed a citywide ban on indoor cooking after the disaster. But this came later, long after the Ham and Eggs Fire. Why was one woman accused of burning down the Western Addition (especially when that particular fire was like dozens of others that ignited on the morning of April 18)?[124] This tale is reminiscent of that of Chicago's legendary Mrs. O'Leary, who, with the help of her ornery cow, was held responsible for burning that city down. San Francisco's gendered fire story curbed fears of the city's vulnerability to disaster. It was safer to blame the fires on a woman cooking breakfast than to acknowledge that damage from the earthquake and raging inferno might be linked to urban infrastructure that had suffered ruptured gas lines and failed water mains.

Evacuating was a difficult decision for many Western Addition residents; homeowners were reluctant to abandon their property prematurely. As on Nob Hill, earthquake damage in the Western Addition was minimal. Ernest and Bella Lilienthal watched as the "chandeliers swayed back and forth, and part of the molding of the ceilings cracked and dropped. The grandfather clock in the upper hall fell on its face."[125] Residents had plenty of time to survey their own property damage and check on their neighbors. They even had time to prepare for the fire. Helen Hillyer Brown, who lived on Van Ness Avenue, found that her home "stood the blow and wrench" of earthquake

San Franciscans watching the fires from Lafayette Square, circa April 18, 1906.
Lafayette Square later became one of the city's twenty-six relief camps. (See
Chapter 5.) (Courtesy of the San Francisco Virtual Museum.)

"exceedingly well." The Browns stayed home that day and "from time to
time" they "went on the roof to watch the progress of the fire."[126] Charles
Elkus, who lived on Pacific Street, recalled, "In the later afternoon people
in our vicinity began to wonder whether they would stay in their houses or
go up to Alta Plaza and stay there overnight. A great number of people did
go."[127] The Browns believed their home would protect them from the distant
inferno. But they gave up hope at 2:00 A.M. on Thursday, May 19. One last
check from the roof convinced Helen Brown that "everything was looking
pretty bad [and] we decided to pack. . . . Everybody was pretty discouraged
and blue by this time."[128]

As they walked away from their property, some Western Addition homeowners did not feel an immediate sense of loss. Loyal servants who stayed
behind allowed families to depart for safer ground with the confidence that
someone was watching their property. Charles Elkus and his family, for example, were safely ensconced at Alta Plaza while their "Chinese cook remained
home to take care of the house."[129] Homeowners could also count on military
troops for protection. Under consultation with Mayor Schmitz and Chief of
Police Dinan, General Funston sent troops to the Western Addition every
evening to "patrol the wealthy residence district west of Van Ness Avenue, in
order to prevent robbery or disorder by the vast throngs being driven thither
by the progress of the fire."[130]

Unlike those in South of Market, some Western Addition residents had
a second home to fall back on. They left San Francisco for the safety of their

Refugees walking down Market Street to the Ferry Building. Many encountered panic on the piers as thousands flocked to the ferryboats that ran nonstop to Oakland and Marin County. (Courtesy of the San Francisco Virtual Museum.)

summer homes, both north and south of the city. But getting there was not easy. There was panic on the piers as thousands of San Franciscans flocked to the ferryboats. The ferry docks may well have been one location where the general fear of social disorder was accurate—but not the kind of social chaos associated with South of Market's working-class refugees. When the official call rang out for women and babies to board first, some abandoned social etiquette. "'Oh, the women and babies—the women and babies!' We are tired of hearing this kind of thing," was a collective cry heard on one ferry landing. "This brutality was not displayed by people of rough exterior," recalled one woman waiting for East Bay transport, "but by well dressed men and women."[131] Some wealthier San Franciscans were able to avoid the ferries altogether. Robert Hall boarded a steamer acquired "through the aid of influential friends." In a letter to his sister, he described being spared from two dangers, the fires and the crowd of refugees: "Our party went on board the steamer, the whistle blew, and we were saved. Water separated us from the fire and the mob." Safety was attained at his family country home north of San Francisco, where, he reassuringly wrote to his sister, he was "breathing pure air, drinking pure water, smelling the aroma of flowers, [and] hearing the birds sing."[132]

The Western Addition was well poised for full recovery. First, much of the neighborhood was spared from the fires. Second, homeowners had financial resources for rebuilding. Further, Western Addition's Polk Street briefly enjoyed commercial prominence as the "new Market Street" during the rebuilding period. Nearby in the Mission District, social class tempered a Western Addition–style encounter with calamity. In this area, residents stayed and fought the flames, knowing it was their best chance at preserving their way of life.

The Mission District

> Florence Sylvester was on duty at the San Francisco Maternity Hospital when the earthquake struck. "It was a long, wavy back and forth movement, nothing jerky about it" was how she described the seismic event. This was a community, not an individual, experience. "South of Mission Street propriety would not over-rule fear as it might in other parts of the city, and the women stood around in front of their doors half dressed, with a big shawl, or warm petticoat and kerchief around their head, talking and gesticulating, and telling of their experiences."[133] Soon these Mission District residents banded together to protect their neighborhood from fire as well as shelter their friends and relatives escaping South of Market.

The Mission District, like South of Market, had pockets of made ground. The ill-fated Valencia Street Hotel was built on swampland at Valencia and Eighteenth Streets. After the first seismic tremors, the hotel sank three stories into the earth, leaving only the fourth floor aboveground. The few survivors who escaped onto the roof said that at least two hundred others were trapped below.[134] James D. Phelan, former San Francisco mayor, witnessed the horrific scene.[135] But there was nothing that could be done for anyone on the first few floors. Fortunately, most of the Mission District was built on solid ground, making the neighborhood more vulnerable to fire than earthquake.

The encroaching inferno posed a serious threat to the Mission District. Firefighters tried dynamite, but to no avail. "I saw the fire at Mission and 15th Streets," recalled James Phelan. "Dynamite was being used to blow up buildings in the path of the flames, on the south east side of Mission Street, but the dynamiting was done too close to the actual fire, and the wreckage, caused by the dynamite, soon ignited, and the fire went on."[136] Local residents did a better job. Thousands of volunteers used water and wet sacks to stop the fire from crossing Dolores Street. Residents passed milk cans filled with water and broke down small houses along Twentieth Street to create an invaluable firebreak.[137] Their ability to work in unison to stop the fire had everything to do with the neighborhood in which they lived.

The Mission District was a few blocks west of South of Market and a step up for Irish and German working-class families. By 1902, streetcars running up Mission Street allowed families to venture farther from work to buy or rent single-family and two-family homes. Despite sharing its western border and many relatives with the South of Market District, the Mission was a different sort of neighborhood. Skilled jobs in the trades or low-level white-collar positions brought more money in the door for many residents. Most families could afford to live on their own, avoiding the overcrowding that came with sharing mortgage or rent costs. Working-class families forged new lives as they moved out of South of Market and into the Mission. There was a high proportion of two-parent households (81 percent) in which most women did not need to work for wages. As in South of Market, residents had everything they needed within walking distance: schools, churches, fraternal halls, and social clubs. But here the schools were a little nicer and the parks a little bigger. Although Catholics constituted a religious majority in the Mission District, the area included a variety of churches. This was a place for families. Not only were there fewer single men than in South of Market, but they were of higher economic standing. For the most part, single men in the Mission were downtown professionals who were busy saving money before starting a family. Thus the Mission District offered a different male social world. Instead of regular meetings at the local saloon, for example, men gathered at the local fraternal or Masonic hall.[138]

Unlike the Western Addition's experience, in the Mission District the active social networks checked the spread of fire. Neighbors met in the street to share personal experiences and decide how to protect their neighborhood from further damage. Mission District resident F. Ernest Edwards led the search for working fire hydrants in the area. "I made my way quickly along 19th to Dolores, opening every hydrant I came to," read Edwards's statement. As he walked up Twentieth Street, he told everyone he met that he was looking for water to fight the fires. This was when Edwards learned that "people had been getting water on the side of the hill."[139] Edwards discovered the Mission District's most important working hydrant. He notified the fire department by sending a note to a fire chief by "a man on a big black horse" and urging a friend on a bicycle to "tell any fireman he saw with a white helmet where the water was."[140] Residents worked side by side with firefighters to pump water from that single hydrant at Church and Twentieth Streets as well as draft water from a cistern on Nineteenth and Shotwell Streets.[141] As a result, the conflagration made little headway into the Mission District. After burning a four-block path from Dolores to Folsom Streets, the fire was extinguished at 7:00 P.M. on April 20.[142]

Mission District residents had several advantages that mitigated fire damage. First and foremost, they had time and distance from the seat of the blaze. Aside from the surprising earthquake tragedy at the Valencia Street Hotel, people had time to plan their fire attack. Unlike residents of the Western Addition, most could not flee to their summer homes or rely on servants to watch their property. They had little choice but to stay and fight. Their success ultimately created a neighborhood refuge. Not surprisingly, the Mission District's largest park sheltered exhausted disaster survivors. But neighborhood residents welcomed refugees as well. Peter Maloney, who owned a horse-shoeing business, opened his home on Twenty-fourth Street to disaster

A man dragging salvaged possessions. San Franciscans grabbed what they could before they escaped from the fires. (Courtesy of the San Francisco Virtual Museum.)

survivors. After spending the night of April 18 sleeping "out on the street," Minnie Coleman heard about the Maloneys and knocked on their door. She was invited to stay even though the women and children had to sleep sideways across the mattresses in order to fit four or five to each bed.[143] The Mission District's organized response to the fire presented a stark contrast to the last neighborhood to succumb to the flames. While North Beach's Italian enclave had plenty of time to prepare, the neighborhood was nevertheless surprised by a conflagration that had, at first, passed them by.

North Beach

> *The Tarantinos prayed the fire would not come. There was nowhere to run when half of their Italian neighborhood was beachfront property. And even if they could, it would not be an easy task to lead their entire extended family to safety. From grandmothers to babies, they counted dozens in their San Francisco clan. But they were the lucky ones—not simply because they survived the fire but because Mr. Tarantino owned a fishing tug that carried the family far away from the burning city.*

North Beach's rocky terrain protected it from earthquake, but not fire. The loss of Nob Hill created a panic, with fire suppression leaders calling for more dynamite to stop the inferno in its tracks. Soldiers ran west to dynamite buildings well ahead of the fires. But they paid a steep price for stopping the flames on Van Ness Avenue. Dynamite and winds pushed the blaze east, and the fires left the Western Addition for the previously unscathed North Beach.[144] Hidden safely behind Telegraph Hill and Russian Hill, most of North Beach's residents remained in or near their homes during the disaster. Few Italians anticipated that the fires would reverse course and race toward their neighborhood on the night of April 20. Unfortunately, North Beach's poorly constructed wood-frame housing, which had offered the lowest rents in San Francisco since the 1860s, provided ample fuel for the blaze.[145] More than thirty thousand Italians awaited their fate on the waterfront as exhausted firefighters turned their attention to their neighborhood.[146] Regrettably, hundreds lost their lives as flames devoured property from Mason to Battery Streets.

North Beach was clearly Italian by 1906. At first the neighborhood was called the Latin Quarter because it attracted immigrants from Italy, Mexico, Peru, and Chile.[147] But skyrocketing Italian immigration at the end of the century transformed the area. Men, not families, came to San Francisco, and women tallied only one in every ten Italian immigrants during the nineteenth century.[148] Most men fished in the bay waters just off North Beach or farmed undeveloped parts of San Francisco. Each profession was associated with a particular region in the home country (Sicilian fishermen, Ligurian farmers, and so on). North Beach had a distinct regional spirit, or "*campanilismo*," with immigrants from the same region, and even the same village, living and working together.[149] *Campanilismo* shielded them from the negative stereotypes assigned to Italians. The meaning of race was the topic of turn-of-the-century national debate and was subject to local interpretation. Nationwide, Italian immigrants were marked by racial difference.[150] Such views permeated San Francisco as well, and strong unions pushed the Italian laborers out while urban elites gave them the cold shoulder. This, in turn, made it easier for the tight-knit neighborhood to band together to face the disaster.

North Beach residents and city firefighters struggled to protect the neighborhood. As the fires approached, soldiers were directed to evacuate residents. Residents on Russian Hill, a small residential area just above North Beach, fought both the fires and the soldiers to save their homes. Henry Lafler, assistant editor of the San Francisco newspaper the *Argonaut*, was highly critical of the military's response. He documented how homeowners used "wet blankets, rugs, and carpets with small quantities of water that had previously been collected in pails and bath-tubs" to save their homes. But in doing so, they defied soldiers, who had ordered them to leave the area.[151] By April 20, city firefighters were exhausted. Lafler also reported seeing a fire hose with "its nozzle pointed up by means of a box and two bricks, playing uselessly into the middle of the street." The firefighters stopped to rest and took "cheese and olives and canned goods, and plenty of alcoholics to drink" from an abandoned grocery store.[152] Navy crews continued to work and pumped a new water supply from the bay, saving a few waterfront warehouses and piers. The navy, and the bay water supply, eventually tipped the firefighting in the city's favor and smothered the fires in North Beach. This brought an end to the fires not only in North Beach but in the city as well. After three days of fire, San Francisco's greatest catastrophe was officially over on Saturday, April 21.

The calamity exposed yet another isolated ethnic enclave in San Francisco. Many fled north, using their fishing vessels for transport.[153] However, they were met with suspicion in Sausalito, the first town north of the city. Sausalito residents organized a coast watch due to "fear of the crowds escaping from San Francisco."[154] They cautiously greeted four thousand refugees, who quickly outnumbered the town's residents. "The morning of the earthquake they came over in droves!" recalled one Sausalito resident. "Every shelter that was available they filled." Many Italian families fled to a cove called Seafirth, where they returned to their daily routines, starting work early each morning, the husbands fishing in the cold bay waters and the wives baking loaves of bread from dough left rising in the night.[155] Meanwhile, town leaders closed the saloons and deputized their male citizens for protection.[156] The *San Francisco Chronicle* reassured its readers that most of the North Beach refugees in Sausalito were "quiet and tractable" once they were relieved "of the strong red wine."[157] The newspaper report's association of red wine with Italian refugees, like the response of Sausalito civic leaders, recapitulated popular ethnic stereotypes.

Not everyone from North Beach remained along the shores of Sausalito. The Tarantino family went farther north to the inland town of Fairfax. Mr. Tarantino, who supplied fish and poultry to a local hotel restaurant, approached the hotel owner and asked permission for his family to camp in the yard outside the establishment. After securing approval, Tarantino surprised the hotel proprietor by transporting eighty relatives from North Beach by fishing tug and train. "It was like a circus," the hotel owner's daughter recalled. "It was an army of children—mothers ready to bear children—fathers, grandfathers, very old, old, weeping people scared to death. . . . Well we had no room for accommodations. But they were smart, they brought tents."[158] For three months, the Tarantinos lived outdoors in the Marin County countryside. By temporarily relocating their extended family outside San Francisco, the Tarantinos avoided the scrutiny of disaster relief policy makers. This strategic move helped them return to and rebuild in North Beach with their family network and ethnic ties intact.

The Italians who remained in San Francisco met with a very different experience. These Italians, the elderly and the poor in particular, sought refuge in San Francisco's relief camps, where they faced a whole new array of hardships under new relief policies. Meanwhile, more-fortunate Italians turned to relatives and North Beach business leaders for financial help. The astute banker Amadeo Peter Giannini was instrumental in funding North Beach's recovery. The speed with which Giannini opened his Bank of Italy for business after the disaster and made loans to locals helped many, especially the Italians in North

Beach, to rebuild their businesses and homes. The well-known success story of Giannini's Bank of Italy—later, Bank of America—reveals how *campanilismo*, not disaster relief, would bring the vibrant North Beach back to life.[159]

After the smoke cleared, reporters and observers alike put a positive spin on the catastrophe. Most agreed that the disaster was a social equalizer and that class and racial barriers had crumbled alongside San Francisco's buildings. Emma Burke, writing for *Overlook Magazine*, idealized disaster survivors: "All artificial restraints of our civilization fell away with the earthquake's shocks. Every man was his brother's keeper. Everyone spoke to everyone else with a smile."[160] Such musings over the benefits of disaster were hardly new. In 1871, both journalists and religious leaders proclaimed that the Chicago Fire burned away social barriers and sin.[161] Another San Francisco reporter's vivid anecdote suggested that the disaster bridged the gap between ethnic differences. The *San Francisco Examiner* story described how an Italian mother, desperate to soothe her crying infant, called out in broken English, "'No milk here since the earthquake scare me so hard.'" Aid soon arrived, the story went on, in the form of a "fat, motherly young Irishwoman with a bouncing boy on her arm [who] stopped on her weary journey to the ferry. 'I've got enough for two,' she laughed. 'Give me the kid. There darlint [sic], take your dinner.' And Italy drained the milk of human kindness at Erin's fount."[162] The journalist played gender and ethnic stereotypes to the hilt to show how women's maternal roles bridged social differences after the disaster. The outlandish story reassured readers that their city, like the hungry infant, would be nursed back to health. But in 1906 San Francisco, the social equalizer narrative masked the persistence of social segregation that existed before and after the calamity. If anything, the catastrophe accentuated pre-disaster social differences while emergency response reified them.

A close examination of earthquake damage and burn patterns reveals that the 1906 earthquake was as socially stratified as the city of San Francisco itself. Nature, urban construction, and social attitudes conspired to make it so, and emergency response added yet another layer of loss. This helps to explain why the disaster played out so differently in each residential neighborhood. Chinatown refugees undoubtedly faced the greatest difficulties as they lost the invaluable physical protection of their neighborhood to fire. Without their familiar neighborhood boundaries in place, they became walking symbols of racial difference in a city already uncomfortable with their presence. The disaster heightened social class fears as well. The working class and poor who dragged their few possessions out of South of Market, as well as the poor Italians who lost their homes in North Beach, raised a general alarm of social disorder.

The San Franciscans who witnessed the failed attempts at fire suppression by trained professionals must have wondered if disaster relief would come to their aid after the city stopped burning. Yet despite a nonexistent disaster plan, an organized relief effort cleaned up after the earthquake and fires when the American National Red Cross sent scientific experts to assess damage, investigate need, and write relief policy. In many ways, relief policy reinforced pre-disaster social hierarchies by advantaging property owners over non–property owners, failing to support Chinese survivors, and evaluating poor and working-class refugees by middle-class standards. Consequently, many disaster survivors faced another sequence of social dislocation as they encountered disaster relief.

CHAPTER 2

Disaster Relief

Local Troubles, National Solutions

San Francisco became a city of the homeless in a matter of days. Residents scattered everywhere; the 100,000 who refused to leave the city camped in their yards or dragged their belongings to parks, vacant lots, and beachfronts. Some of those without family and friends nearby took refuge in old trolley cars, voting booths, and empty cisterns. The mayor declared martial law while soldiers struggled to guard property and hand out the relief supplies that poured into the city. At first, giving aid was nearly as chaotic as dealing with the disaster. The breadlines stretched for blocks, and thousands, residents and visitors alike, made daily trips to the city, which only added to the confusion. While hundreds volunteered to assist refugees, most of San Francisco's newest arrivals came not to help but to take pictures and collect disaster souvenirs.

Like San Francisco, the United States was unprepared for the 1906 catastrophe. Federal disaster relief had been either ad hoc or negligible for the preceding century.[1] In the absence of a standard relief policy, disaster survivors initially turned to family and friends instead of seeking state or federal support. But local political, business, and charity leaders, all of whom worked closely with the American National Red Cross and social work experts, soon formed San Francisco Relief and Red Cross Funds, an organization that brought order out of chaos. In the end, this relief policy altered San Francisco's physical landscape almost as much as the earthquake and fires had.

The 1906 calamity was a watershed moment for the recently reincorporated American National Red Cross. President Theodore Roosevelt dispatched Red Cross leaders from Washington, D.C., to distribute the $2.5 million congressional emergency appropriation.[2] Red Cross experts brought a Progressive

Era agenda to San Francisco, where they pushed new scientific social work methods into the cracks and crevasses of the post-disaster city. Scholars continue to debate a precise definition of Progressivism, but most agree that it had political, intellectual, and cultural strands focused on ameliorating the effects of industrialization.[3] As Daniel Rodgers describes Progressive reformers, they "swam in a sudden abundance of solutions" in their attempt to humanize and regulate the conditions of industrial life.[4] Indeed, the disaster zone provided a valuable laboratory to test new scientific social work theories. And the power to do so only expanded as the pool of relief donations swelled to $9.5 million. The underlying goal of the reformers was straightforward: create social order by funding the return of San Francisco's property owners and its professional workforce to their pre-disaster social status. Financed by millions and facilitated by experts, San Francisco's 1906 disaster relief was heralded by many as a victory for the emerging field of social work.

The professionalization of social work was well under way by the time the 1906 disaster occurred. The founding of the U.S. Sanitary Commission in 1862 marked the first major shift in the philosophy and structure of antebellum charity organizations. The Sanitary Commission departed from idealistic antebellum philanthropy by replacing empathetic volunteers with efficient paid agents. As George Fredrickson describes it, the commission's often "hardhearted" approach to philanthropy used science to justify its emphasis on discipline and efficiency.[5] Professionalization made a leap forward in the 1870s with the charity organization movement, which systematized social services to the poor by minimizing material aid and replacing it with spiritual and moral uplift. Middle-class white women served a dual role as friendly visitors, investigating need and offering moral support and self-improvement encouragement to the poor.

Yet another shift came in the 1890s, when charity organization leaders explored the idea that poverty was caused not by moral failure but by economic forces.[6] The settlement house movement, in which reformers worked within the boundaries of impoverished neighborhoods, shed new light on poverty's causes and cure. This work coincided with opportunities for formal education in social work, which used new social science research methods to turn friendly visitors into well-educated caseworkers.[7] The 1906 earthquake struck as this transition was in progress, and what transpired in the disaster zone provides insight into the conversion of nineteenth-century approaches to charity to twentieth-century social work methodologies.

Disaster relief leaders and volunteers arrived in the smoke-and-dust-filled disaster zone where soldiers and recently deputized men carried loaded rifles, making their adaptation of Progressive relief methodology difficult. In the translation from policy to practice, the objective, bureaucratic standards of twentieth-century scientific social work were blended with nineteenth-century notions of charity that included moral assessment and personal involvement. San Francisco provides an illustrative example of what Robert Crunden calls "innovative nostalgia," or the tendency among Progressive reformers to cling to nineteenth-century ideas of moral reform even as they espoused the objectivity of twentieth-century scientific methods.[8] Even though the 1906 disaster acted as a catalyst for scientific social work, relief policy nonetheless supported a subjective approach toward aiding those in need.

THE BROKEN CITY

The mayor of San Francisco, while working closely with the military, continued to take direct action after the conflagration ended. Within days of the catastrophe, Mayor Eugene Schmitz denied access by ferry or train to sightseers and supported the military's division of the city into seven emergency districts. The military guarded property and pushed refugees out of the disaster zone and into military relief camps. At that point, few publicly protested the military's presence in the city. William James, who was a visiting scholar at Stanford University at the time, applauded the "rapidity of the improvisation of order out of chaos" that he observed on his expedition to the disaster zone.[9] The military presence was reassuring for anyone concerned that the catastrophe had created social disorder. But military intervention was a temporary solution. Civic leaders turned to relief experts, and Progressive disaster relief, to inculcate a new sense of order.

One of the mayor's first responses to the disaster was his infamous shoot-to-kill proclamation. The stark order to "KILL any and all persons found engaged in Looting or in the Commission of Any Other Crime" was posted on unburned edifices throughout the city as well as printed in local newspapers. Almost every historical and popular account of the 1906 catastrophe cites this order as evidence of criminal activity and social chaos after the disaster.[10] A cursory reading of the city's major newspaper headlines would seem to justify the mayor's denial of civil liberties—"Looters Busy Among the Ruins," "Looters Overrun Ruins of Burnt San Francisco," "14 Men Shot and Killed."[11] Yet Schmitz issued his shoot-to-kill order prior to any reports of criminal activity. The mayor envisioned the proclamation as a preventive measure to protect the city from the social chaos he assumed was inevitable. When he first arrived in the disaster zone on April 18, the pragmatic Schmitz justified the order by saying, "We would have no place in which to keep prisoners if we arrested any."[12]

The new military zones reinforced the mayor's command over civic order. San Francisco's distinct neighborhoods became the template for seven emergency districts. South of Market, North Beach, and the Mission District were converted into three emergency districts. This meant that military personnel controlled how, and sometimes when, refugees accessed the burned sections of their neighborhoods. Post-disaster redistricting was more complicated for Chinatown. Military leaders eliminated Chinatown's distinct neighborhood boundaries by merging the area with Nob Hill and the Western Addition. This was in keeping with popular anti-Chinese sentiment. Even before the fire, local political and business leaders sought to eliminate Chinatown's fifteen-block habitation of prime real estate.[13] The emergency district, then, was a precursor to a raging post-disaster battle over Chinatown's place in the rebuilt city. Brigadier General Frederick Funston reassured the mayor that soldiers maintained a careful watch over city neighborhoods by ordering his seven district commanders to "protect the property and keep order in [their] district[s]."[14]

Protecting property and maintaining order was, at times, a subjective exercise. Along the sandy northern shoreline of Black Point, near Chinatown and Russian Hill, refugees made beds from the blankets and bedsheets they had dragged to the beaches filled with their prized possessions.[15] Once safe on the beach, they faced armed soldiers shouting for them to vacate the area. The evacuation order, however, was not intended for everyone. When questioned, one soldier admitted that "these demonstrations were really intended to frighten the Chinese and Japanese into moving." A native-born refugee noticed that "after each session of such vociferation a few more orientals abandoned their stopping places and crept away."[16] White homeowners, on the other hand, camped on the beach near their earthquake-damaged homes without comment from the soldiers. This simple privilege during the disaster was later reinforced by relief policy that strongly favored native-born property owners.

Army and National Guard patrols made returning to the disaster zone lethal for some. Stories of looting and social chaos were sensational front-page news, which put anxious soldiers on high alert. One National Guardsman wrote to his father, "They kept us busy breaking into saloons and putting the liquors into the St[reet]s, and keeping the Italians in order." On patrol in the South of Market District, he shot at a suspicious-looking man who was searching for something on the ground. The shot missed its mark and the frightened refugee ran. The National Guardsman looked on as another soldier aimed and fired. "When the two of us reached the fallen man," wrote the National Guardsman, "we found he had been shot through the neck and was stone dead. It proved to be a negro." An officer ordered them to throw the unidentified body into "the still burning ruins, so in it went."[17] For the most part, events such as these escaped the public record. Only the candor of a young National Guardsmen writing to his father suggests the possibility of escalating violence against racial and ethnic minorities in San Francisco at that time. That his duties included keeping "the Italians in order" and burning the remains of an African American civilian illustrates how soldiers and armed guards had the means and opportunity to suppress far more than fire.

The battle to maintain social order moved almost as swiftly as the fires. Mayor Schmitz convened the city's first official emergency relief organization, called the Citizens' Committee or the Committee of 50. With the loss of City Hall, this ad hoc committee became the symbolic seat of political order.[18]

A government-based relief committee was not novel. Urban catastrophes, from Chicago's 1871 Great Fire to Galveston's devastating 1900 hurricane, employed similar ad hoc committees to address urban recovery.[19] In a matter of days the Committee of 50 ballooned to 134 members who staffed

Men and boys clearing debris as ordered by soldiers deployed to the disaster zone, 1906. (Courtesy of the San Francisco Virtual Museum.)

twenty-one subcommittees.[20] The male-dominated leadership relied on contemporary social hierarchies to reestablish order as they tackled everything from restoring utilities to the resumption of the judiciary. For example, they gave all qualified male citizens the responsibility of protecting their neighborhoods. All "able bodied" men were required to register "for patrol duty in their respective blocks." And when men were not policing, they were put to work. Soldiers ordered "every available man" to help repair downtown streets.[21] As one survivor wrote to her sister, "All the men that pass are grabbed by soldiers and forced to go to work. So Pa and Mr. Sport are always very busy fixing bricks, sweeping the streets and taking our ash barrels out. (Regular scavengers.) All the men are working this way."[22] New civic responsibilities were not limited to adult white males; they included boys as well. Boys became a critical information network for the Committee of 50, which asked them "to distribute circulars in their own neighborhoods."[23] By turning to male citizens to protect and repair the city in this way, the mayor's committees reinforced pre-disaster social hierarchies.

As the military set to work building relief camps, family and neighborhood networks continued to offer support to refugees in need. As one working-class refugee wrote, "We collected a committee on our grounds to get food for the people in our camp, The Camp Bryant, after the street we are on and we are getting along nicely."[24] But the new military camps allowed officials to shut down the informal encampments throughout the city. Near the end of May, Red Cross representative Edward T. Devine cut off relief rations to Jewish families camping on San Bruno Road and forced their relocation to Golden Gate Park, "where the others are that came from the same part of town."[25] Public health inspectors joined military personnel in policing refugees. Since the nineteenth century, public health had provided an effective means to regulate urban social order.[26] This was also the case in San Francisco, and within one week of the earthquake, the Board of Health appointed five hundred volunteer physicians as sanitary inspectors.[27] As one relief administrator later summarized, they lent "sanitary and moral protection to a large body of persons living under abnormal conditions."[28] "Moral protection" was a loosely defined goal left to the individual interpretation of sanitary inspectors. One public health inspector, for example, recommended relocating "a camp composed of 45 people, mostly colored" to Fort Mason despite the fact that the camp passed inspection.[29] City inspectors initially assumed that sanitary conditions on Telegraph Hill would "not be entirely satisfactory until the Mexicans and Italians on top of the Hill are removed from their present quarters."[30] However, these refugees were spared eviction by a Spanish-speaking military guard who translated sanitation requirements. When the inspectors returned three days later, they found that the refugees had "at least heeded their instructions."[31] It is likely that the Telegraph Hill camp remained until the completion of additional military camps. Throughout May and June, relief leaders questioned the autonomy of refugees camping in the city and did what they could to bring an end to family and neighborhood encampments.

A family living in one of the many temporary encampments in San Francisco, 1906. Once the military built official relief camps, refugees came under increasing scrutiny. (Courtesy of the San Francisco Virtual Museum.)

Despite military backing and a growing relief fund, initial relief efforts were deficient in many ways. The Committee of 50's general orders, for example, promised meat, fresh vegetables, and staples to all refugees starting May 1, 1906, less than two weeks after the disaster.[32] But the rations hardly lived up to this description. A disappointed mother walked her rations to the chief sanitary inspector's office and confronted him with her weekly allotment for a family of seven: a handful of vegetables that were either bruised or covered with "coal oil or some oily substance," one package of contaminated tea, and one three-pound piece of meat "which has been fly-blown and is in an advanced state of decomposition."[33]

Inadequate supplies were the Achilles' heel of early relief efforts, as they served to strengthen existing family and neighborhood networks that the Committee of 50 sought to subvert. Refugees who gathered at the homes of their friends and relatives pooled their resources and cooked collectively. During the citywide ban on indoor cooking, makeshift outdoor kitchens lined the streets in front of undamaged homes. Some families joined together for their outdoor meals, and for a period of time, some slept outdoors. Residents on Ashbury Street wrote a humorous newsletter about their experiences. "Since we have become 'quakers,'" read one newsletter item, "the residents of Ashbarrel St. have built very unique kitchens in the middle of the street." They shared recipes for pancakes ("they can be used as post cards if not eaten"), threw card parties, and took note of how "a great number of our charming neighbors" left the city to live elsewhere.[34] Their humor perhaps reflected their fortunate status as homeowners distant from the disaster zone. Most refugees, on the other hand, felt less secure about where their next meal was coming from. As one San Franciscan explained to her sister about why they stood in line for relief rations, "Not that we need it, personally, but we can never tell when somebody that we know will apply to us for shelter and so we take all the food that we can get."[35] This approach to relief foreshadowed events during the summer of 1906, when refugees confronted disaster relief officials and demanded control of the entire relief fund.

THE POLITICS OF DISASTER RELIEF

The city's political elite soon began to view the disaster as an opportunity. Mayor Eugene Schmitz used the catastrophe to increase his political power and his bank account, but the new disaster relief policy and programs challenged his political potency. Former mayor James Phelan's Finance Committee tethered the provisions for emergency relief—food, clothing, and shelter—to a Progressive vision of social and political order. Phelan's committee united business leaders and Red Cross social work experts in a common goal: help disaster refugees while improving the environment in which they lived. They envisioned disaster relief as extending beyond basic needs to alterations to San Francisco's social and political landscape.

The ideological and personal differences between Schmitz and Phelan were readily apparent in their responses to the disaster. A third-term Union Labor Party (ULP) mayor envisioning life in the governor's mansion, the well-groomed, affable Schmitz was a deft politician. He had replaced James Phelan as mayor in 1901. Phelan, a pro-business, Progressive member of the "lace curtain Irish" (or Irish immigrants who found economic success in San Francisco), had temporarily won the support of labor; however, his working-class political base crumbled after he authorized police protection for strike-breakers in the 1901 City Front strike, a violent confrontation that would eventually give rise to pivotal trade union reforms.[36] Phelan felt the heat of 16,000 angry teamsters and waterfront workers, who joined the ranks of the newly formed Union Labor Party during the summer of 1901. They put Eugene Schmitz, a German and Irish Catholic president of the Musicians' Union, on the ballot and he won his first of three mayoral elections (1901, 1903, 1905) with support from the working-class South of Market neighborhood.[37]

While the Schmitz era of San Francisco politics is well-traveled terrain, the earthquake's timing warrants a brief synopsis in these pages. After the 1905 election, the ULP controlled the mayor's office and claimed all eighteen seats of the Board of Supervisors.[38] Although the major county officers were elected (district attorney, sheriff, county clerk, assessor, and superintendent of public schools), members of the board of public works, police commissioners, and education served at the mayor's discretion. In 1906, all of the city's major services—water, electricity, gas, and public transportation—were privately run. Under the guidance of Abraham Ruef, the mayor's close personal friend and political confidant, Schmitz amassed a small fortune from his municipal contracts. The Schmitz-Ruef regime appeared invincible through the 1905 election. However, change was afoot. James Phelan and *San Francisco Bulletin* managing editor Fremont Older, who often criticized the ULP administration in print, won support for a federal graft investigation.[39] But then the 1906 earthquake incapacitated the graft investigation, and Schmitz seemed indestructible.

San Francisco's misfortune increased the mayor's power, freeing Schmitz from legislative accountability to the Board of Supervisors and relieving him from the scrutiny of his political enemies. Even the newspapers once so highly critical of him were impressed by his post-disaster command. As one editorial declared, "Schmitz met it manfully, energetically, and wisely."[40] Astonishingly, Fremont Older's *San Francisco Bulletin* temporarily suspended its scathing attacks and declared that the mayor's leadership "merited unqualified admiration."[41] But Schmitz did not need to read the daily press to measure public support for what he imagined as his single-handed rule of the burning city. He proudly recited an incident during the fire when he ended the "conflict of authority" between the fire department and federal troops to stop the fires along Van Ness Avenue "amid cheers."[42] For the orchestra conductor turned mayor, the catastrophe was the performance of a lifetime.

"In the months after the earthquake," one writer recalled, Schmitz "often said that his life began on the 18th of April."[43]

But the mayor struggled to maintain control of his city when emergency response ended and disaster relief began. While Schmitz was basking in his role as city savior, his political nemesis, James Phelan, was returning to political power riding on the back of disaster relief. Schmitz gave control of the relief Finance Committee to Phelan, perhaps in hopes of curtailing Phelan's support for the federal graft investigation.[44] Schmitz could hardly foresee that the Finance Committee would become the most influential organization in the city.[45] As Phelan later recalled, "We did not anticipate, at that time, that the city would be the recipient of large donations of money and supplies from all over the state and country."[46] Managing millions in relief dollars made Phelan a worthy rival for the mayor, giving Phelan the opportunity to offer a Progressive counterpoint to Schmitz's ULP San Francisco.

Phelan's Finance Committee was the hub for all major relief policy decisions. Undoubtedly he benefited from the nonexistence of federal relief legislation. In a letter to his uncle in New York, Phelan clearly outlined his control over the relief fund: "Our policy is to have the money [donations] deposited to my credit as Chairman of the Finance Committee of Relief and Red Cross Funds before we definitely plan for its beneficial use for the relief of San Francisco."[47] At first, Phelan prohibited any relief expenditures without his direct approval. One Red Cross official called it "red tape run mad. . . . Before a payment could be made it required the support of sixteen signatures and if Chairman Phelan of the corporation happened to be inaccessible, all payments stopped because his signature was imperative; without it, all the other fifteen signatures were worthless."[48] Phelan often refused to leave the city because, as he told a fellow committee member, "if I absented myself from the City, something would be attempted in a way of turning over the funds to the Board of Supervisors, whose integrity was seriously questioned."[49] But the politically astute Phelan used a different explanation of his role on the Finance Committee when corresponding with Schmitz: "If I went away, the Committee would absolutely be without a head and my absence would reflect discredit not only on me, but upon you and the administration of this fund."[50]

Thus Mayor Schmitz slowly lost his solitary grip on the vulnerable city during the transition from emergency response to disaster relief. The Committee of 50 required collaboration between local political and business leaders. After Galveston's massive hurricane (1900) and Baltimore's fire (1904), ad hoc committees in those cities shared a Progressive outlook and easily agreed upon solutions for urban recovery.[51] But Mayor Schmitz's pro-labor stance and Phelan's disdain for the mayor in general created a strained alliance between municipal government and Progressive interests. As the *San Francisco Newsletter* commented, "Who would have believed it possible for . . . Abe Ruef, James D. Phelan and Mayor Schmitz to stand shoulder to shoulder in a common cause? Earthquakes make strange bed fellows."[52] But standing "shoulder to shoulder" meant that there would be quite a bit of shoving. James Phelan was quick to use his control over relief to push for a Progressive political and social agenda.

The 1906 disaster inaugurated a new Red Cross era of disaster relief marked by scientific social work. This was in sharp contrast to the iconic Red Cross that Clara Barton started in 1882. The original Red Cross mission was infused with female moral leadership associated with nineteenth-century benevolence work. Barton's 1904 resignation from the Red Cross at age eighty-two marked the institution's transition to a federally monitored organization steeped in the science of modern social work. As the 1906 San Francisco catastrophe set the new Red Cross administration in motion, Barton reluctantly remained in her home outside Washington, D.C., scanning newspaper headlines and waiting for news from loyal Red Cross insiders. Without a doubt, Barton's exclusion from San Francisco symbolized the organization's ongoing attempt to cast aside older notions of benevolence in order to align itself with more-modern methods.

As a woman who had worked at the intersection of two historical trends, female benevolence and scientific philanthropy, Barton found her entry into relief work paved by antebellum domesticity.[53] An elite, unmarried, well-educated woman from the North, Barton immersed herself in the war, living through what George Fredrickson summarizes as a "large-scale suffering [that] was a new experience for Americans."[54] But even as Barton was aiding soldiers on the battlefield, a bureaucratic philanthropic organization, the U.S. Sanitary Commission, was altering both the philosophy and the structure of antebellum charity efforts. Founded in 1862, the commission run by elite Northern men brought a different social philosophy to their work than did Barton.[55] The Sanitary Commission departed from idealistic philanthropy by replacing empathetic, zealous volunteers with efficient paid agents.[56] "Scientific philanthropy," which emphasized discipline and efficiency, was the new game in town.[57] The strong-willed Barton refused to work within the new organization and began searching for her own solution to relief work.

Clara Barton became devoted to founding the American Red Cross after an introduction to the International Red Cross (IRC) on a postwar trip to Europe. She petitioned the federal government to endorse this new organization that emphasized peacetime disaster relief.[58] Barton lobbied tirelessly for the Red Cross, petitioning the federal government for approval starting with the Rutherford B. Hayes administration. Finally in 1882, during Chester A. Arthur's presidency, Barton's American Red Cross was approved along with the Treaty of Geneva ratification.[59] Barton retained control over the organization, carefully selecting the disasters to which the Red Cross would respond. As Barton wrote in 1882, "we must hold ourselves *dear* and *rare*, gather and husband our resources, and be ready to move like the winds when the true moment comes. . . . I think we should *never* move until the need or shock is so great as to annihilate *political* considerations, which are of all things the greatest abomination."[60] In short, Barton picked catastrophes that allowed her to dispense disaster relief with a personal touch and a dramatic flourish.

The American Red Cross created its own relief philosophy. Barton distinguished two disaster relief periods: first, immediate post-disaster relief; second, restoration of basic community functions. The Red Cross focused on the first period. Two catastrophic floods, one in Johnstown, Pennsylvania (1889) and the other in Galveston, Texas (1900), gave Barton the chance to test her relief methodology. After the Johnstown Flood, Pennsylvania governor James Beaver noted how Barton used "such wisdom and tenderness that the charity of the Red Cross had no sting, and its recipients are not Miss Barton's dependents, but her friends."[61] For Barton, a bureaucratic organization was incapable of such compassionate care. Disaster relief was a personal experience, which placed enormous demands on the shoulders of one woman. But Clara Barton relished the strenuous work at the heart of the disaster zone, aiding countless "friends" and leaving well before they had a chance to become Red Cross "dependents."

Starting at the turn of the century, the federal government became more involved in the Red Cross, and Clara Barton less so. Congress incorporated the American Red Cross in 1900, the same year that floodwaters washed over Galveston.[62] Incorporation gave federal protection for the Red Cross insignia and minimal federal support during major emergencies. A significant change, from Barton's perspective, was that incorporation empowered the War Department to audit Red Cross expenditures.[63]

The Red Cross began to slip out of Barton's fingers in 1900. When the Galveston Hurricane struck, the seventy-seven-year-old Barton rushed from Washington, D.C., to lead the relief effort, later explaining, "It was naturally my work to go."[64] Meanwhile, new Red Cross executives, like Mabel Boardman, challenged Barton's sole authority. Only about half Barton's age, the unmarried Boardman exuded Progressive Era ideals and brought an impressive array of business, political, and social connections to her philanthropic work.[65] Boardman's passion for large hierarchical organizations and major fund-raising drives clashed with Barton's personal, hands-on approach. It may have been Boardman's suspicions of such an approach that prompted an internal investigation that examined Barton's leadership all the way back to her Civil War days. Boardman misread Barton as "an adventuress from the beginning and a clever one," and became obsessed with removing her from office.[66] Unfortunately, Clara Barton did not possess business acumen. One Barton biographer described her as "casual in her accounting of exact debits and credits, but she knew that the organization had taken far more from her than it had ever contributed to her income."[67] Over the next few years, Barton was asked to produce financial accounting dating back to the 1889 Johnstown Flood. Although she was exonerated by the Red Cross of any wrongdoing after a trying hearing, she resigned from the organization in May 1904.

The post-Barton American National Red Cross focused on increasing its membership and fund. The Red Cross continued its close relationship with the federal government, which was validated when President Theodore Roosevelt signed its reincorporation papers in 1905. President Roosevelt appointed his secretary of the War Department, William H. Taft, as Red Cross president. Mable Boardman later celebrated 1905 as "the first time the American Red Cross became truly national in its scope and standing."[68] "Since 1905 the American Red Cross has entered into so many active fields of relief," wrote Boardman, "and has so greatly developed, both in organization and efficiency."[69] Organizational efficiency was exactly what would be tested in 1906 San Francisco.

The 1906 disaster in San Francisco thus struck at a crossroads in Red Cross history. On the one hand, it presented a great opportunity for national publicity for the new Red Cross. But on the other, it came distressingly quickly on the heels of Barton's departure. In 1906, the organization was cash poor, inheriting approximately $10,000 from the Barton administration, and had a lackluster relationship with the states because Barton ignored the state-based auxiliary societies.[70] But the organization undoubtedly missed Barton's four decades of field experience. For the first time in Red Cross history, it did not employ a single administrator who had actual disaster relief experience.[71]

After the 1906 earthquake, President Roosevelt called the Red Cross into service without consulting its governing committee. The president then appointed a social work expert, Dr. Edward T. Devine, instead of a Red Cross administrator as the on-scene Red Cross director.[72] Devine, professor of social economy at Columbia University as well as the general secretary of the New York Charity Organization Society, was well known in Progressive social work circles. And Devine was not a fan of Barton. He had publicly criticized her failure to produce post-disaster reports on her work, "or, indeed, anything that can be properly called a report or financial statement." (But when asked if she knew Edward Devine, Barton commented that she had "never heard of him till the appointment by Pres. Roosevelt.")[73] Devine's philosophy was very much in keeping with the Progressive-minded Red Cross, and he endorsed efforts to "bring about a reorganization of management, especially on the financial side."[74]

During his three months in the disaster zone, Devine scripted relief policies while Boardman monitored expenditures from the Washington office. Also at this time, Barton orchestrated the delivery to San Francisco of a single railroad car filled with relief supplies. Sending relief supplies while the fires still burned showed that the eighty-four-year-old Barton's passions had not diminished, but her belief that her supplies "will stop hunger and want and the city will revive" was wishful thinking.[75] The Red Cross did not ask for Barton's help, and she remained at home, reading "the California news [that] is all engrossing."[76]

By early summer 1906, the American National Red Cross and James Phelan's Finance Committee joined forces and formed the San Francisco Relief and Red Cross Funds (SFRRCF).[77] The organization bureaucratized relief to "stop waste, to bring all the independent efforts under centralized control and to prepare for the constructive work of restoring the refugees as rapidly as possible to self-support and approximately normal life."[78] The SFRRCF's scientific evaluation of "normal life" was based on pre-disaster social status. In this relief logic, need was based on the potential for self-sufficiency; self-sufficiency was linked to pre-disaster status; and pre-disaster status was determined by, in part, gender, class, and race social norms. Red Cross experts argued that unlimited disaster relief created dependency and its corollary, moral depravity. This put poor refugees, who lacked additional resources such as insurance, savings, and property, in a tenuous position. In most cases, relief left these disaster survivors worse off than they were the year before.

Instead of distributing relief monies equitably among all disaster victims, the SFRRCF focused on San Francisco's property- and business-owning classes. "Rehabilitation," a non-emergency classification that based relief on pre-disaster social status instead of immediate need, distributed approximately one-third of the organization's funds to 20,241 individuals and families.[79] According to a report by Stanford economics professor James Motley, business rehabilitation grants were "confined almost entirely to re-establishing families in a line of business in which they had been engaged as proprietors."[80] For example, single women received a majority of the business rehabilitation money to return to domestic businesses such as boarding- and rooming houses, dressmaking and millinery shops, and seamstress work.[81] Thus in the very act of giving aid, relief monies reinscribed normative class and gender hierarchies. In addition to these grants, a "bonus plan" added more than $400,000 to post-disaster housing development by offering up to $500 to property owners rebuilding in the disaster zone. Relief grants favored applications by native-born families and two-parent households, who, in the case of the bonus plan, won 80 percent of the funds.[82] As the bonus plan clearly demonstrates, financial need was measured in terms of pre-disaster class and marital status. Devine approved of the plan as the most efficient way to restore social order, saying baldly, "We pay them [relief workers] to discriminate."[83]

By the time disaster victims applied for rehabilitation, relief policy guidelines had already sorted them into categories of eligibility on the basis of class, gender, and race. A temporary transportation program, for example, shipped undesirable refugees out of the city. Officials believed "that families should be kept together" but gave one-way tickets to anyone they considered "on the whole, lacking in physical vigor or mental qualities of courage and initiative, or in attachment to their city."[84] The relief camps later played a similar role by segregating refugees by race and gender before offering food, shelter, and clothing. It was clear that rehabilitation funds were not earmarked for the high proportion of ethnic working-class and poor refugees waiting inside these camps.

San Francisco's relief policy followed Edward Devine's disaster theories with textbook-like precision, and his latest publication, "Relief in Disasters," was a veritable policy template.[85] But it is one thing to theorize disaster relief and another thing to implement it. Outside the classroom and in the disaster zone, Devine relied on Katharine Felton and the San Francisco Associated Charities to transform his theories into practice.[86] Felton was an easy ally for Devine, having brought "scientific advancement" to California after completing studies at the University of Chicago's social welfare program and training at Jane Addams's famed Hull House.[87] The Associated Charities welcomed Felton's expertise, considering her 1901 appointment to be "fortunate" because "she has taken up, as her life's work, the study and administration of modern charity as her profession, and therefore comes to us equipped and prepared to enter upon a broader and more progressive work than the Association has ever done."[88] Devine and Felton were both what Paul Boyer called "positive environmentalists," reformers who shared the belief that economic and social conditions, not hereditary factors, created poverty. Turn-of-the-century social work fell into two camps: coercive and positive environmentalism. The coercive platform adhered to the nineteenth-century notion that poverty was embedded in hereditary factors and thus improvements to the lower classes were made by coercive programs. Positive environmentalists, on the other hand, focused on environment, visualizing a "more subtle and complex process of influencing behavior and molding character through a transformed, consciously planned urban environment."[89] However, Felton's social work practice differed from Devine's theory in significant ways.

Felton softened relief's new scientific and bureaucratic methods. Despite her professional training, she was concerned about a scientific approach that denied empathy for individuals in need. In a 1905 speech to social work professionals, she explained, "Expenditures, moreover, are to be judged not by the amount of relief distributed but by the *value of the work done*; that is, the social and spiritual services rendered."[90] Further, she taught Associated Charities caseworkers that "efficiency in charity work" depended on their being "trained in a knowledge of local conditions, knowing the languages spoken by the poor of the city and thoroughly understanding how to deal with people in trouble."[91] Felton did not stand alone in such views. Elizabeth Agnew's study of the Progressive social work leader Mary E. Richmond reveals nuances within the "scientific and bureaucratic advance" of twentieth-century social work. In practice, Richmond also "developed a holistic, civic vision of social work and an understanding of practitioners as artists as well as scientists."[92] In Felton's case, she did not cast aside the scientific philosophy in which she was trained. She knew that "careful investigation" by her caseworkers was a prerequisite "to restor[ing] the family to independence." However, she also believed that the lives of relief recipients should be "permanently and materially" improved.[93] This goal put her at odds with Devine, who argued that disaster relief should return victims to their pre-disaster social status.

San Francisco relief work illustrates how tidy scientific theories played out in the messy disaster zone. Working-class and poor refugees relied on investigations by Associated Charities representatives to garner financial support. A personal letter of recommendation vouching for their character would not suffice. Here San Francisco took a lesson from the Great Chicago Fire of 1871. Chicago's relief policies required that applicants submit a letter of recommendation from clergy, and it was widely known, at least by 1906, that Chicago's clergy wrote glowing recommendations for almost anyone who asked.[94] San Francisco's Rehabilitation Committee, whose mission was to provide selected disaster survivors "a reasonable lift" toward pre-disaster status, labeled clergy recommendations as "valueless in the vast majority of cases" because "some of the clergy of the city had manifolded [sic] a stereo-typed form of recommendation to give to any one who might apply."[95] Policy makers wanted objective standards, and thus all investigators asked the same set of questions: "What the family had to say about its previous income; what its present income was; what its plans were and how it hoped with the aid of a grant to carry out these plans." A general lack of scientific training, however, made it difficult for investigators to maintain the requisite objectiv-ity. With 100,000 refugees in San Francisco, there simply were not enough trained investigators to make the rounds. As a result, 150 San Francisco schoolteachers, local university students, and charity workers imported from several cities in the East were trained as relief investigators.[96] Although Red Cross experts instructed their newest inspectors to avoid looking "closely into the moral character of the applicants," one wonders how the field inves-tigators interpreted this directive. Felton's advocacy of personal involvement and moral assessment may have gained traction because she was responsible for training the new investigators. Relief officials depended heavily on their investigators, using each report as "a sort of rough-and-ready gauge" of refu-gee need.[97] As we shall see, the gap between policy and execution meant that moral evaluations—based on nineteenth-century definitions of the "deserv-ing" poor—crept back into disaster relief.[98]

MEASURING RELIEF BY GENDER AND CLASS

The relief investigator's observations weighed heavily in the determination of aid. Felton humanized the process, meeting daily with her caseworkers to remind them that "no one *likes* filling out forms. . . . You are dealing with human beings; your treatment and respect of a fellow human will usually be reflected in his cooperation, his attitude toward this organization, and the maintenance of his own self respect."[99] At the same time, Felton's relief evalu-ations included moral assessment. In one case, Felton reviewed the rehabilita-tion request made by a young woman on behalf of her elderly male cousin. Felton concluded that "the young woman, if she had the ambition, could not only earn her own living, but could also support the old man." After several failed attempts to secure employment for the "young, able-bodied woman," Felton summarized that "they both take the attitude they should be supported by the community." The grant application was denied, "since another grant would only be taken to pay current expenses."[100] Two assumptions lay at the heart of Felton's conclusions: first, industriousness was a distinguishing mark of worthy relief recipients; and second, working-class women should work to support themselves.

That relief investigations embraced subjective, moral assessments is evident in a case that personally involved James Phelan. In the summer of 1906, Phelan, while driving his car through the city, struck Mr. Lane, a teamster who lived in the Mission District. Mr. Lane's injuries to his back and leg required hospitalization, and Phelan agreed to pay for the weeklong treatment. Two months after Mr. Lane's recovery, however, Mrs. Lane paid James Phelan a visit. She wanted a rehabilitation grant. Mrs. Lane, who was supporting her family until her husband "could go to work again as [a] teamster," wanted to build "some sort of business (notion store, bakery or grocery store)" at their Mission Street storefront.[101] The personal visit to Phelan initially helped Mrs. Lane because he opened a rehabilitation grant case file on her behalf. But the Lanes' luck ran out once the Associated Charities investigated the case. The investigator spoke to a hospital clerk who tended to Mr. Lane's injuries and learned that the "applicant's injury was slight . . . and when discharged, it was considered that after a week's rest he would be able to go to work." Thus the investigator concluded that the Lanes had a "decided inclination to embellish and exaggerate the accident." The Lanes lost all hope for business rehabilitation after the home investigation. Even though they slept on the floor at the back of an empty store, the investigator reported that "both man and wife, as well as the children, look well fed, and there is no evidence of distress." Business funds, the investigator believed, would be wasted on the Lanes: "From the men who were loafing in the empty store, I imagine that it will be a saloon when 'they get a start.'" The case was closed with a single seventy-five-dollar furniture grant, most likely to purchase much-needed beds.[102]

Relief officials and reporters alike fretted that unemployed working-class women would grow dependent on disaster relief. Working-class women, more so than men, were singled out for reprimand most likely because paid work for men—from cleaning bricks to rebuilding—was plentiful in the post-disaster city. In one of her *San Francisco Examiner* articles, "All Women Can Have Work for the Asking," writer Lillian Ferguson insisted that all women who worked for wages before the disaster must return to work. Ferguson spoke for many San Franciscans when she wrote, "Nobody who is penniless and able bodied has any right to eat the bread of idleness a day longer than is absolutely unavoidable."[103]

The absence of female domestic servants was particularly troublesome because it marked the simultaneous disruption of home and work. Their newfound autonomy started during the fires, when servant girls left employers to find family and friends. One wealthy couple could not convince the household servants to stay and sweep up debris; as they explained it, "They wanted to find their sisters, and would not go with us so we let them go."[104] Female employers frequently commented on their abandonment. One woman, thankful that her cook had returned, noted that the less fortunate of her class were "deserted by help, to go to friends."[105] Losing servants changed, albeit temporarily, the roles of middle-class women in the home. As one female employer wrote to a friend, "The cook came back to us last night—the housemaid gone away with friends—we shall have enough to eat—and can get along all right. . . . [O]h its [sic] awful but sweetheart *we* are safe . . . but we *all* have to work now."[106] From the viewpoint of San Francisco's upper classes, the loss of female domestic workers was yet another casualty of the catastrophe. "Every one had wondered where the cooks had gone," reported the *San Francisco Chronicle*. "They had been lost since the fire."

San Francisco's female domestic worker crisis encompassed more than a potential drain on relief funds. Their absence from the workforce threatened both class and gender systems that required the contribution of domestic servants. Relief officials demanded that female domestics return to their employers.[107] As the *San Francisco Newsletter* described it, women domestics "were loafing . . . when families needed help."[108] Even Red Cross leader Mabel Boardman was alarmed by reports of "the great difficulty of securing maid servants without paying almost prohibitory wages." Believing the cause was that "the women [domestics] prefer to live in the [relief] camps," Boardman reiterated the belief that prolonged disaster relief was wasted on the poor and working classes. Forcing female domestics to return to work not only aided the wealthy and employed the laborer but also ensured the reestablishment of pre-disaster gender and class roles.

A woman standing in a relief camp with her sewing machine by her side, 1906. Refugee women living in the camps took in sewing and laundry to generate income. (Courtesy of the San Francisco Virtual Museum.)

In contrast to their treatment of domestic workers, relief leaders paid close attention to single women, especially single mothers. "Unsupported women and children" received special treatment, with single women earning 37 percent of the rehabilitation grants.[109] Widows with children were a top priority. "Quite naturally," one assessment of Felton's disaster relief work read, "she began work with the widows and their families."[110] Felton's work with disaster widows may well have driven her later advocacy of widows' pensions, a welfare plan that supported single mothers. The 1906 catastrophe acted as a catalyst for what Linda Gordon describes as "widow discourse," or the singular focus on aiding innocent widows and their children.[111] Felton's relief work coincided with the expansion of widow discourse in social work circles. As early as 1907, her organization earmarked funds for widows with children, with the goal of keeping a mother "at home so that she can give her time and strength to her children."[112] By 1913, the campaign for a mothers' pension bill in California was under way. The California League for the Protection of Motherhood lobbied for a "mother's pension bill which will provide a sufficient amount to keep children with their mothers; to have the state do for mothers what it does for institutions."[113] The relationships Felton built during relief work seem to have sustained these later efforts; she turned to James Phelan, who supported the league by "generously responding" with "liberal cheques."[114] In August 1913, California's State Aid Law was amended to fund widows with children.[115]

Policy makers set out to protect pre-disaster class status, believing that professionals "suffered the most in proportion to [their] resources."[116] In Finance Committee meetings, Edward Devine argued, "Exception[al] consideration should be given to professional men and women. . . . The loss of libraries, implements, and other means of livelihood for such people is in many instances, even more serious than the loss of their homes, household furniture, or other property."[117] But the committee, including Devine, recognized that this philosophy would be hard to sell in a city known for its affection for the working class. He agreed to table the proposal, advising that he "would not recommend any public announcement at this time of any such intended disbursement."[118] Nonetheless, relief officials found ways to aid the upper classes. At a subsequent meeting, Devine suggested a philanthropic pawnshop where "people who saved their jewelry could be rehabilitated by having such a place to go where they would not have to pay too much interest." The committee approved the idea, but the local press lambasted it. Policy makers quickly learned to keep quiet about their preferences and confer special treatment to San Francisco's professionals and elites by means of "Confidential Cases."

Relief officials discreetly distributed funds to hand-selected disaster victims, loosely defined as those who were in need but too proud to ask for help. Confidential case procedure circumvented regulations by eliminating the required Associated Charities investigation. In other words, confidential cases were "peer reviewed" in the sense that a recommendation by one relief official was all it took to hand out hundreds of dollars in aid. Instead of a home investigation, "two trusted clerks" reviewed the cases and kept the records "separate from the others."[119] Perhaps more importantly, confidential cases were more likely to receive higher financial awards than the average rehabilitation grantee. Not surprisingly, relief officials kept confidential case data private, and a complete file of confidential cases does not exist. However, the meticulous James Phelan saved thirty-three requests for confidential cases submitted between December 1906 and April 1908. These records reveal another form of social bias embedded in scientific relief. Even as relief officials publicly endorsed the evenhandedness of scientific methodology, they privately favored the financial recovery of their social peers.

As head of the Finance Committee, James Phelan submitted numerous confidential case applications to shield grant recipients from investigation. It remains unclear if confidential case subjects completed applications for aid or if Phelan did so on their behalf. Once such an application was completed, Phelan submitted the case directly to the Rehabilitation Committee, sparing the applicant the discomfort of a home investigation. In an interesting turn of events, Phelan discovered a policy loophole so that his confidential case applicants also avoided review by the Rehabilitation Committee employees. As Rehabilitation Committee member John Emery explained to Phelan: "You will notice that some of the cheques for parties you bring to the notice of the Confidential Committee are made out for $495. instead of $500. This is because of a standing order of the Rehabilitation Committee. That all grants for 500. or over must be signed by *two* members—and as one of the chief objects . . . is to have these cases strictly confidential—I make the grants a little less."[120]

Phelan's personal involvement not only ensured success—only one of his requests was refused—but also guaranteed the recipient a more lucrative grant than other rehabilitation applicants received.[121] While more than 75 percent of successful rehabilitation applicants received less than $200, 75 percent of Phelan's confidential recommendations received more than $200 in aid.[122] In fact, confidential applications submitted by Phelan were more than seven times more likely to receive grants greater than $400 than relief applications that refugees submitted on their own. Phelan was careful to shelter his charges and, in many cases, the final relief payments were endorsed directly to Phelan rather than to the recipient of the award (in one instance, Phelan received a blank check).[123] Phelan's only rejection came after an investigation by the secretary of the Rehabilitation Committee, Charles O'Connor, in 1908. For unknown reasons, investigators took the time to interview Phelan's referral. Secretary O'Connor denied the grant because the recipient "had never lived in San Francisco nor owned property here, having been a resident of San Jose more than three years."[124] Though Phelan had doled out dollars to confidential cases for two years, this incident may well have brought an end to his work in this regard; it was the final case listed in Phelan's records.

After 1908, the Red Cross handed the remaining relief work to Katharine Felton's Associated Charities.[125] As a result, Felton controlled a hefty budget to support her work in San Francisco. Before the earthquake, the Associated Charities annual budget rarely exceeded $5,000; after the disaster, the budget swelled to just over $80,000.[126] The Associated Charities reported in 1913 that the disaster caused a "force of circumstances" that transformed the organization from "mainly an investigating and advising agency" to "the principal social service organization of San Francisco."[127] As one of Felton's colleagues, Anna Pratt Simpson, assessed: "Handling a considerable portion of the relief money after the days of emergency disbursements has shown the tremendous possibilities for good in the machinery of the Associated Charities."[128] With her expanded funds and influence, Felton continued to infuse scientific social work with the gendered empathy of benevolence. A few years after the disaster, she wrote that the "conventional view of scientific charity" was not enough. Instead, "a sympathetic insight into the needs of those in trouble must be at the heart and core" of social work.[129]

Modern social work methods underwent rapid incubation in the 1906 disaster zone. San Francisco's catastrophe clearly punctuated the end of the Clara Barton Red Cross era, which valued a nineteenth-century approach to charity work, by sending Edward Devine and his scientific methods to the distraught city. In fact, one social work expert summarized 1906 San Francisco as "the greatest piece of charity work (for the time being) in the world."[130] San Francisco Relief and Red Cross Funds' non-emergency funding—rehabilitation, bonus plan, and confidential cases—undoubtedly offered a new prescription for relief to the ailing city. Although purportedly based on objective criteria, these funds nevertheless reinscribed normative class and gender hierarchies. For example, the "bonus plan" home grants favored native-born families and two-parent households, while a significant portion of rehabilitation funds was reserved to aid single women's resumption of domestic-related work. Thus as Progressive policy makers envisioned the future, their new policies repackaged the past by reinforcing contemporary social norms.

Despite the scientific veneer of modern relief policy, a benevolent sentiment reminiscent of the nineteenth century lingered just below the surface. This moral assessment of "deserving" and "undeserving" refugees further reinforced class and gender social boundaries. A closer look at Felton's practical approach to social work, however, reveals some positive aspects as well. Felton's criteria made it possible for some investigators to become advocates for San Franciscans in need. Several letters written by caseworkers to James Phelan reassured him and his associates that the relief recipients were "well known to us." Using phrases like "this family has been known to us for many years," "is well known to us," and "has been known to us for a number of years," Associated Charities caseworkers' familiarity with relief clients often helped procure funding.[131] Although that occurred on a case-by-case basis, the approach humanized—with middle-class moral values—the objective, bureaucratic formality of relief policy. In this regard the 1906 disaster presents a fascinating case study of the evolution of Progressive social reform during the early twentieth century.

By the summer of 1907, the SFRRCF had allocated the majority of its multimillion-dollar relief fund, aiding relief policy leaders as well as their chosen disaster survivors. The catastrophe was a shot in the arm for Mabel Boardman's Red Cross, bringing unprecedented publicity that in the end tripled its national membership.[132] Boardman must have been pleased by a run of positive press, such as the *Leslie's Magazine* article that proclaimed, "The Red Cross had become the most talked about society in the United States."[133] Dr. Edward Devine's role validated the social work theories he taught at Columbia University and advocated at the New York Charity Organization Society. Further, Ernest Bicknell, who joined Edward Devine in San Francisco, also benefited from his disaster zone experience by earning the American National Red Cross presidency in 1908. When SFRRCF leaders terminated their projects and turned the remaining cases over to the Associated Charities, they made Katharine Felton one of the most powerful, though overworked, charity leaders in the city. Her annual budget would never again dip to its pre-disaster levels. The disaster served James Phelan as well. His Finance Committee leadership placed him at the center of disaster relief, where he pursued his Progressive plans for San Francisco's future. "Don't doubt the ability of San Francisco," Phelan wrote to one reporter, "to recover its lost ground."[134] Phelan's prediction applied to Progressives in San Francisco, who continued to push hard for reform during the rebuilding period. Relief policy, then, brought advantages both to those who administered the millions in donations and to those who received them. As we shall see in Chapter 3, disaster relief created an array of opportunities for some individuals and groups that were excluded by these new policies.

CHAPTER 3

Disastrous Opportunities

Unofficial Disaster Relief

Disaster relief flooded the city with money and conferred a newfound authority on policy makers as they apportioned millions of dollars in relief funds among those they deemed the most productive and promising citizens. The weeks spent in organizing and streamlining official disaster relief left most refugees in dire straits. Local residents—middle-class women, Catholic nuns, and Chinatown leaders among them—took charge and did what needed to be done while officials scrambled to put a centralized relief effort in place. In a sense, the catastrophe created new opportunities for those local residents and communities who responded to thousands of San Franciscans in need. When middle-class women mobilized their social club networks to create and disseminate emergency supplies, they gained valuable political experience working in the public sphere. The disaster also bolstered Chinatown's merchant elite, whose community relief programs fortified important national and international relationships with Chinese business and political leaders. In fact, their Chinese-funded relief system helped ensure Chinatown's permanent place in the rebuilt city.

This chapter searches out a variety of unofficial relief efforts and investigates how these activities challenged San Francisco Relief and Red Cross Funds (SFRRCF) policy, scripted to first and foremost aid elite and middle-class citizens. Chinatown's merchant elite posed the greatest threat because it cut SFRRCF-enforced racial segregation to the quick. Further, Chinese relief called on outside resources, which further developed San Francisco Chinatown's ties to United States–based Chinese merchant groups and Chinese diplomats alike. Unofficial relief also challenged the scientific social work methods espoused by Red Cross experts. Middle-class women volunteers and Catholic nuns, for example, offered relief that was unfettered by bureaucratic regulation when they handed out supplies without first registering or investigating refugees. During the summer of 1906, another challenge to official relief policy surfaced among working-class and poor refugees. Thousands of San Francisco's homeless banded together to protest relief policy, pointing to social bias as they contested scientific social work methods and Progressive visions of the twentieth-century city. While massive donations gave SFRRCF leaders the ultimate authority to influence post-catastrophe urban society, the SFRRCF was not the only group to discover the power of disaster relief.

WOMEN IN RELIEF

A group of nuns at a retreat just north of San Francisco took the earthquake and fires as a sign from God. The Sisters of Mercy witnessed the "dense column of thick black smoke" hovering above the city as the unmistakable shape of the "body of the cross."[1] "Some of the sisters thought the figure was a sign of God's displeasure, others, of His Mercy," wrote Sister Gerard. "Let us hope the latter."[2] These nuns and other religious women from the city's convents took immediate action by organizing medical aid and relief supplies for refugees. The work brought the nuns into the city's public sphere, which expanded their spiritual influence over the refugees for whom they cared and, consequently, strengthened their own religious communities.

Middle-class women went to work in the city as well, handing out relief supplies and nursing injured refugees. For many women in California, the destruction of San Francisco's domestic sphere granted them the authority to mend the social fabric that had been rent by the disaster. Beryl Bishop, a Stanford student at the time, explained that the city needed a woman's touch: "I was sure there was a large place of service in the needy city for a woman's heart and hands; it should be my labor to discover this and open the way for others who were waiting to help."[3] Or as the president of Berkeley's Twentieth Century Club explained, "This is an opportunity to show the kindness we must all feel toward other women."[4]

Women's clubs were poised for immediate and efficient disaster response. Paula Baker tells us that during the Progressive Era women's clubs shifted their agendas from self-improvement to public betterment through educational and legislative change. After the creation of the General Federation of Women's Clubs in 1890, the focus of women's clubs on labor, health, educational, and court reform brought "the benefits of motherhood to the public sphere."[5] The 1906 catastrophe occurred in the midst of this transition, giving California women's clubs an additional lesson in public work as they assumed responsibility for a critical condition to which the state was unprepared to respond—the massive displacement of urban residents.

At first, women's clubs in San Francisco were better organized than the American National Red Cross. At his initial meeting with the Committee of 50, the Red Cross's Edward Devine insisted that "it was necessary that this voluntary force of [women] relief workers be continued."[6] Relief work meant that state and local women's clubs worked in unison. The California Federation of Women's Clubs collected clothing donations, then sent these directly to their San Francisco sister organizations for distribution. Local California club members met at a home in the Western Addition to manage these donations.[7] All of this was without Red Cross involvement. These women were so efficient that the Red Cross tapped the women's club network for volunteers. A few local California club members set out on foot to visit their San Francisco constituents, thus recruiting new volunteers to work for the Red Cross initiative. Later on, the women's club used Red Cross headquarters inside the disaster zone to distribute the Federation of Women's Clubs donations "to the needy who had been burned out."[8] While Progressive administrators debated relief policy, local clubwomen were already at work on the ground serving the thousands of San Franciscans struggling to piece together their daily lives in the desolate city.

Women's clubs were particularly adept at disaster relief because so much of it involved domestic tasks. Handmade clothing could be produced by club members at low cost and then shipped to the San Francisco relief committee free of charge. The well-publicized catastrophe prompted an outpouring of donations from across the country. But while most cities and towns collected cash from their citizens, women's clubs prepared and sent products of the domestic sphere. The women's club in Elkhart, Indiana, for example, collected only $50 of the $3,000 donation sent by their town. Rather than money, the clubwomen focused on restoring the comforts of home. "Warmest sympathy accompanies this offering," read the letter attached to their gift of blankets, bedding, and clothing, "and the hopes that it will, in some small degree, give help to those who are suffering in this great calamity."[9] In Portland, Oregon, an estimated two hundred women gathered and "faithfully plied needle and thread all day long, making garments ready for those who have not even the simple necessities of needle and thread."[10] In nearby Palo Alto, women's organizations purchased their own materials to sew "mother and infant outfits of the daintiest and most useful sort and these were sent out in large numbers to the relief stations in the City."[11] As they plied needle and thread, wives and mothers became active participants in the nationwide relief effort.

Women's relief work was not limited to blankets and clothing. California women who lived along the state's train routes organized relief workers to cook and sew for refugees traveling through their towns. In small towns such as Gilroy, a "bevy of ladies were at every train, passing food to the passengers."[12] In Fresno, women prepared lunches for refugees on the trains.[13] Florence Sylvester, a third-year medical student on a hospital rotation in San Francisco, took advantage of the free train transportation to stay with an aunt in Los Angeles. The train was made up "entirely of day coaches and was crowded to the last seat with non-paying passengers from San Francisco." They made one stop for food on the fifty-three-hour trip, where "the ladies of the town had instituted a relief corps." At that stop, "the ladies went through each coach with baskets on their arms, seeking to supply any who might need it with fruit, baby clothes, bottles of malted milk, and nipples, lemons, little home remedies for car sickness, etc.," wrote Sylvester. "There seemed to be nothing they had not thought of."[14]

Women's volunteer efforts successfully united the public and domestic spheres far from the disaster zone. Palo Alto mothers who could not leave their homes to "serve in person in the church" remained in their "own kitchens, beating tirelessly back and forth between table and stove" to prepare relief supplies.[15] At the same time in Oregon, "hundreds of Portland wives and mothers who were unable to be there [working at the Armory] render[ed] as effective service in their own homes by ransacking closets and drawers and making up bundles to send to the Armory."[16] In Utah, Mormon women baked bread and sewed clothes for San Francisco refugees, which reinvigorated their own religious women's organization. Disaster relief provided an opportunity, as the group's president fittingly summarized, to "prove their benevolence."[17]

But the "valiant relief work" of San Francisco women, as a *San Francisco Examiner* editorial phrased it, required constant negotiation with relief administrators.[18] Dr. Adelaide Brown, a female physician in San Francisco, organized an emergency clinic at a private home near the Presidio.[19] Dr. Brown had her clinic donations mailed directly to the San Francisco relief committee in order to avoid shipping charges. (Donations sent to the relief committee were not charged shipping fees.) This required the approval of the Finance Committee chair, James Phelan. When she appeared before the committee to explain her medical work, Phelan agreed to release the donations "for the purpose of distribution in her judgment."[20] But the relief committee's decision to allow Dr. Brown to administer private donations may well have been an exception to the rule.

When shipping their goods to San Francisco's relief committee, most women's groups acknowledged their loss of control over the final outcome. The women from Buffalo, New York's Lafayette Avenue Presbyterian Church, for example, at first hoped that a female friend in San Francisco would hand out their church group's clothing donation. However, the logistics proved daunting, and instead they urged the relief committee to "kindly use the articles where they will do the most good."[21]

The San Jose Woman's Club provides another example of the SFRRCF's increasing control over relief. The group contacted James Phelan to offer support, requesting that he send either funds or fabric so that they might sew clothes for refugee women and children.[22] While relief administrators welcomed donations from women's organizations, they refused to open their coffers to fund these efforts. Phelan's unwillingness to subsidize the San Jose Woman's Club highlights the differences between official and unofficial disaster relief. As the SFRRCF bureaucratized its policies and personnel, it simultaneously reduced its reliance on women's clubs. And as women's clubs lost their independence to relief bureaucracy, they changed tactics and volunteered directly for the SFRRCF. Women volunteers found a new role in the SFRRCF relief camps, where they had direct contact with refugee women and children during the summer of 1906.

San Francisco's Catholic nuns represented another kind of women's group that found new opportunities for service after the disaster. San Francisco and Catholicism were nearly synonymous terms at the turn of the century. The city was a place where Irish and German working classes, Italian immigrants, and the "lace curtain Irish" elite all shared in communion. As a result, the San Francisco Catholic experience incorporated social, cultural, and political characteristics.[23] The nuns, who represented several orders, had served the city well for more than half a century by working in convents, schools, and hospitals. Their long history in San Francisco put the parishes and convents in an excellent position, in both location and staff, to offer immediate relief.[24] The Sacred Heart Presentation Convent, located at Taylor and Ellis Streets just north of Market Street, was in a prime spot to serve refugees fleeing the South of Market District. "The door bell continued ringing," recalled Mother Superior Xavier Hayden, "friends in hysterics seeking shelter and comfort at the convent."[25] Like the city's clubwomen, the sisters responded to widespread human need by working in the post-disaster public sphere. "God preserved us," wrote the Dominican Reverend Mother Pia Backes on April 20. "How can we ever thank Him?" They expressed their gratitude through relief work and became some of the earliest Red Cross volunteers. Reverend Mother Backes wrote of being "loaded down with articles of food provided by the 'Red Cross' for distribution among the needy." Disaster relief became intertwined with religious work as the sisters continued to "visit the poor and the sick and share with them our supplies."[26] In this fashion, the sisters saturated their relief work with religious meaning and gave simultaneous material aid and spiritual comfort to San Francisco refugees.

The experienced San Francisco nuns did not shy away from SFRRCF authority. The Sisters of Mercy were so efficient at collecting and distributing bundles of clothing for the predominantly Irish St. Peter's parishioners that the parish became an official relief station. However, the relief committee kept a close watch over the nuns by regularly sending police officers to supervise parish relief work. One nun questioned this practice after the scheduled officer failed to appear at St. Peter's one morning. She announced, "A Sister is as good as a policeman. You may open the gate. There will be no disorder."[27] The nuns fed the waiting refugees while "those in charge were more than surprised at the order and quiet that prevailed."

The nuns' integral role in a predominantly Catholic San Francisco may have helped them establish their place in the city's emerging relief system. Indeed, much of their labor focused on the spiritual needs of disaster survivors. In addressing such needs, the nuns helped preserve neighborhood and individual social identity. For example, the Sacred Heart Presentation Convent not only ran a relief station but also reconstructed a place of worship for the Italians who remained near North Beach.[28] "You cannot imagine how strange it is to be here," Sister Genevieve commented on the Italian neighborhood. "We feel as though we were in some foreign country." The Irish sisters and Italian San Franciscans worked side by side to turn a local school into a sacred space for mass. Although the school lacked pews and altar, two Presentation sisters "fixed it up very grand. The poor people brought large pictures to hang up. We even had a very nice little side altar of Our Blessed Lady."[29] For the Italians still living on Telegraph Hill, the sisters built a bridge to their pre-disaster lives through religious practice, as "the former routine was kept alive as nearly as possible."[30] Their work presented a sharp contrast to official relief policy that would soon establish relief camps to more closely monitor refugees. In the meantime, the nuns played a critical role by bringing some continuity of religious experience to Catholics in the post-disaster city.

Like the women's clubs, San Francisco's convents accessed a national support network to sustain their relief work. The Sisters of Mercy, who lost their hospital on South of Market's Rincon Hill, built a tent hospital on their undeveloped property near Golden Gate Park. Their medical work united the Convents of Mercy across the country, which reinvigorated their sense of community as servants of the ill and impoverished. Under the direction of Mother M. Pius, eight sisters slept without bedding and "got up rested" each morning to care for injured refugees.[31] The local sisters collected money, materials, and letters of support from convents in major U.S. cities, including New York, Chicago, Los Angeles, Pittsburgh, Cincinnati, St. Louis, and Portland.[32] At the end of summer, St. Mary's Hospital moved to Sutter Street, near San Francisco's temporary post-disaster business district. The Sisters of Mercy were key players in San Francisco's medical infrastructure, and St. Mary's Hospital continued to have "a great run on emergency work." It may even be the case that their ability to maintain uninterrupted medical care increased their influence; the Sisters of Mercy became a permanent part of the expanding urban landscape when they built a new hospital near Golden Gate Park.[33]

Women led this initial disaster relief endeavor, quickly filling that void in the relief system. As women's clubs and women-dominated relief groups gathered to cook meals, bake bread, sew clothing, or provide medical care for survivors, they used relief work to transfer their domestic values to the public realm. And their volunteer experiences undoubtedly improved the effectiveness of their organizational structure and internal communication. In addition, their relief efforts offered tangible proof, to themselves and others, of the urgent need for their presence in the public sphere. As the SFRRC formalized its relief policy, however, administrators discouraged this vital independent wave of women's relief work in favor of a centralized relief distribution network that screened refugees before offering aid. Still, many of these women continued their work, but within the SFRRCF organization. The successes of women's relief efforts lingered long past the summer of 1906, as middle-class clubwomen became more deeply involved in San Francisco politics.

Revising Relief in Chinatown

Disaster relief heightened racial fears and, simultaneously, empowered the Chinese community. After the earthquake and fires destroyed Chinatown, civic officials and residents publicly worried about the uncontained Chinese. The first attempt at social control occurred during the disaster, when civic and military leaders forced Chinese residents to evacuate Chinatown and the disaster zone. Within days of the earthquake, Oakland papers cautioned that "Oakland's Chinatown will spread and tend to be the same menace to this city as Chinatown was to San Francisco unless measures are promptly taken to check it from doing so."[34] San Francisco's policy makers managed the Chinatown "menace" by segregation, building Chinese relief camps in both San Francisco and Oakland to reestablish Chinatown's racial boundaries. In the meantime, San Francisco's Chinese Consolidated Benevolent Association (CCBA) refused to kowtow to SFRRC's racially based polices and created an independent Chinatown relief committee to care for their community. Their relief effort was twofold: directing aid to Chinatown refugees and generating support for rebuilding. Chinatown relief efforts carried the hidden benefits of increasing the CCBA's economic and political power and accelerating the development of Bay Area Chinese communities.

Chinese residents found it difficult to remain in or near Chinatown after the calamity. The experiences of Ella May Clemens, an idiosyncratic missionary worker who built her own relief camp in Chinatown, illustrate why. Self-described as an independent Catholic missionary, Clemens founded a camp for Chinese survivors after her exposure to blatant disaster relief racism. When she first requested supplies for some of the few remaining men in Chinatown, a relief worker told her, "'Dear lady, you can have anything you want, but we will carry the chinks nothing.'" Upset by his declaration, Clemens demanded tents and bedding. She later wrote that she had "carried these things, how I do not know, for they were so heavy, to them on my back."[35] Donaldina Cameron's Presbyterian Chinese Mission Home, built to protect Chinese women and girls, provided a new form of security when Clemens scavenged the mission home's iron gates and screens for her camp.[36] Clemens used her property to create a religious relief camp that she named Dragon Hill, which consisted of her missionary tent, chapel, and four large tents occupied by twenty Chinese laborers. Ella May Clemens somehow managed to bridge the gap between white officials and Chinese refugees, and Dragon Hill is the only known site where Chinese residents remained in Chinatown after the disaster. San Francisco relief leaders supported Clemens's direct supervision of Chinese refugees by allocating a steady stream of relief supplies to Dragon Hill. As one military commander wrote to Clemens, "I am glad that the food issued to you for the destitute Chinese, under your supervision, held out for so long."[37]

Ella May Clemens's life choices reveal some of the complexities of racial identity and race relations in turn-of-the-century San Francisco. Her experiences in post-disaster Chinatown caused her to lament that "they [Chinese people] are neither understood nor appreciated." Believing that matrimonial ties bridged white-Chinese cultural differences, Clemens married one of the camp's Chinese refugees in late September 1906. "My marriage will make me one of them," she declared. "I shall know them from the inside of their lives—the side the world does not see."[38] Although a local news story made her marriage appear to be a strange, if not scandalous, choice, Clemens did not lose her standing as a Chinatown relief provider. Perhaps her marriage to Sun Yue Wong helped to mitigate the perceived danger of Chinese men to the post-disaster city. Ella May Wong and her husband took up permanent residence in the rebuilt Chinatown, where they participated in the tourist trade by running a curio shop that sold relics from the 1906 disaster. They later developed their own tour of Chinatown, which Ella May Wong advertised in her 1915 guidebook. As Wendy Rouse Jorae points out, Wong created a sanitized, "romanticized vision of old Chinatown" that simultaneously highlighted "the development of a new and respectable Chinese American community."[39] While her marriage may have combated stereotypes of dangerous Chinese men, the couple's choice to remain in Chinatown may well reflect how the neighborhood continued to create a safe space for Chinese residents in San Francisco.

Chinese refugees fared better when they remained within their own community. As evidence in Chapter 4 demonstrates, the SFRRC relief camps lacked stability—in location, supplies, and sanitary conditions—to support the Chinese community. The Wong family, for example, quickly realized that the San Francisco Chinese relief camp could not meet their needs. Instead, they pooled their money and, once they had enough for boat fare, traveled east to Vallejo. They chose the East Bay town with its small Chinese community because they had "previous acquaintances there."[40]

Bay Area Chinese fishing and shrimp camps also attracted refugees because they promised the security of a pre-established Chinese community. In addition to heading for the shrimp camp near San Francisco's Potrero Hill, refugees went north to the Marin County camps or east to the shrimp camps in Richmond, knowing they would find Chinese residents there to help them. Leland Chin described Richmond as "nothin' but shrimp camps. There was a lot of shrimp in the bay, and at least thirty shrimp camps in Richmond. Sure, all Chinese! Everything was Chinese in those days."[41] The arrival of even a few dozen refugees significantly altered these locations. In Marin County, for example, refugee relocation boosted the small Chinese community by 13 percent, a dramatic reversal of the 73 percent decline after the 1882 Exclusion Act.[42]

Even outside the Bay Area, Chinatown refugees remained within their own community. In Fresno, for example, the three hundred to four hundred Chinese refugees who stepped off the trains decided to live in Chinatown rather than seek assistance from the town's relief committee. They were first subjected to a Board of Health medical examination in a quarantine tent at the Fresno depot, after which they walked to Fresno's small Chinatown.[43]

The post-disaster story of native-born Hugh Kwong Liang illustrates one of the rare instances when a Chinatown refugee traveled alone. A teenager at the time, Liang was left alone by a foreign-born cousin who told him he would survive without difficulty because he was "American." Liang trekked as far north as Napa and then east to Vallejo looking for family relations before settling with Chinatown refugees in Oakland. In general, Chinatown refugee relocation patterns followed an unspoken rule of survival—travel in groups to Bay Area Chinese enclaves.[44] The collective impact of their individual journeys, which is discussed further in Chapter 5, expanded Bay Area Chinese communities.

Bay Area Chinese-owned businesses became a vital community resource for Chinatown refugees. In Berkeley, relief officials noted 115 refugees who boarded with Chinese residents or businesses in their East Bay town.[45] Relief investigators found refugee groups ranging in size from 15 to 30 clustered in the Chinese-owned businesses and homes along Berkeley's Dwight Way. The 15 refugees who slept at the Lee Yaik Company and the 30 who stayed at Hong Wo's home next door on Dwight Way typified the group size and location for at least 350 Chinatown refugees in the area.[46] Berkeley was a departure point as well as a destination for hundreds of Chinatown refugees who regularly moved in and out of the small city. As one Berkeley historian noted at the time, "Many Chinese left daily for places in the interior looking for work, and every day more came in and settled."[47] In fact, Chinatown refugees who remained in Berkeley boosted the Chinese population by 66 percent.[48] One of the benefits of relocation to these Berkeley homes and businesses was that it created a dense population of Chinese and reestablished some of the social networks familiar from pre-disaster Chinatown.

The faith of Chinese Christians unlocked another resource for some refugees, specifically missionaries and religious leaders. Religion bridged perceived racial differences; white Christians did not question the worthiness of Christians from Chinatown. Not surprisingly, Christian-based aid for Chinese refugees maintained a safe distance from official disaster relief. In Oakland, Reverend J. H. Laughlin organized a meeting for "all who are interested in the welfare of distressed Chinese Christians" to plan a relief fund for Chinese Christian families, schools, and rescue homes.[49] But there were also cases of individual white Christians' acting as advocates for Chinese refugees. For example, Mrs. Hannah A. De Voe Wilkins, a Christian woman from New York, sent a recommendation to the Berkeley Relief Committee on behalf of a Chinese refugee family. Wilkins promised the relief committee that it could trust the family's oldest child, saying, "She is a practical Christian and you can rely upon every word she says."[50]

Local discrimination was held in check by national politics. China's empress dowager wisely supported both the CCBA and the Red Cross. As a result, China's financial contributions to San Francisco's official relief fund resulted in new political bargaining power. Though diplomatic relations between the United States and China were already strained by a 1905 anti-American boycott in Shanghai (as well as decades of U.S. government restrictions on Chinese immigration), the $40,000 donation to the SFRRCF smoothed the situation. Private Chinatown disaster relief further unified the Chinese community in the United States as nationwide donations from Chinese merchant associations poured into the Oakland headquarters.[51] The relief effort was endorsed by the Chinese consul of San Francisco, Chung Pao Hsi, who urged all Chinese merchants to send relief: "Chinatown is entirely destroyed and our people are in great distress. Send whatever money you can collect for our people."[52] As it collected donations for "our people," the Chinese aid effort solidified its place in post-disaster San Francisco and the nation.

Chinatown relief circumvented racist SFFRC policy while enhancing CCBA authority. A powerful fifty-member relief committee comprising diplomats and CCBA members was formed.[53] Chinese relief focused on four areas: registering refugees; distributing food and clothing; monitoring placement into relief camps; and searching San Francisco for surviving residents.[54] The West Coast branches of the CCBA rushed money, provisions, and delegates to the new Chinese relief organization.[55] From its headquarters, the relief committee supervised nearly 6,000 Chinatown refugees in Oakland.[56] However, Chinatown relief was not without its own form of social bias: class was the foundation of new policy. The committee encouraged successful merchants to rebuild in San Francisco and transported Chinatown's sick and poor populations to points outside the city, "where friends will take care of them."[57] Chinese relief officials negotiated train fare reductions and put hundreds of Chinese refugees on trains departing the Oakland terminal. They also lobbied to deport some refugees to China. The *San Francisco Call* reported that the committee intended to send 1,000 "aged and destitute Chinese who were rendered homeless by the fire in San Francisco back to China to spend the rest of their days in peace at home."[58] At least 1,500 Chinatown residents left for China after the disaster.[59] In general, most refugees fared better under Chinese disaster relief than under official relief policy. Alice Sue Fun, for example, successfully escaped Chinatown with her family only to watch her father die from typhoid in an official relief camp. Her experience is a stark reminder of the dangers of Chinese isolation under segregated relief policy. Despite China's $40,000 to the SFRRCF, the Chinatown relief committee encouraged refugees to rely on their own community for aid. "If the Chinese don't immediately find a way to earn a living and remain on relief," warned the Chinatown daily newspaper *Chung Sai Yat Po*, they "will be driven out."[60]

The calamity created a distinct opportunity for Chinatown leaders. First and foremost, disaster relief funds increased CCBA's scope and power. The disaster was also a boon to Oakland's Chinatown, which became the temporary headquarters of Chinese disaster relief and grew by at least 46 percent after the disaster, ending the decade with approximately 3,600 residents.[61] Before the catastrophe, CCBA authority was limited to the San Francisco peninsula and did not extend to other Bay Area Chinese communities.[62] The

CCBA's response to the disaster, however, pushed its influence well beyond the boundaries of San Francisco's Chinatown, meaning that the Chinese had greater political influence in the Bay Area than ever before.

DISASTER RELIEF AS PERSONAL GAIN

San Francisco's calamity created new prospects for some clever individuals. William Randolph Hearst, for example, used the catastrophe to enhance his public image and promote his political aspirations. Hearst, who was in New York at the time of the earthquake, envisioned himself as the personal savior of San Francisco's refugees: "Tell the people of San Francisco not to worry," he telegraphed a friend on April 18. "I am starting West."[63] Hearst ignored the American National Red Cross in San Francisco and set up a variety of relief efforts and photo opportunities in the East Bay. A local editorialist, who applauded Hearst's work, commented, "The distress of his fellow man, no matter in what quarter of the globe, has always appealed to him."[64] But others were more suspicious. One local writer was intentionally sardonic: "Although the Hearst earthquake and the Hearst fire which followed the seismic upheaval in Hearst's city of San Francisco constitute the greatest catastrophe in America's history of disasters, Hearst has been equal to the task."[65] Indeed, Hearst's own newspaper, the *San Francisco Examiner*, put the owner, not the Red Cross, at the center of the catastrophe. When the *Los Angeles Examiner* sent doctors, nurses, and relief supplies by train to San Francisco, it draped the locomotives with banners proclaiming "Examiner Relief Trains." Hearst's competitors speculated that the allegedly empty railcars were intended only to boost Hearst's political image.[66] But such criticism did not stop him. Hearst continued by naming a relief camp and maternity hospital after himself. When newspapers reported that lost children were stepping aboard trains bound for Oregon, he opened the W. R. Hearst Children's Reunion Camp. The camp was intended to reunite refugee children with their families, and his newspaper reporters stood ready to record their stories.[67] Hearst's private relief campaign was unusual in that some citizens donated to Hearst instead of to the Red Cross. *Examiner* subscribers, like one reader from New York, entrusted their donations to Hearst: "Trusting to God you will please send them to San Francisco."[68]

Hearst's relief policy, however, did not help everyone; he prioritized white, male-headed households. Oakland's W. R. Hearst Tent City segregated its one thousand refugees by ensuring that women and families lived apart from single men and African Americans.[69] Most of Hearst's work made great copy, and his *Examiner* was filled with success stories about his relief efforts. Upon the visit of Mr. and Mrs. Hearst to their own relief camp, the *Examiner* reported: "They were stopped by a representative of the tenants, who presented a resolution of thanks, signed by nearly 1,000 persons who have enjoyed the hospitality at the camp."[70]

Hearst's agenda was most transparent at the refugee maternity hospital, where he enticed pregnant women to the delivery room by finding employment for their husbands and giving $100 for the birth of each baby. The *Examiner* waited patiently for the birth of a boy. Reporters passed up the first four births, all girls, and wrote about a male baby who was the fifth to be born. Baby William Randolph Hearst Eby made for a great headline and personified Hearst's use of disaster relief to expand his public image.[71]

John D. Rockefeller provides another example of how some used private disaster relief to their own advantage. At the time, Rockefeller's Standard Oil Company was reviled by the press as an evil trust. In fact, the headline proclaiming, "The Standard Oil Is the Vilest Trust on Earth," ran in one San Francisco daily during the disaster.[72] Rockefeller combated such negative press with his massive relief donations. First, he contributed $95,000 to the San Francisco relief fund.[73] Next he sent his employees into the streets of San Francisco to hand out another $100,000 to the needy. Rockefeller put Colonel E. H. Merrill, department manager of the Standard Oil Company, in charge. Rockefeller's money first went to "a number of clergymen" so that they could buy books and "a decent suit of clothes."[74]

There is little question that Rockefeller used the donation to combat his negative public image. Before giving the clergy money, Colonel Merrill informed them it was "tainted money—tainted through and through" and gave them a chance to decline Rockefeller's donation. Rockefeller got good mileage out of their responses when Colonel Merrill explained, "In response to this statement one of the clergymen said: 'The taint wears off the moment it passes from your hands into ours.' Another said, 'It's the motive that makes money tainted or not.' The third said, 'All money is tainted.' The fourth one said, "Taint 'nough.'"[75]

Many of Rockefeller's charity cases tugged on the public's heartstrings. He was careful to use most of his money for women and families—he funded 355 families, 303 women (independent of families), and only 25 men (in addition to the clergy).[76] He gave money to "a hunch-back, a girl about eighteen years old, [who] before the fire had supported her invalid mother and an aged grandfather," and the "trained nurse [who] allowed her clothing and household goods to burn up while she remained on duty in a refugee camp hospital during the fire, working until she dropped."[77] Perhaps the donation with the greatest positive impact on Rockefeller's image was a host of Bibles, each signed by Rockefeller. "To Mrs. _____ from the John D. Rockefeller Relief Fund, San Francisco, Calif. 1906," read the flyleaf of each free Bible.[78]

As discussed previously, the disaster occurred at a time when formal relief efforts were in their nascent stages and unable to draw private funding. As a result, the San Francisco calamity created opportunities for wealthy Americans, like Hearst and Rockefeller, to use their financial largesse to influence turn-of-the-century politics and bolster their public images.

A relief line, 1906. Photographs of San Franciscans standing in long relief lines reassured outsiders of San Francisco's post-disaster social equality. (California Historical Society, FN-34109/CHS2011.468.tif.)

PROTESTING OFFICIAL RELIEF

The Flour Riot: "Let Them Eat Bread"

Many of San Francisco's working-class and poor disaster survivors adamantly opposed SFRRC disaster relief. "Kickers," as these male and female relief protesters were named by relief officials and the local press, organized a variety of protest groups that demanded financial control over all donations. Women were the driving force behind these protest movements for two reasons: first, post-disaster labor opportunities favored working men, and second, the necessities of domestic life—food, shelter, and clothing—were accorded heightened priority after the disaster. A powerful critique of official relief policy gained salience as sporadic refugee protests turned into an organized protest movement called the United Refugees.

The most publicized example of female protest was the July 1906 "Flour Riot."[79] As was typical on almost any weekday after the disaster, women waited in a long line for flour rations outside the main relief warehouse. Women in San Francisco were fed up with cumbersome regulations and, after months of waiting in such lines, some demanded more than their allotted flour. When warehouse guards refused to comply, the women stormed the building and walked off with two thousand pounds of flour. As one warehouse guard recalled, a woman blocked the warehouse doors and shouted to all within earshot that "everybody connected with the work of relief . . . [was] engaged in a colossal and far-reaching graft to defraud deserving refugees of the flour that was rightfully theirs."[80] This proclamation incited a riot and the women who had been waiting in line "berated the guards and demanded their rights as American citizens, and threatened to return to-day with sufficient women to tie up the guards and help themselves to the flour." According to one news report, the women "made a rush on the stack of flour, tore the coat from the back of the storekeeper . . . and scratched his face."[81] This was not the first time in U.S. history when women organized protests over food, thereby transcending their prescribed gender roles as docile creatures in order to care for their families.[82]

Organized female protest had been brewing under the hands of Mary Kelly, an Irish working-class refugee. A middle-aged mother with an invalid husband, Kelly was a recent convert to protest work. After witnessing the plight of her fellow refugees, she vowed to fight "for the cause of justice and right, come what would, even though it might cost me my life." Years later, one Red Cross administrator still remembered Kelly as "a constitutional agitator. She was violently critical of conditions, no matter what they were. Loud, aggressive in voice and manner."[83] Before the Flour Riot, Kelly sought out Edward Devine to discuss the relief policy on flour distribution.[84] Unsatisfied with Devine's response, she "marshaled a hundred or more of her followers in a noisy and threatening mob and led them to relief headquarters," where relief officials immediately handed out fifty bags of flour to avoid the "most embarrassing . . . newspaper publicity which might follow." This outcome represented a decisive victory over relief committee bureaucracy, and as the women left with the flour, they shouted "their triumph over Devine and the relief committee."[85]

To Devine's dismay, his fifty-bag donation did not stop the women's momentum, but perhaps encouraged it. The infamous Flour Riot erupted only a few days later and resulted in a grand jury investigation and a criminal trial. As the grand jury sent delegates to interview "several women, among them some who had been in the flour line," a female protester, Maude Brown, filed battery charges against Captain Kilian, a warehouse guard.[86] Maude Brown used her body as evidence, showing the police how her arm "was still black and blue from the alleged rough treatment." A warrant for Captain Kilian's arrest soon followed. In the courtroom, it became clear that the trial was about SFRRCF leadership as well as Brown's encounter with Captain Kilian. The local press sided with the women, arguing that Red Cross experts ignored the needs of local residents and refugees. "Dr. Devine . . . has written a book on methods in charity," read one San Francisco Chronicle article. "They use that book in Eastern colleges, and the ideas of [presiding] Judge Conlan . . . and Mrs. Brown are not to be found in its pages."[87]

Did disaster survivors have a right to control donations sent on their behalf? The Flour Riot trial, which ended in a guilty verdict for Captain Kilian, put female disaster survivors at the center of a national debate over the

Red Cross. Flour was a tricky issue during the summer of 1906. Supposedly a 70,000-barrel donation from the Minneapolis Committee for California Relief resulted in a surplus.[88] In late May 1906, the relief corporation, whose administrators believed that women in San Francisco would not use all the flour, wanted to sell 4 million pounds of it.[89] James Phelan advocated the sale to the Finance Committee, insisting, "Our information is that they [the women] have not applied for flour. What they wanted was bread."[90] The outraged Minneapolis donors demanded an investigation by the American National Red Cross.[91] San Francisco relief administrators quickly put the flour out to bid and sold it at a competitive rate to avoid the appearance of a back-room deal.[92] Even though the proceeds were added to the relief fund, the flour sale failed to resolve the debate about donations. The furious donors demanded that the Red Cross rewrite donation policy in order to protect San Francisco's refugees.[93] Indeed, control over the relief fund would soon become one of the most important issues facing San Francisco.

The Flour Riot was about much more than flour. The successful riot inspired women to ask for money instead of supplies. After the riot, one woman surprised relief supply warehouse workers when she said: "No, I don't want flour. . . . The papers say the money [relief donations] belongs to the people, and I want mine."[94] New demands for direct access to the relief funds led residents and refugees to form the Committee of Friends of Refugees, with its first agenda item being mounting a protest of the SFRRCF banquet honoring Edward Devine. The refugee committee's printed broadsheet high-lighted the stark differences between the elaborate banquet for relief officials and the food allotted to refugees: "Let the whole world know that while we are starving they are feasting. Such infamy was never known."[95] The poorly timed banquet on July 31, which was held just a few weeks after the Flour Riot, was surrounded by several thousand refugees "assembled with ban-ners and torchlights" to listen to speeches that challenged both Devine and Red Cross scientific methods.[96] The group first met at Mary Kelly's camp in Jefferson Square before marching down to the banquet. "At the head of those who marched in a body," reported the *San Francisco Examiner*, "was a little elderly woman, wearing glasses." This was Mary Kelly, who "headed the procession with a small American flag in her hand. She was the central figure of the occasion."[97] Kelly spoke at the rally and galvanized the crowd with her rousing rhetoric. "Food is given us that a dog would revolt at," she told the roaring crowd. "We have protested and where is the result?—a banquet to a man who was sent here to distribute charity among us." Kelly struck a nerve when she pointed out that "a very good time" was being had at the banquet while "we are out here having a very poor time."[98] She later recalled:

> We made appropriate speeches, telling the general public how the poor refugees, made destitute by the fire through no fault of their own, had been made to suffer and go hungry and cold after having lost every-thing, while the staff of the Relief Corporation were banquetted [*sic*]

Mary Kelly, standing at her relief cottage door, 1906. An adept protest leader, Kelly gave speeches, led marches, and lobbied state legislators. She believed that refugees, not officials, should control the relief fund. (Courtesy of the California History Room, California State Library, Sacramento, California.)

to the finest of everything that money could buy, not at their own expense, oh, no, but from the very funds which were sent here with which to rehabilitate the sufferers and victims of the great disaster.[99]

News coverage of the protest posed a serious threat to relief officials. Dr. Devine attempted to clear his name when he told reporters that "some mistakes have been made in the last hundred days. I do wish to say that myself and those under me have been actuated by the best motives of intelligent sympathy to try to help refugees on their feet."[100] But little could be said or done to stop the momentum of protest. One SFRRCF employee complained that the banquet protest incited refugees to further action: "They refuse to believe that the leaders at the office at the corner of Geary and Gough streets are alone responsible, and they begin to think that I am a party to the plot to keep them out of 'their share of the relief fund.'"[101] What started as a women's protest for flour took root and bloomed into a full-fledged protest movement. Mary Kelly played a prominent role, politicizing her fellow refugees and becoming a thorn in the side of many relief officials during the summer of 1906. After one of Kelly's rally speeches in early October, for example, "many of the refugee women went into headquarters demanding relief and they refused to leave. About half a dozen police were kept busy."[102] It would not be long before Mary Kelly and relief administrators would face a very public showdown in the disaster camps.

United Refugees

The well-publicized Flour Riot trial and SFFRC banquet protest created momentum for a bigger protest group of men and women. This group, the United Refugees, filed incorporation papers in July 1906 and made a direct run for the relief fund. Its primary objective was full financial control in order to purchase property to be held in common for working-class and poor refugees. The group was most likely inspired by an enormous relief fund that was administered by "outsiders." Refugees did not protest after the Great Chicago Fire, for example, where a much smaller fund was managed by a local charity agency.[103] In 1900 Galveston, most locals approved of Clara Barton's personalized Red Cross, which meshed nicely with the relief efforts sponsored by local women's clubs.[104] And the recent Baltimore Fire in 1904 did not incinerate enough residential property to generate a substantial relief effort or protest movement. San Francisco lawyer Alva Udell chaired the new organization and brought a distinctive mixture of legal training, socialist beliefs, and self-righteous anger to the group.[105] Mary Kelly participated by chairing the Grievance Committee. Kelly and Udell tapped the energy of disgruntled working-class and poor refugees, many of whom were living in relief camps. The organization also capitalized on San Francisco's history, often gaining sympathy in the press by pitting homeless San Franciscans against coldhearted, educated outsiders. The United Refugees effectively used protest rallies and printed grievances to gain the attention of local and national political and relief officials.

Refugee protest emerged from the experiences of the working class in the city's pre-disaster labor movement. At the time of the catastrophe, San Francisco had already earned a national reputation as a pro-labor, "closed shop city."[106] According to Michael Kazin, the city's geographic isolation facilitated union power by inhibiting the influx of strikebreakers. The primary center for organized working life was the San Francisco Labor Council, founded in 1892 as an advisory board to a diverse body of members that included a few women's locals.[107] But the Building Trades Council (BTC), headed by Patrick H. McCarthy, was "the epitome of labor's power in San Francisco." And labor's power, as McCarthy made clear in the BTC's weekly journal, *Organized Labor*, was intimately connected to the political realm.[108]

Working-class interests bridged some ethnic boundaries. McCarthy's *Organized Labor*, for example, launched a successful campaign for "workers to act vigorously to gain power for their class."[109] Dues-paying Irish and German male laborers formed the backbone of San Francisco's unions. Italian immigrant workers, whose North Beach population had been steadily increasing since 1900, "courted a life apart" from the unions as fishermen, bootblacks, and fruit-and-vegetable truck farmers and peddlers. Chinese workers, whose labor was virulently opposed by San Francisco unions, obtained nonunion work in laundries, in small cigar-making factories, and in homes as domestic servants. Whether they were union members or not, most San Franciscans were familiar with union rhetoric.

Interestingly, San Francisco unions were more apt to support relief leaders than refugee interests. According to Kazin, the union leaders and members "both desired a secure, male-dominated family life" and equated self-respect with middle-class domestic ideals.[110] As the wife of BTC president McCarthy later recalled, "Men who fight outside need some place in which to rest."[111] McCarthy's post-disaster union agenda dovetailed with the relief administrator's conceptions of both gender and race, as he worked closely with Mayor Schmitz's reconstruction efforts to control new building opportunities for the city's male labor force. The United Refugees appealed to those excluded by the SFRRCF and left out of the BTC's windfall. A brief recap of Mary Kelly's predicament sheds light on that point. Mary's husband, William Kelly, arrived in San Francisco in 1881 and worked as a rigger. At some point after their 1888 marriage, William was injured and stopped working. This left Mary, who worked as a cleaning woman at St. Ignatius School, as the sole wage earner for their family of five. The disaster put the Kelly family out of work altogether (St. Ignatius School burned), with few prospects for employment. Not surprisingly, the United Refugees' promise to give refugees direct access to relief funds offered hope to many who shared dire circumstances similar to Mary Kelly's.

Yet post-disaster conditions disturbed the close relationship between San Francisco's workers and its political leaders. When Mayor Schmitz fostered contacts within San Francisco's business elite during the emergency, he threatened his working-class constituency. In addition, the mayor's anti-looting and anti-liquor orders appeared to be designed to protect the city from working-class residents.[112] Father Peter C. Yorke, the outspoken and unorthodox advocate of Irish and working-class interests, launched an attack on Schmitz's organized relief methods before the end of April. Outraged at finding "old women" who were "sleeping on the floor," Father Yorke demanded the immediate delivery of two hundred cots from the mayor's initial relief Committee of 50. The pro–United Labor Party Yorke, whose ecclesiastical endorsement of the bloody 1901 strike helped bring down Mayor Phelan, threatened to hold Mayor Schmitz "personally responsible if with red tape [he] strangle[d] American charity."[113]

The United Refugees also gained momentum by tapping into growing public dissatisfaction with relief bureaucracy. Local news was rife with criticism of red tape. As one *San Francisco Newsletter* editorial made clear,

> Dr. Devine and the other professional charity workers know that personal experience doesn't count in such matters. They know that a theory is the only thing to work on. Of course, the kitchens may be bad, people may go hungry—but as long as the theory is adhered to, the system is worked out on scientific principles, there should be no kick [protest]. Anyone should prefer a scientifically empty stomach to one filled by unscientific methods.[114]

Scientific social work theory, according to the press, came at the people's expense. The authors tacitly endorsed refugee protest by stating that unsanitary kitchens and hungry people coexisted with relief theory and scientific principles. The sarcastic argument that a "scientifically empty stomach" was preferable to "one filled by unscientific methods" may well have convinced many San Franciscans that local refugees were justified in their actions.

Further, the timing of the United Refugees, which dovetailed with women's spontaneous activism, was flawless. A critic from within the ranks of the Associated Charities, for example, lent credence to the cause. Dr. Margaret Mahoney, a San Francisco physician and Associated Charities Central Council member, published a scathing attack on SFRRCF bureaucracy in late July. Mahoney believed that the relief corporation "undertook to pauperize a self-respecting community" by refusing to distribute freely all relief supplies and funds.[115] The doctor printed her opinions in a pamphlet, arguing that modern relief methods "brought disaster to a self-respecting, industrious, prosperous people. . . . The only way to obtain supplies was to fill out cards containing humiliating and impertinent questions. Investigation, elimination, statistics were the order of the day where food and clothing were needed."[116] That Mahoney had her say at the expense of her position with the Associated Charities was yet another example of the politicizing effect of disaster relief.[117]

United Refugees success hinged on controlling the multimillion-dollar relief fund. The group's ambitious plans included "co-operative stores, factories, bakeries, restaurants, commission houses, farms, poultry growing, cattle, sheep and horse raising."[118] The new organization also asked its members to pledge their property to the organization for the "mutual protection of its members."[119] While Alva Udell's connection to other socialist movements is unknown, it is likely that he was influenced by the growing U.S. socialist response to industrialization.[120] The 1906 calamity may have awakened dormant concerns about social inequities for Udell, as it had for Mary Kelly. In the legal battle against the relief corporation, Udell used alternate means to secure Red Cross funds. Part of the United Refugees campaign was the distribution of preprinted loan applications to refugees, encouraging families to apply for $250 home loans from the American National Red Cross.[121] This perplexing legal document represented capitalist means to socialist ends. Refugees who accepted the United Refugees terms applied for a loan from the Red Cross but, in turn, used the loan to buy preferred capital stock in United Refugees—which planned to use this fund to purchase land for refugee housing in San Francisco.[122] Although the success of the loan program was never recorded, it represents a creative alternative to disaster relief.

United Refugees also turned its attention to state and national legislative action. By midsummer, refugees had organized committees and elected delegates to represent their interests, sending a female-dominated delegation to Phelan's Finance Committee to debate refugee housing in early December.[123] In 1907, the group went a step further as Udell and Kelly traveled to

Sacramento to lobby for an assembly bill that would create a "public relief commission."[124] The bill required each city to appoint five citizens to the panel, which would have the "power to receive, distribute and disperse of the real property and all moneys . . . given or bequeathed for the relief of any sufferers from any earthquake, conflagration or other disaster heretofore or hereafter occurring in the State of California."[125] Section 3 of the proposed bill targeted Phelan's favorite "Confidential Cases," prohibiting the secret distribution of relief funds. Udell also sent letters to Senate and Assembly leaders sprinkled with the passionate prose of protest. In one letter to a state representative, he proclaimed that the bill's passage would ensure that "idiots, incompetents and knaves may be known and punished as traitors to the poor people."[126] But Udell's and Kelly's polarizing presence in Sacramento may have hindered the passage of the bill, which swept the Assembly but failed in the Senate.

Despite the failure at the state capitol, the United Refugees pursued federal intervention. The group appealed to President Roosevelt for help and regularly updated the Red Cross national headquarters with news from the West.[127] Its protest activity prompted two investigations, one by the Massachusetts Association for the Relief of California during the fall of 1906 and a second by the American National Red Cross during the spring of 1907. The Massachusetts investigation brought a temporary halt to relief donations. But the East Coast investigators soon concluded that the United Refugees members were simply "organized and systematic stirrers-up of discontent," and resumed funding the relief corporation in November 1906, though cautioning that United Refugees "ideas [were] harmful in making others, badly enough off now, discontented with their lot."[128]

The American National Red Cross neither endorsed nor ignored the United Refugees. At first, Red Cross Executive Committee member Mabel Boardman dismissed their claims, arguing that reports on the United Refugees had "not been a surprise to us for no such work of magnitude could have been carried out without criticism and the only marvel is that it has been as unworthy of consideration as it has."[129] Nonetheless, the Red Cross responded to steady complaints from the United Refugees by sending General G.W.W. Davis to San Francisco in May 1907. After meeting with Udell and other protest leaders, Davis determined that the United Refugees claims were "without merit" because they were "not supported by proof." Davis admitted, however, "that mistakes have been made by the officers of the Corporation in applying relief." He concluded that these were simply "errors in judgment, and that no charge of negligence, graft or prejudice can be laid at the feet of those who have been administering relief work." Davis's report upheld the principles of modern philanthropy, arguing that such methods prevented the misappropriation of relief funds. "In the application of relief, the greatest possible care has been taken to investigate every case by disinterested inspectors," read Davis's report, "and whenever the relief was not evidently needed, it has been withheld."[130]

To be sure, refugee protest called attention to the class and gender biases of scientific social work. And organized protest gave voice to refugee women in particular. By asserting their right to control the relief fund, protesting refugees inserted themselves in San Francisco's public realm. Although they logged more defeats than victories, their protest created solidarity among many of San Francisco's poor and working classes as they challenged the conception of social order held by relief policy makers.

The 1906 disaster created chaos and opportunity. The far-reaching need for relief was a catalyst for the groups, and sometimes individuals, who quickly responded to alleviate suffering. Refugees were not the only ones to benefit from the women's organizations that offered aid. For Catholic religious women, volunteerism brought spiritual reward or, in the words of one Catholic sister, "Our dear Lord will no doubt reward the labors of the Sisters."[131] For middle-class clubwomen, relief work firmly opened the door to the public realm, giving them the valuable experience to disseminate domestic values for the public good. It may be that such relief work also buttressed future political activism for California clubwomen: not long after the disaster, the well-organized clubwomen entered San Francisco politics and in 1911 made a successful bid for state suffrage.

Disaster relief ultimately strengthened the Chinese community in San Francisco and the Bay Area after SFRRCF racial discrimination reenergized Chinatown's social and political networks. Disaster relief brought additional economic and political leverage that helped the CCBA to reestablish San Francisco's Chinatown, while refugee relocation expanded the Chinese presence in the Bay Area. The Chinese community was also built up by a disaster-inspired increase in immigration. With the destruction of San Francisco's City Hall and its entire collection of birth certificates, thousands of Chinese declared their rights as "native born" and claimed immigration privileges for their families. As the national and international Chinese community rallied to aid "our people [who] are in great distress," they sketched the borders of a Chinese community that extended well beyond the boundaries of San Francisco's Chinatown.

Unlike the varied, informal relief efforts, refugee protest confronted official relief policy head-on. While ultimately unsuccessful, organizations like the United Refugees presented an important counterpoint to official policy. The 1907 bill that passed the state assembly, for example, banned the secret distribution of relief funds, which would have ended James Phelan's preferred "Confidential Cases." The United Refugees envisioned a city where refugees lived on common land and the $9.5 million relief fund went to cooperative enterprises. In the end, by battling the city's business and political elite and unwittingly challenging working-class people who stood to benefit from reconstruction's high labor demands, the United Refugees failed to draw enough supporters to its cause.

Official disaster relief prevailed in the city for two main reasons: its massive relief fund and its influential leadership. By maintaining control over relief, the SFRRCF had the power to influence the recovery of refugees and residents alike. This power was realized by the relief camps, which became the public home for thousands of refugees and, as we shall see, were integral to the relief agenda and rebuilding efforts in post-disaster San Francisco.

CHAPTER 4

Disaster Relief Camps

The Public Home of Private Life

The 1906 catastrophe removed physical boundaries between public and private property in San Francisco and literally pushed domestic life into public space, giving both politicians and Progressive reformers unforeseen access to private life. If the public is, as Mary Ryan argues, "situated analytically so as to exercise decisive authority over the private world and over its female inhabitants in particular," then the San Francisco earthquake and fire amplified that authority.[1] Refugees recognized it by another name: disaster relief. Responding to real (destroyed neighborhoods) and imagined (non-elite refugees) social disorder, relief policy reinforced gender, race, and class norms. As discussed in Chapter 2, programs like the "bonus plan" home grants prioritized native-born families and two-parent households. The policy-backed social hierarchy took firm root in the relief camps, which became a public household for refugees and the linchpin of disaster recovery.

With San Francisco property titles reduced to a pile of ashes under City Hall's skeletal dome, disaster zone evacuation prevented potential squatters from interfering with civic rebuilding. A segregated camp for Chinese refugees, which in essence reconstituted the city's racialized boundaries, was a critical part of a larger plan to excise Chinatown from post-disaster San Francisco. The racially segregated camp was but one example of how this relief program reestablished the social boundaries that had been annihilated by the catastrophe.

The relief camps illustrate the centrality of gender to post-disaster policy as well. The camps were the city's new public household, headed by camp commanders who determined the fate of the refugee families under their supervision. Approximately 40 percent of San Francisco's 100,000 homeless lived in twenty-six camps that served up social order along with meals, tents, and blankets. Camp policy physically separated families from single men and all Chinese refugees, giving native-born two-parent families, especially those with property in San Francisco, additional relief dollars to rebuild their homes and businesses in the city. Only working-class families whom relief officials deemed "deserving," based on middle-class values, found rebuilding assistance. A new relief cottage program, which replaced camp tents with small wooden homes, extended the camp experience into the rebuilding city. As the camps closed, "earthquake cottage" occupants relocated these structures throughout San Francisco. Once again, relief policy determined who had the right to claim such homes. Thus the future of thousands of refugees hung in the balance as they were evaluated and categorized by relief standards.

Yet the disaster created a strange array of opportunities as well. The usual privacy of domestic life was now public, and the resulting "politicized" domesticity had a direct impact on women in two ways. First, middle-class women gained a stronger foothold in the public sphere by providing relief supplies and, later, moral influence inside the camps. Second, camp residency made working-class and poor women public agents, and they actively negotiated for relief benefits for themselves and their families. In 1906 San Francisco, post-disaster material conditions forced many women to exceed their prescribed gender roles in order to obtain the materials necessary to

A building on Sacramento Street, 1906. The missing façade is a visual reminder of disaster relief's powerful influence, which—because of the destruction to both public and private property—allowed policy makers to reach into the private lives of San Franciscans. (Courtesy of the San Francisco Virtual Museum.)

resume those very roles.[2] Politicized domesticity was the means by which they could both secure immediate disaster relief and define the rights of citizenship.

Public Housekeeping: Physical Needs and Moral Order

During the summer of 1906, forty thousand refugees considered their small tents and fly-infested dining halls home.[3] The men, women, and children were nearly equally divided, tallying 39 percent, 31 percent, and 30 percent of the population, respectively.[4] Relief camp demographic data pointed to the dual goals of relief policy: the camps funneled native-born middle-class and working-class refugees back to private life in the city and created a public home to contain poor and working-class refugees during the city's initial rebuilding period.[5]

Progressive leaders hoped that this public home would provide both physical and moral shelter. Military personnel created the physical space when they pitched army tents, dug latrines, and stocked dining halls for more than two dozen relief camps in May and June. But they did not have the staff or the time to supervise moral conditions. Presidio military commander and relief camp supervisor General A. W. Greely admitted that his troops were not trained for this endeavor. "We are not handling the Relief business," the general reported to the Committee of 50. "We are simply supervising it."[6] On July 1, 1906, Greely withdrew his troops from the camps, leaving fertile ground for San Francisco's relief agenda to take root. However, supply shortages and substandard camp conditions challenged policy effectiveness. As a result, policy makers turned to middle-class women volunteers to create a positive, moral camp environment. Gathering women from their various clubs and church groups to undertake the task of municipal housekeeping, the Women's Alliance for Reconstruction put them to work in the post-disaster public sphere. Although relief officials never acquired the unmitigated social control they desired, women volunteers breathed life into the relief organization's gender ideology.[7]

Relief leaders used two criteria to select the locations for the twenty-six military camps: pre-disaster urban spatial arrangements and post-disaster rebuilding plans. These camps, in city parks or undamaged public squares, removed a majority of refugees from the disaster zone.[8] By taking control of all public square encampments, relief leaders assumed new regulatory authority over San Francisco's homeless. In other words, refugees residing in public squares temporarily forfeited their privacy as domestic life became the property of the city.

Dust, wind, and hordes of flies were staples of everyday life in the relief camps. Even if the thin canvas tents blocked the chilly early-evening winds, they provided little protection against the dirt and insects swirling about the camp grounds. Most of daily life happened outside the thick rows of pitched tents, as refugee families trekked across the grounds to use the latrines, eat in the kitchen and dining area, or collect new supplies. The best feature of a

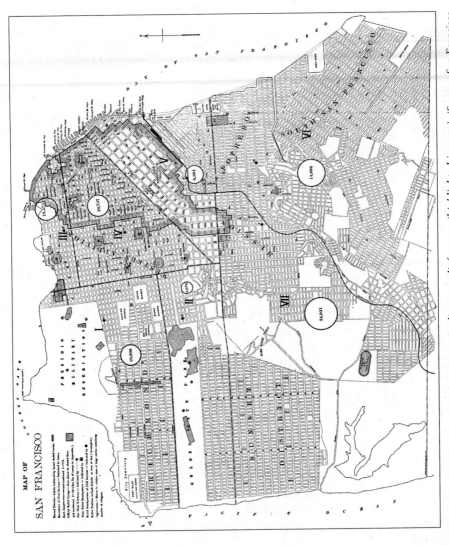

Map showing San Francisco's twenty-six disaster relief camps (highlighted in gray). (Source: San Francisco Relief Survey. Russell Sage Foundation. New York: Survey Associates, Inc., 1913.)

camp called Harbor View was aptly described by its name. Nestled on the city's northern shore near the Presidio, the camp offered a stunning panorama of the bay. Later in the century, this Marina District real estate would bring premium prices for its views of the Golden Gate Bridge and beyond. But in 1906 it was a dismal location for three thousand camp residents. One reporter, who had the luxury of sleeping elsewhere, noted that the camp was "swept by fog and raw winds in chilly weather, [and] without shade trees and dusty and warm in sunny, hot weather."[9] But refugees were exposed to more than just the physical elements in the camps.

The relief camps created a new kind of domestic space, with their commanders supervising all aspects of daily life. Not only did they enforce camp rules and regulations; they decided if and when their residents received additional aid. While working-class Irish and Italian refugees may have been accustomed to residing in close proximity to their neighbors, they shared more than hallways or curbsides in the camps. Refugees dined and bathed with their neighbors, all under the oversight of military and civilian personnel. When sociologist Mary Roberts Smith visited the camps, she worried that "the total uprooting of all ordinary habits of life" was an experience that fell "more and more heavily on the women and children."[10] The young refugee Edna Calhan found this out when she used the camp latrines. She recalled her excitement at discovering the new facilities, which could accommodate eight to ten women. But her experience of them quickly extinguished that excitement: "I just got

One of San Francisco's twenty-six official relief camps, 1906. Approximately forty thousand refugees lived in the camps, the last of which closed in 1908. (Courtesy of the San Francisco Virtual Museum.)

seated nicely and there was a knock on the door. . . . An Army officer walked in. . . . He said, 'Never mind me. I'm an Army officer.' He was inspecting, looking down at the seat and writing something in his notes. I sat there. Finally, he went out. . . . I lost all interest in that particular toilet."[11] While refugees experienced a loss of privacy in the camps, relief officials benefited from reconfigured domestic space, since the camps created a public home where they, not the refugees, ran the household.

But camp rules and regulations did not guarantee habitable conditions. The findings of a woman investigative reporter confirmed a deplorable state of affairs at the camps. Constance Lawrence Dean, "one of San Francisco's keenest and most capable newspaper women," spent a mid-July week living in a refugee camp. Dean traded in her shopping dress for old clothes and a worn hat to assume the identity of "Margaret Jennings, refugee." The *San Francisco Call*'s front-page exposé ran the side-by-side photos of the well-coiffed, wide-eyed Dean and "Margaret Jennings, refugee," who glared warily at the camera from beneath her limp hat. "I had dressed miserably, with a show of untidy poverty," explained Dean, "for it was a part of my design to appear utterly, commonplacely [*sic*] uninteresting." Plied with questions and confused by multiple relief forms, Dean found that her "General Supply Card" and "Special Order Card" earned her several days of standing in a relief line, a tent without bedding, and a lantern without oil or wick. Her "Food Card," on the other hand, was accepted at the camp kitchen, but the "distressing odors and the half-musty food dispelled the desire to eat."

Dean's experience of camp life was not far off the mark. Indeed, camp dining facilities were unappetizing and unsanitary places to consume a meal. July camp inspections, months after the earthquake and fires, documented conditions in which refugees waited in line for up to a hour and a half for a seat at a dining table, where they were sure to encounter poor food and dirty utensils and dishes.[12] The flies, which sanitary inspectors found "in every portion of and upon everything in these kitchens," were linked by agar plate testing to 151 cases of typhoid fever.[13] Kitchen employees were another liability, as they had to be reminded to clean their hands and dishes, remove flypaper from the tables before the refugees arrived, and stop poking their fingers into cooked food.[14] Dean called for a Progressive remedy for poor camp conditions. "Forcible, honest executive officials, and plenty of them," she insisted, would bring the "speedy arrangement of a [better] system."[15]

Progressive relief leaders worried that substandard living conditions would destroy their efforts to create a good home for San Francisco's refugees and encourage moral decline.[16] In early July, they sent the following policy memo to camp commanders: "It will not be permitted to have the sense of decency of refugees in your camp shocked by disgraceful or scandalous action on the part of others."[17] The memo instructed commanders to "segregate all moral degenerates in your camps" and to use "moral persuasion" on the remaining refugees. Many camp commanders found it difficult to enforce "moral persuasion." They rarely resorted to eviction, ejecting only 1 percent of all camp residents.[18] In one case, a commander employed a troublesome male tenant in order to put travel money in the refugee's pocket. "I kept him on my roll two weeks so as to get rid of him," admitted the commander.[19] But his strategy did not produce the desired result; the resident in question remained at the camp. Most camp commanders were ill-equipped and, quite simply, outnumbered when it came to using "moral persuasion." As a result, relief leaders sought the input of middle-class women volunteers to address the issue.

Women in California were among the first disaster relief volunteers, springing into action before Red Cross officials boarded trains bound for San Francisco. Middle-class clubwomen brought what Paula Baker describes as "the benefits of motherhood to the public sphere."[20] They turned out in droves, responding to the call for "women everywhere" to defend the city from "the threat of depravity."[21] They cooked meals, baked bread, and collected and sewed clothes for refugees. As shown in Chapter 3, these women were so effective that Red Cross and civic leaders temporarily relied on them for support.

Many women volunteers brought enthusiasm in place of experience. The women who were already trained in social work or nursing worked outside the camps with Katharine Felton's Associated Charities. It was up to Lucile Eaves, a determined former San Francisco settlement house leader, to organize inexperienced women volunteers inside the camps. Eaves ran the "Women's Alliance for Reconstruction," and advertised for "an army of philanthropic women, who will give their leisure time to relief work which will be of both economic and moral benefit."[22] In Eaves's words, "Women everywhere must be made to realize that they are part of a municipal family. The men are too busy with bread winning to do what should be done. We women must work to defend our city from threatened degradation."[23] Thus the camps provided new opportunities for women to work in the public sphere.[24]

Local middle-class women volunteered at the newly constructed camp sewing centers, where refugees stitched both fabric and moral fiber. In the eyes of Progressive reformers, busy women were honest women. Eaves believed that the sewing centers prevented the "idleness of the women of the camps [that] was demoralizing." The Red Cross leadership agreed. Mabel Boardman, the Red Cross's most prominent leader and spokesperson, later wrote that "idleness [in the camps] is a habit easily acquired and difficult to overcome."[25] Consequently, refugee women could no longer expect free clothing after the sewing centers appeared. Instead, new policy required that they take up needle and thread to create their own. Asked to pay for their fabric, many did additional labor beyond sewing their own clothes. According to relief records, this policy held potentially dishonest refugees in check: "those who were disposed to 'graft' were much less apt to do so when they made their own garments, and also in many cases gave a return in labor for the material."[26] These sewing centers were not simply a gendered workplace; they were also a critical social space to inculcate class-based moral ideals. Volunteers taught girls how to sew a literal and metaphorical straight seam when they "gather[ed]

Members of a sewing class at a relief camp in Lobos Square, 1906. Middle-class women volunteered at the sewing centers, where they supervised refugee women and gave sewing lessons to girls. (California Historical Society, Resv. FN-34241/ CHS2011.469.tif.)

the little girls into classes where they could be given much-needed guidance and instruction."[27] In some camps, the centers expanded to include reading rooms, youth and adult clubs, concerts, lectures, and religious services.[28] The centers' broad social agenda embodied the idealism of women volunteers who sincerely wanted to help improve the lives of refugee women.

In the end, the volunteers may have been better served than the refugees. Work inside the camps contributed to local and state clubwomen's networks by giving their members invaluable experience in the public realm. These networks thrived long after the last camp closed in 1908. Nonetheless, the sewing centers remained on the camp periphery and camp commanders, not volunteers, regulated everyday life. Relief officials endorsed a patriarchal structure that allowed commanders to decide where refugees ate, what they slept on, and when they would receive additional funds. There is little evidence to suggest that women volunteers reformed the attitudes or altered the decisions of camp commanders. Most women volunteers, who cared for refugee women on the camp margins, had few opportunities to challenge the authority of camp commanders. For most refugees, a camp commander's opinion was more influential than the social events hosted by sewing center volunteers. At the end of the day, their fate rested in the hands of the commander, the man who determined who was eligible for additional relief funds.

Race and Relief: The Chinese Camp

For relief and civic leaders, plans for social order required racial segregation. The Chinese relief camp reconstituted racialized boundaries to promote two distinct goals: segregating the Chinese and excising Chinatown from post-disaster San Francisco.[29] Citizens' Committee meeting minutes suggest that leaders spent more time discussing Chinatown's real estate than its refugees. James Phelan—relief leader, former mayor, and virulent opponent of Asian immigration—was one of the plan's most prominent promoters.[30] Relief committee meeting minutes reveal a receptive audience for Phelan's ideas to use the Chinese relief camp as an optimal strategy for removing Chinese residents from the city. The segregated camp served an ideological function as well: by clearly demarcating the racial other, it created the aura of possibility for the moral improvement of the city's poor and working classes. All other racial and ethnic groups, including African Americans, lived together in the remaining twenty-five camps.[31]

The first camp was located well outside Chinatown, on several vacant blocks at the foot of Van Ness Avenue near the Bay. "Chinese are being concentrated on the North Beach," reassured a *San Francisco Chronicle* editorial, "from whence they can be moved by water to their permanent location [outside the city]."[32] Phelan endorsed the relocation plan but not the camp location. Temporary residence inside the city limits, he argued, created influential residential ties for Chinatown refugees.[33] As newspapers printed stories highlighting the Van Ness Avenue location, Phelan's committee approved moving the camp to the military grounds of the Presidio.[34] The new camp was outside the city, standing on the Presidio's grassy slopes just inside its east gate. Abraham Ruef, the mayor's close associate, reassured his colleagues that "there were very few Chinese in the city . . . and that these [Chinese] had all been removed to the temporary quarters at the Presidio."[35]

But that response did not satisfy angry property owners living near the Presidio, who forced yet another move. Within twenty-four hours, "a large delegation of neighbors" demanded that the relief committee move the camp.[36] They "objected to the establishment of the Oriental quarter so close to their homes," reported the *Chronicle*, "where the summer zephyrs would blow the odors of Chinatown into their front doors."[37] Hardly describing the thinly populated Chinese camp, the reports in the local press added fuel to the committee's racist fire and the camp was moved to the western edge of the Presidio. Brigadier General Frederick Funston, who selected the final site for the encampment, concurred with the popular racialized view of Chinatown. "His twofold objective was to place a traditionally unsanitary people as remote as possible from the Caucasian camps," reported the local press, "where they would have the greatest attainable natural hygienic aids."[38]

On the national stage, politicians and press showered the Chinese camp with compliments. Even before the refugees made their journey to the final

A 1906 postcard print showing an unrealistic view of a Chinese relief camp. San Francisco relief officials failed to attract many Chinese refugees to the segregated camp. (Courtesy of the California Historical Society, Resv. FN-34054/CHS2010.308.tif.)

camp location, a special presidential investigator determined that all was well in the Chinese camp. "An interpreter informed me there that they [Chinatown refugees] had no complaints to make at all," Roosevelt's secretary of commerce and labor reassured the president. "They were living better than in Chinatown."[39] Later that summer, the national press painted an idyllic portrait of the camp's green fields "washed with yellow, white, violet, and orange of mustard, lupine, and poppy flowers . . . [on the] rolling stretch of country near the bay." A journalist writing in the *Century Magazine* told her readers that "the whole equipment here was noticeably good; from tents and ropes to stoves and shining refuse-cans, the material was new and sound, the best I had seen issued by the government to refugees."[40] Unbeknownst to her readers, however, the Chinese camp was closed two months before this story rolled off the press in August 1906.

The true story was that Chinese refugees refused to submit to camp conditions. Reports from the camp commander and sanitary inspectors were hidden from the press and, until recently, from historians as well. Although the camp was built for 10,000 refugees, internal reports indicate that its population never climbed above 200.[41] By the end of May, the remote camp was down to 120 Chinese refugees.[42] A sanitation report on May 22 revealed the tentative status of the camp: "Three or four in tent. No floors or mattresses. If this camp is to be permanent it is recommended that these be supplied at once. Not yet required by the camp commander in view of this question."[43]

Some camp inspectors believed the multiple relocations discouraged the Chinese refugees. "They were much dissatisfied at having to move again and I think it is probable that many of them will not remain," reported one camp official. "They have been moved so many times . . . that they have lost confidence and do not feel that they will be allowed to stay anywhere."[44] In truth, most Chinese did not rely on disaster relief. Instead they thwarted relief officials' plans for social control by turning to members of their own community of family and friends for support in navigating life outside their pre-disaster homes.

Chinese refugees could not assume that official relief representatives would care for them. Lee Dock found this out all too soon. In mid-May 1906, a city sanitary inspector found Lee Dock "in a tent near the west fence of the Fort Mason," suffering from dysentery and "in a very bad condition." The inspector wrote that the "case should be referred to the proper authorities and should be removed to a hospital."[45] But racialized social norms left Lee Dock a victim of the city's unwillingness to care for Chinese refugees outside of Chinatown. "There seems to be considerable doubt as to who should act in the case of the Chinaman, Lee Dock, mentioned in yesterday's report," the inspector wrote the following day. "In the meantime he is in sad need of attention."[46]

The hope of survival for Chinatown refugees rested on their ability to maintain family and neighborhood ties. Alice Sue Fun's family, for example, suffered from their decision to live in Oakland's Chinese relief camp. After Alice's family made it across the bay to Oakland, her mother gave birth to her sixth child at the relief camp. Shortly thereafter, Alice's father died from typhoid fever. The family was devastated. "There was nothing my mother could do," recalled Fun. "She had six children. At that time, you know, no welfare, nothing." Her mother's only alternative was a hasty marriage to another Chinatown refugee.[47]

So Chinatown organized its own disaster relief. A sizable donation to the relief fund from China's empress dowager obliged President Roosevelt to respond to the Chinese in San Francisco. Roosevelt's directive to relief leaders read: "President directs you furnish same shelter and camping facilities to Chinese as to others . . . and that you cooperate with Red-Cross in relieving suffering or destitution among them."[48] The telegram was in keeping with Roosevelt's June 1905 order that required the Chinese exclusion laws to be carried out "without harshness."[49] Roosevelt, however, tacitly approved segregated relief in the same telegram: "Use your own discretion as to whether special camps shall be established for them."[50] Despite the president's endorsement of the segregated camp, Phelan and his associates never gained control of the camp or of property in Chinatown.[51]

The racist relief policy only strengthened Chinatown's business and political networks.[52] The Chinese disaster relief effort collected food and supply shipments sent by Chinese Consolidated Benevolent Associations (CCBAs) from around the country and found refugees housing in Oakland's small

Chinatown and Berkeley's Chinese-owned businesses. These relief efforts increased their negotiation power in the Chinatown relocation debates.[53] It was not long before San Francisco's CCBA convinced local political and business leaders that the catastrophe had not destroyed their vibrant community. The CCBA's threat to relocate San Francisco's lucrative Chinatown to another city was taken seriously and civic leaders agreed to Chinatown's return to the city.

Relief leaders were more successful in realizing their second goal for segregating the camps. Eliminating Chinese refugees, who were differentiated by both race and sex (with a male population hovering at 85 percent), highlighted relief camp policy class and gender ideals. Relief officials continued to label Chinese residents as the source of San Francisco's social problems, while pinning their hopes on "improving" the working-class and poor refugees living in their relief camps.

REFUGEE WOMEN

Working-class and poor refugee women exhibited two distinct responses to the commanders who managed camp life: patronage and protest. By forging a personal relationship with relief administrators, refugee women gained access to additional aid through their relief patrons. Single refugee women in particular adhered to popular conceptions of gender to reclaim their domestic space in post-disaster San Francisco. Married women, on the other hand, more often challenged relief policy and policy makers. They joined protest rallies in the city and initiated female-based acts of protest inside the camps. To do so, these women defied their prescribed gender roles to obtain access to relief, which, in turn, funded their roles as wives and mothers inside the private household.[54] The following analysis, like that of Michael Katz and Thomas Krainz, shifts the focus away from the rhetoric of leaders to spotlight the everyday experiences of those on the receiving end of reform.[55] This perspective shows how relief recipients constantly negotiated, and sometimes transformed, policy regulations.

The records left by a young camp commander provide a rare view of how refugee women adapted to life inside the camps. The commander of Harbor View, Dr. Rene Bine, was a local physician who supported the Progressive agenda of national Red Cross and local relief leaders. As Paul Boyer aptly summarizes, relief policy makers used "professional expertise and technical skill, rather than class dominance or an assumed moral superiority, as justification for their manipulation of the urban environment."[56] But this did not prevent moral evaluations from finding their way into relief policy. When it came to those who applied relief guidelines, nineteenth-century definitions of the "deserving" poor crept back into disaster policy.[57] The unmarried Bine, for example, took his paternal role seriously and was devoted to finding and helping deserving refugees. He maintained personal contact with camp tenants, acting as both their advocate and their judge. As the first civilian to serve in a military relief camp immediately following the disaster, he was already adept

Harbor View Relief Camp, staff photo, 1906. This camp of three thousand refugees was located in the present-day Marina District. (Courtesy of the San Francisco Virtual Museum.)

at interceding in refugee domestic life. According to one local newspaper story on the military camp, Bine was "the social and domestic arbiter of the 1150 souls whose health is in his keeping. If housewives quarrel—which housewives sometimes do, even when under military control—he is called upon to decide the right and wrong of the dispute, and if children disobey their parents, he it is to whom appeal is made by the latter."[58] He brought this experience to Harbor View, where he was convinced that refugees would be best served by following his judgment. "The sooner you realize that I am here to be of assistance to all," read his memo posted for camp occupants, "the sooner will you help me in keeping the camp as I want to have it."[59]

Bine's opinions were indispensable to refugee women who had difficulty navigating the system of relief on their own. Like the social worker who made a home visit, Bine interviewed refugees in their tents before submitting brief reports to headquarters. His support was necessary for a favorable response. A. K. Sheehan, for example, was relieved by Bine's assessment that her "case soon be taken up, if on no other grounds than priority application." Although "a real good-hearted woman," the single Irish refugee came across as "very hard to handle, as she always feels that somebody meant other than [what] was . . . really said."[60] The rough edges of Sheehan's noncompliance with gendered expectations of docility were smoothed away under the pen of the paternalistic commander.

Even hardworking mothers needed assistance in gaining visibility amid the seemingly endless piles of protocol paperwork. "Application for rehabilitation filed weeks ago and nothing done," read another Bine report that painted a sympathetic portrait of Allie Bailey. With a son suffering from tuberculosis and a "daughter-in-law with baby on her hands," Bailey continued to work "on and off at whatever her appearance allowed her to apply for." Bine's character assessment was the most important part of his report. Two simple words guaranteed financial aid for Allie Bailey: "is deserving."[61]

Many single female refugees forged personal relationships with male relief administrators to circumvent the relief system's emphasis on two-parent households. These relationships were a matter of survival and, as a result, they often traversed relief camp boundaries. One woman wrote a series of letters to Bine about her difficulties with the relief system after leaving the camp. "You sent for me the other day to tell me that $100 had been granted to me on my application and expected me to feel very grateful etc.," she wrote to the commander. "That $100 will not tide me through the three months treatment, it will not pay rent, furnish the food necessary to build me up, buy clothing and other absolutely [sic] articles and provide transportation."[62] Without Bine's intervention, the $100 was the last relief payment that she could expect. Women often appealed to Bine as a male authority figure by emphasizing their social isolation, physical helplessness, and poverty. In the dramatic words of another former refugee who continued to write for help, "I hope that you will take a little interest in this my case and advise me, what to do as well as how to send an aplication [sic] in, for my share of the Relief money, Because I am friendless, and poor, and persecuted."[63] It was obvious that gender and marital status dictated the amount of aid granted by the relief system. Perhaps more important, gender ideology also provided the tools with which to work the system.

The campaign for help was not limited to camp commanders. Some women took their cases directly to the man in charge. Even James Phelan was not immune to their demands. Agness Menzer called on Phelan's office and residence before resorting to the following letter: "I am the lady who called to try and see you one morning so very early at your home. I knew afterward it was wrong to call so early so please excuse me. . . . I had been trying for a long time to see you at your office and could not."[64] The chief of police fielded another request by a single female resident at Harbor View: "We ppor [sic] helpless, stranded refugees feel we are still entitled to protection day and night," wrote A. L. Pascoe. "Robberies and assaults occur so often that we women fear to sleep at night, especially those who are without protectors."[65] Although her letter emphasized her helplessness, she was quite specific about the solution. She told Chief Dinan to hire a male friend who lived nearby in Tent 14 for the job. But she masked her assertiveness by highlighting her vulnerability as a female refugee "without protectors." Women like Pascoe walked a fine line. Their credibility depended on appealing to the gender and class belief systems of male leaders. Yet in the act of delivering their message, they stepped beyond those expectations of docility and fragility.

Not every woman fit neatly into the camp's gendered description of need. Some defied traditional gender roles and used other means to secure aid. Stealing was one way to do so. Speaking out against physical abuse was another. Ida Boyne lost $150 in rehabilitation money to another refugee woman who, posing as Boyne's mother, claimed and cashed the check.[66] The success of this crime hinged on the maternal role; gendered assumptions about motherhood gave the thief legitimacy in the eyes of the relief administrator. The relief system, not Ida Boyne, suffered the loss. She was issued a second check because officials considered her to be a deserving refugee.

With a police force stretched thin to cover the city and few civilian guards inside the camps, women were undoubtedly exposed to crime and physical violence. Public accusations of physical abuse were a clear transgression of popular gender ideology.[67] Refugee women who spoke out against violence usually found support in the local press. Relief officials, on the other hand, were harder to convince. Women found favorable press during the prosecution of a warehouse supply officer for assault during the June Flour Riot, but the guilty verdict did not hurt the assailant's career. His supervisor, Edward Devine, remained convinced of his innocence and offered the warehouse officer a new position as a camp commander. Relief officials labeled women who spoke out against violence as troublemakers. Sometimes their peers did as well. Camp residents turned on Alice Lastra, a refugee who often complained about the relief system, when they told a reporter that she had "been studying to become proficient in the art of stage fainting and falling" so that "if a commander attempted to eject her . . . she would have him arrested for abuse."[68] While the truth of this claim is questionable, the vulnerability of refugee women is not. Women made vulnerable within the relief system might garner the sympathy of the press, but they were also likely to face repercussions from relief administrators and, sometimes, peers.

Few women challenged the paternal foundation of the relief camp and won. This is evident in the experiences of another Harbor View camp resident, Johanna Dohrman. The relationship between Dohrman and Commander Bine followed a paternalistic story line not unlike the relationships between Bine and other female residents. Even Bine recalled how, at first, the two had become "great friends."[69] But their alliance soon ended over a tin of milk. Dohrman and her elderly female friend, identified only as Mrs. Martin, accused Bine and the camp nurse of violently throwing Martin to the ground after refusing to issue a ration of milk. Dohrman called in local reporters and testified to Bine's "cruel treatment."[70] According to the commander, this was all in the imagination of a disgruntled refugee. "Dohrman, although not within 200 yards of Headquarters was the 'chief witness,'" Bine wrote to his superiors, "and I was still further from the scene of my alleged deeds."[71] And the elderly Martin was not helpless in Bine's story. Instead, she struck "the nurse on the head with her milk tin, when informed by this most gentle of nurses, 'that to get milk, she would have to get an order from Bine, in the Headquarters tent.'"[72] At stake was not Martin's right to a tin of milk, for her age guaranteed a milk ration under current policy. Rather it was her failure to follow the protocol established by her commander. Johanna Dohrman never fully recovered from this public confrontation. She sent a futile letter to Bine's supervisor to rectify the situation. "I beg you to inform me as to why I cannot receive any aid from the relief and red cross funds," she wrote. "If that is the case that they have reported me as a meddler as I have been told, I wish you would let me know at once."[73] Already known as a member of the United Refugees and a friend to refugee activist Mary Kelly, Dohrman found that her credibility within the relief system was further tarnished by her commander. Such an episode only reinforced the need for women to comply with relief policy as well as please their camp commanders.

As refugee women battled for control over their homes in the relief camps, substandard relief supplies gave them the upper hand with officials. The camp dining hall policy illustrates this point. Bine easily enforced a new meal policy that eliminated food preparation in tents despite refugee objections that the dining hall broke "up the privacy of the home circle."[74] One refugee woman, M. Hefferman, wanted to eat in her tent, and she lodged a complaint with Bine's supervisors over the "lack of food" available to her.[75] Bine countered the complaint with plenty of free meal tickets, which left Hefferman no choice but to eat the food prepared in the outdoor cafeteria. But his victory was short-lived; general supply shortages threatened the commander's authority. In August 1906, a camp nurse noted the refugees' growing discontent, saying, "The supplies are short in every department, and consequently the refugees are neither fed nor clothed. . . . In fact, they are hungry."[76] Bine confirmed the real threat of disgruntled refugees. Later that month, he informed his family that he had "changed his tactics, and now carried a cane, a revolver, and a police whistle, which he used frequently."[77] Regular supply shortages, relief application delays, and unsanitary kitchens and latrines ultimately challenged a commander's authority. The threat of disorder was, however, abated by new housing policies geared toward transitioning refugees to life outside the camps.

ALTERNATIVE HOMES:
THE COTTAGE PROGRAM AND INGLESIDE MODEL CAMP

The canvas tents left refugees exposed to the elements and relief officials vulnerable to their discontent. But by the end of the 1906 summer, more than five thousand wood-frame cottages replaced just as many tents. "Earthquake cottages" or "refugee shacks," were the closest that thousands of working-class and poor refugees had come to living in a single-family dwelling.[78] These small cottages were a privilege, not a right. Horse stalls down at the local racetrack were another option. At Ingleside Model Camp, refugees slept in renovated horse stalls, ate in a common mess hall, and worked for small wages. Most refugees could not choose their homes; they depended on the favorable

Ingleside Model Camp, Women's Section. Refugee women are shown outside their bedrooms, which were renovated horse stalls at a local racetrack. The camp remained open until January 1908, when residents were sent to the newly built Relief Home in San Francisco. (Courtesy of the Bancroft Library, University of California, Berkeley.)

opinions of relief investigators. Ingleside was the elephant graveyard for aging and invalid refugees who did not have extended family to care for them, and their classification for either cottage or Ingleside became an important battle for home and identity.

The Ingleside Model Camp was the antithesis of the family-centered camps.[79] The Ingleside racetrack, located several miles southwest of downtown San Francisco, opened its gates to "the aged, the infirm, and the handicapped," as well as to refugees lacking family or community support networks. Ingleside's "no children" policy ensured that only "chronic" dependent refugees entered its gates. The camp stayed open until January 1908, when residents were sent to the newly built Relief Home in San Francisco. Every inch of racetrack space was converted to refugee accommodations for the often elderly residents. The track's twenty-six stables morphed into dormitories, a dining hall, a hospital annex, a religious center, and a social hall to accommodate refugees' physical, social, and spiritual needs according to relief standards.[80] Refugee bedrooms were limited to the dimensions of a horse stall, which numbered as many as forty per stable. In ironic homage to the man who donated the racetrack to the city, California Jockey Club president Thomas H. Williams, residents called their bedrooms "Tom Williams' horse boxes."[81]

The camp created a prisonlike atmosphere in both spatial arrangement and social organization. A horse stall created a space even more regimented than the grid layout of the other relief camps. Officials were not optimistic about the futures of Ingleside refugees. As Stanford sociologist Mary Roberts Coolidge explained, they were "the last precipitate of the social confusion." Some inmates, she wrote, "were a semi-vicious, irresponsible, and idle lot who were at Ingleside only because they could not find food and shelter in their old disreputable haunts."[82] Before remodeling the Ingleside stables for human tenants, camp commanders sent refugees who were "not capable of self-support or who had no relatives to care for them," to the unoccupied and unappealing army barracks in Golden Gate Park. Housed in quarters considered unsuitable for refugee families, they waited to be "sent to Ingleside when it should be ready."[83] Ingleside's camp commander was charged with creating social order defined by "good feeling, health, and discipline" and he had free rein. Far from the city and the other camps, Ingleside took the underlying principles of the relief camps to their worst extreme.

The first camp commander, military Captain Kilian, ruled with an iron fist. It is noteworthy that Captain Kilian was the same officer convicted for battery after the Flour Riot. After the trial, he found work at Ingleside, where he closely supervised every meal. Anyone found grabbing food was "summarily relegated to what became known as the 'hog table.'" Any residents found in a state of "drunkenness" were ejected from Ingleside after a single warning. Intoxication was an employee problem as well. The authorities found it "necessary to discipline and finally discharge for intoxication a considerable number of employes [sic] as well as refugees."[84] The only camp to discharge employees for intoxication, Ingleside seemed to be the last resort for both refugees and relief workers.

Refugees worked hard at Ingleside; it was the only camp that ran a labor program for men and women. The January 1907 policy required "a definite amount of inmate labor, varying according to the physical condition of each inmate." Men were reintroduced to the benefits of wage work by farming vegetables, running a dairy, and working in tailoring, carpentry, and shoe repair shops "that afforded work at a fair wage." Women labored in the sewing center. Unlike the sewing centers at other relief camps, this one was mandatory: "Every woman who could sew was expected to be in the sewing room twice a week." Following a regimented production schedule, residents produced more than six thousand garments and 754 curtains. The number of items produced, rather than the moral betterment of refugee women, became the marker of success. Ingleside's labor program and low cost per inmate was, in subsequent reports, held up as a model of efficiency.[85]

But Ingleside's residents were reluctant inmates. "Besides being old, infirm, or incapacitated to some degree," read one report, "the classes assembled at Ingleside were inevitably the most discontented of all the refugees."[86] Fear that Ingleside was a potential breeding ground for refugee protest raised the ire of relief administrators. Such behavior was the least tolerated in women, who were depicted as "more exacting, lazy, and termagant."[87]

Officials knew that the prospect of living at Ingleside forced some refugees to end their dependence on relief, reporting that many of those ordered to Ingleside "managed to find friends or work at the last moment."[88] Other refugees turned to patrons and asked them to intercede on their behalf. Nelly Spreckels (sister of San Francisco millionaire and relief leader Rudolph Spreckels) wrote a personal letter to James Phelan telling him to "loosen up on that fund" and give $500 to aid her friend's former cook. "I think that she would not want to go to Ingleside," Spreckels explained. "I would not advise sending her, as she would keep every one out there stirred up—she is such an excitable creature her influence would be bad."[89]

Some refugees convinced their women caseworkers to help them by forming friendships during their interviews and engendering sympathy for their plight. This strategy is yet another example of how nineteenth-century charity notions of moral assessment and personal involvement became entwined with twentieth-century scientific social work. One caseworker called for a new classification of refugees to account for the ones that were "too nice to go to the almshouse." The report explained, "A number of feeble persons who had been decent and hardworking before the fire . . . very evidently, could never again be self-supporting. . . . No decent person of this borderland class should be prematurely relegated to an institution."[90] Those refugees who fell into the final relief category, chronic dependents, lost their opportunity for relief-sponsored independent life. The high level of state control over this group is evident by the reluctance of caseworkers to classify refugees they had befriended as chronic dependents. Disadvantaged refugees, especially women, used everything in their power to avoid sleeping in the horse boxes at the racetrack.

For those outside the racetrack, finding good housing was not easy. The relief housing program had multiple tiers: top candidates received grant money for building new homes, those at the bottom were sent to almshouse-like boarding, and those in the middle lived in refugee cottages. The housing system ranked refugees by class status framed as moral status, with previous property owners and "resourceful" non–property owners (those demonstrating the potential for self-sufficiency) at the top of the list. And these rankings mattered. The higher the ranking, the shorter the time spent in the camps. Money went to previous property owners for rebuilding and to "resourceful" non–property owners for purchasing new property.

Anyone falling in one of the final two aid categories, "unresourceful" non–property owners and "chronic dependents," rarely received money. As housing officials reviewed and filed refugee applications, they defined this new, "borderland class" of San Franciscans. While both groups lacked financial resources, those deemed "unresourceful" held the potential for self-sufficiency. As one relief administrator described this group: "They were not

Refugee families living in relief camp earthquake cottages, 1906. (Courtesy of the California History Room, California State Library, Sacramento, California.)

the vicious or really indolent, but the inept, the people who could not initiate anything for themselves, those who through misfortune and circumstances had lost moral courage."[91] For the "inept," relief officials believed that a moderate amount of supervised assistance both reinvigorated moral courage and promoted self-sufficiency. Relief officials believed that these refugees could be saved. The difficulty, of course, lay in determining which refugees would be able to rise to the occasion.

Relief administrators showed their support for male heads of households by putting them first in line for the new cottages. A survey of 680 cottage families shows that nearly 60 percent belonged to married couples.[92] The typical cottage dwellers were thirty to forty years old, were married with children, and were laborers or those trained in domestic service. Before the catastrophe, most of them lived with their children in four-to-seven-room sublet flats without private bathing facilities.[93] The cottages presented a sharp contrast. Most refugee cottages were no more than fourteen by eighteen feet, with three windows, a rough board floor, a shingled roof, and a single exterior door. They were arranged in tight rows, like a book of matches, and some camps required the installation of sliding windows because there was no room for casement windows to swing open. Officials hoped that the color of the structures would compensate for the congestion. Thickly applied park-bench-green paint helped the shacks blend in with the grassy lawns of the city's parks and squares.

The cottages were intimately connected to the rights of citizenship. Following the disaster, the Board of Election Commissioners ruled that male relief camp residents lost the right to vote. "The parks, squares and streets of a city are not places where any person can acquire legal residence," declared the board on May 24, 1906. "A person must not be considered to have gained a residence in any precinct into which he comes for temporary purposes."[94] Ironically, the city's electoral board disenfranchised male citizens even as refugees were climbing into the city's voting machines for shelter. To the dismay of George Adams, the registrar of voters, refugee occupation prevented his repossession of city voting booths that had been donated for temporary shelter. "They [voting booths] are scattered, and attachments built on to the same, and patched almost beyond recognition in many cases," Adams reported to the mayor, "and almost every attempt to retake one is met by a piteous wail of the occupants, which is of a nature to excite sympathy and practically prevent us from steps of forcible ejectment."[95] At the end of the summer, the cottage program prompted the reversal of the electoral board's ruling. On August 17, 1906, the vote was reinstated to adult male relief camp refugees.[96]

The high demand for affordable housing in San Francisco placed a premium on camp cottages. As one man wrote to his mother in Ireland, "It is impossible for any Poor Man to get a house to live in here now, as there are a very few houses left, and they have raised the rent of those houses so high that no workingman can afford to pay the rent."[97] Thus the thin-walled shacks were anything but temporary. They became a point of reconnection to life in San Francisco when they were removed from the camps during late 1907 and 1908. Relief officials endorsed this transition because they saw it as an important moral lesson. They hoped that carefully chosen camp dwellers would become responsible home owners and, by extension, better citizens.[98]

Relief administrators in San Francisco were not the first to believe in the moral value of single-family dwellings. After the 1871 Chicago Fire, civic leaders complained that temporary refugee barracks were infested with "idleness, disorder, and vice."[99] Previous home owners, instead of being consigned to such conditions, received prefabricated shanties to ensure social order. Relief housing after the 1889 flood in Johnstown, Pennsylvania, also reaffirmed the moral benefits of single-family dwellings. Clara Barton's Red Cross used donated lumber to build three "Red Cross hotels."[100] Before long the Red Cross hotels were drowned in "rumors of excessive fees and drunken brawls" and given the epitaph "the bummer's retreat."[101] If these history lessons were not enough, 1906 relief officials witnessed their own failed experiment in communal living. Early on, army personnel hammered together two wooden barracks in Golden Gate Park, an inhospitable location. In their haste to build housing, soldiers and their officers failed to consider that barracks in the center of the park would be out of reach of street sewers and fire hydrants. But relief experts worried about moral, not physical, safety. They pulled refugees out of the barracks as quickly as possible, fearing that "refugees were [being] brought into an association so close as to be either demoralizing or humiliating."[102] Communal housing blurred boundaries between families and, as a result, threatened the integrity of the family unit. In the view of relief officials, building single-family dwellings was worth the expense.

But these new homes were not built for most single women. Relief records confirm that after married couples, widows with young children were the most likely recipients of aid.[103] Prioritizing this group after the calamity paved the way for state support for widows with children. In 1906, the general understanding was that "single women could provide for themselves."[104] At the same time, however, administrators recognized that "nothing more pathetic had to be considered by the Associated Charities than the plaint of the middle aged unmarried women."[105] The case of one Mrs. Coleman, a childless woman living in Lobos Square, illustrates this point. "She is unfortunate & in great distress," a local clubwoman wrote on Coleman's behalf. "She does not want to be sent to the *house* at Ingleside [Model Camp], & I do not blame her, as I know the conditions that exist there, & no self respecting person could endure."[106] But Katharine Felton denied Coleman's application for a relief cottage, arguing, "The rules under which we are working allow us to consider applications only from widows who have families to support. . . . [This] does not apply to women who have no one depending on them."[107]

When the relief camps closed, refugees took their relief cottages from the camps to use as permanent homes.[108] In January 1907, the Associated Charities paid moving expenses and installed sanitary plumbing "for families who were unable on account of illness or low earning capacity to meet these expenses for themselves."[109] These funds came with a watchful eye. Associated Charities director Katharine Felton assigned caseworkers to help refugees adjust to their new lives as home owners, such as "the foreign families [who] had never been out of North Beach and did not know their way from one part of the city to another."[110] This practice gave social workers new access to and influence over burgeoning post-disaster neighborhoods. As one reviewer described the cottage home visitor's influential role, she was "an arbiter, an adviser and, in short, something of a ministering angel."[111]

Creating a home in the post-disaster city may have been thornier for single women than for married women. In fact, Katharine Felton believed that single women could not maintain their cottage homes without the help of husbands or sons. "If they are taken by a family where the husband or sons can do this necessary repair work they can be made into suitable homes," opined Felton. "If taken by single, aged women and left unrepaired, they will be almost uninhabitable after the first storm."[112] One resourceful refugee, Sarah Brastow, proved otherwise. As a single woman without extended family in the area, Brastow relied on her personal relationship with a relief administrator for support. After her cottage was relocated to the Richmond District, Brastow sent a personal note to James Phelan: "This is the most grateful refugee you ever housed. . . . I am so happy and feel so independent."[113] Brastow turned to Phelan for help as she faced life on her own. "I have discovered a very disheartening experience that the sewers to the houses were never connected to the street," read a subsequent letter from Brastow. "I don't know what I am going to do about it all. It looks like a muddle I can't untangle."[114] Brastow's personal appeals to Phelan blurred the boundaries between bureaucratic efficiency and personal involvement. She, like other refugee women, created new ways to circumvent relief policy shortcomings in order to forge their place in San Francisco.

Inside the camps, officials continued to supervise cottage residents by charging rent instead of giving away or selling the small homes.[115] They considered rental fees a bargain in comparison to San Francisco's high rents. As one camp commander explained to his tenants, "All of you paid rent before the fire, and $6 per month for a cottage is certainly, or should be within the means of every working person."[116] But refugees believed they had a right to own their homes. Mary Kelly, a resident of the Jefferson Square camp, led the battle for cottage ownership. Kelly called for a boycott while the lawyer who founded the United Refugees, Alva Udell, threatened to file extortion charges for the collection of rent by "wrongful use of force or fear."[117] Mary Kelly went so far as to accuse relief officials of creating "governments of their own" inside the camps. Kelly asserted her private rights within the camp's public sphere and argued for control over the most basic aspect of life: a home.

Mary Kelly combined the battle over cottage rents with the fight for a cottage of her own. At the time, Kelly was living in a "very bad tent" in Jefferson Square with her invalid husband and children. Her reputation for protest and dissent preceded her application for a cottage, and she found it impossible to qualify for one. "I had made repeated application for one of them [cottages]," lamented Kelly, "and every time I was turned down."[118] She then took matters into her own hands. On a chilly October evening, Kelly led a small group of refugee women to several newly built and still unoccupied cottages near their tents in Jefferson Square. She "gave" a cottage to each of her friends before claiming one for herself. Then she "had locks attached" to the doors, securing both their physical homes and their personal privacy.[119]

Home had become a very public matter for Mary Kelly. Before the disaster, she considered herself to be "a very quiet woman, thinking I had about all I could do to keep my home and family . . . minding my own work and affairs." But the "terrible disaster" transformed her, with "so many lives and homes lost and destroyed, my own included with the others, [that] I was heartbroken and driven almost crazy." Once inside the camps, she found that her politicization soon followed. She was horrified by the struggles of a "hard-working class of people who never asked for charity from any one and always paid their own way." By the time Kelly stole a cottage, she justified her actions with the language of citizenship:

I stated that I had a perfect legal right to the cottage, as it was built out of the money which had been sent here to San Francisco to rehabilitate the suffering and destitute refugees, and besides that the cottage was built on public ground. . . . If there was any law by which they could put me out of the cottage I was willing to submit to the law as laid down by the court, as I had always been a law-abiding citizen.[120]

Although women in San Francisco waited another five years for the vote, Mary Kelly's rhetoric of citizenship secured her residency for the next month. Her cottage possession challenged a policy that determined which refugee women had the right to create a home. First, she made her cottage a symbol of relief policy class bias by posting "anti-relief committee banners" in its windows.[121] Second, she refused to leave. Third, she snubbed the rent collector. This was not simply a personal issue for Kelly; it was a political one. Kelly occupied cottage No. 7 in Jefferson Square, from which she demanded that the relief funds be distributed among refugees before anyone paid rent. According to the papers, "The nominal rent placed on the refugee cottages at Jefferson Square has been paid by all except Mary Kelly. She alone denounces the rent rule as an injustice and has undertaken to 'fight it to the finish.'"[122]

In response to Mary Kelly's stance, officials silenced both person and place. They issued an eviction notice for nonpayment of rent in November 1906, one of only twelve documented evictions during the entire relief period. When she refused to abandon her home, the cottage was slated for

An earthquake cottage being moved from a camp to an owner's lot, July 28, 1907. More than five thousand cottages were moved from the relief camps to become permanent housing for refugees. (Courtesy of the Bancroft Library, University of California, Berkeley.)

transportation to the Ingleside Model Camp.[123] Despite the fact that ten men arrived to put the shack on the back of a hay wagon for the drive to the racetrack, Kelly refused to leave. She hung a placard out of one window that read: "We demand a share of the Relief Fund. We demand a distribution of food and relief supplies."[124] One news account quoted her as calling to the crowds, "I'll stay with the house if they take it to the end of the earth," while weaving through San Francisco's neighborhoods on the back of the wagon.[125] She certainly was aware of the symbolic significance of her removal from the city. Later, she recalled that their route to the camp traversed the "most thickly populated parts of the city to exhibit me as an example to the other poor refugees and show them what they might expect should they themselves fail to come up to the demands of the Relief Corporation as to paying rent for their cottages."[126] On that November morning, relief administrators literally reasserted their control over refugee domestic space. The removal of both Kelly and her cottage defined the cottage program as a place where women like Mary Kelly had no home.

Relief officials, however, failed to realize the post-disaster power of domestic rhetoric. The camps and the cottages allowed female refugees to claim their place in the public realm, and in Kelly's case her presence in the public realm was not easily shaken. As she made clear to the press, "They are moving me to Ingleside because I won't pay rent, when the money was sent out here to me and to other refugees, and not to Jimmy Phelan and Rudolph Spreckels."[127] When she arrived at Ingleside, in her cottage and on the hay wagon, she was personally greeted by a familiar and unfriendly face: that of Captain Kilian. The camp commander undoubtedly remembered her from their encounter earlier that year when Kelly and a group of angry women had supported his conviction for assaulting a refugee woman. Understandably, the captain refused to allow Mary Kelly in his camp. One report stated that "for the good of his camp, [he] refused to admit Mrs. Kelly, a recognized agitator."[128] He left her, in the cottage and on the hay wagon, outside the gates for three days.[129] Although she was brought food from the camp, she was not permitted inside the gates "unless she promised to observe the rules of the camp, which she would not do."[130] Even James Phelan visited the camp "but claimed to have no knowledge of the affair."[131] Mary Kelly was undaunted. "I shall remain right here," she said, "until my house is taken back to Jefferson Square or I am taken out by force. I am still contented; I am still easy in my mind; I have done no wrong."[132] On November 7, the commander ordered the cottage destroyed. The fate that eventually befell Kelly's cottage is perhaps not as remarkable as the fact that the cottage remained on the truck, with Mary Kelly inside, during its demolition. She never fully relinquished her stolen cottage. Rather she picked up a few of the remaining floor planks and returned to Jefferson Square, where she "still had that leaky tent."[133]

Mary Kelly continued to battle cottage rents from her tent in Jefferson Square. The press called her "a factor to be dealt with. She is not cut down by any manner of means. . . . Little Mary Kelly commands respect."[134] Indeed, the issue was unresolved until the mayor and the Board of Supervisors intervened. After an investigation, the mayor "declared that he was opposed to any one being allowed to collect rents on public property and particularly was he opposed to allowing the Relief Committee to aggrandize itself by collecting rents from refugees."[135] In December 1906, Mayor Schmitz signed a board-approved ordinance replacing rents with a lease program that granted home ownership after the lessee found land on which to relocate the occupied cottage.

Refugees like Mary Kelly, who staked their claim to home on public ground, entered the realm of public discourse for the first time. "My case is the case of every refugee in San Francisco," Kelly boldly told the press.[136] For her, this was an assertion and experience that lasted much longer than the relief camps. She would go on to enter politics, traveling to the state capital to support a relief reform bill in 1908. In 1911, after women gained the right to vote in California, Mary Kelly was one of the first to register as a "labor unionist in politics."[137] Mary Kelly's post-disaster story, particularly the account of her cottage theft and eviction, reveals the politicizing potential of disasters. The disruption of the public/private boundary opened up debate over the meaning of space, place, and gender in post-disaster San Francisco.

As a laboratory of sorts for new scientific policies, the relief camps provide a window into Progressive Era reform efforts. At their most basic level, the camps redrew social boundaries by delineating spaces outside the disaster zone to contain poor and working-class refugees. Further, racist relief policy segregated Chinese refugees, forcing them to rely on diplomatic and business leaders to successfully pressure relief and civic leaders to rebuild Chinatown in San Francisco. Meanwhile, relief policy screened "deserving" refugees for rebuilding assistance. For those who remained in the camps, an experimental cottage program extended their public home experience into private life when cottage occupants relocated these small wooden structures to vacant lots in the post-disaster city. As we see in Chapter 5, disaster relief influenced urban design by supporting the rebuilding of homes on the basis of socioeconomic status. The delayed reentry of the working class and poor into the rebuilding city ensured that the homes they found would be distant from their old neighborhoods.

While relief policy espoused twentieth-century scientific methods, not everyone agreed with such calculations. As Linda Gordon showed in her study of social control in Boston's child welfare agencies, clients often used the agencies of social control to their own ends.[138] Similarly, many refugee women in San Francisco openly defied the class and gender biases of relief and used the system for their own purposes. Like the women in Drew Gilpin Faust's study of the Civil War, earthquake refugees went beyond their prescribed gender roles in order to obtain the materials necessary to resume those very roles.[139] Politicized domesticity altered the public sphere, at least temporarily, and allowed women a newfound agency. Although their ultimate goal was to protect their roles as wives and mothers within the private household, the disaster had a ripple effect on San Francisco's political landscape. The politicized lexicon of domesticity, coupled with the presence of women in the post-disaster public realm, brought gender ideology to the political forefront in the recovering city.

CHAPTER 5

The New San Francisco

Like disaster relief, reconstruction widened the economic divide between the city's social classes. Rebuilding also exacerbated racial divisions when political and business leaders demanded Chinatown's permanent removal from the city. Despite the loss of land titles and insurance records as well as buildings in the fires, the power-hungry mayor—armed with new land title legislation, insurance protocols, and relief grants—rapidly began reconstruction. Fire insurance was a boon to wealthier property owners who tapped into top compensation rates.[1] Insurance payouts covered half of the reconstruction costs (approximately $250 million), while relief grants added more cash to the rebuilding effort. Relief policy favored property owners and more than half of these grant recipients owned additional, undamaged property.[2]

The catastrophe spurred "disaster suburbanization" and stretched the boundaries of San Francisco. Residential rebuilding followed a predictable pattern in most neighborhoods: wealthy home owners were the first to reestablish their homes, followed by middle-class home owners and, finally, working-class home owners and renters. The total urban population bounced back after only three years, growing from 342,700 in 1900 to 416,900 in 1910 (most agreed that the city reached its pre-disaster population in 1909).[3] Urban growth continued and reached 506,600 by 1920.[4] Favoring business, the city allowed commercial construction projects to commence without permits. Local political and business leaders wasted no time in returning San Francisco to her previous glory as America's ninth-largest city and the economic center of the American West.

San Francisco's Progressives saw the disaster as a watershed for reform. Baltimore's recent recovery from fire in 1904, which brought physical improvements and Progressive Era reform, provided a promising example. But Progressive success was threatened by the demand for rapid rebuilding. As Kevin Rozario points out, Eastern investors exerted increasing influence over urban development as both business and building boomed with their dollars.[5] Eastern influence, coupled with a new alliance between local business owners and labor, thwarted the grand plans of Progressive reformers. Yet Progressives successfully battled municipal government corruption and advanced women's participation—specifically that of middle-class clubwomen, who were so active in disaster relief—in the political realm. Thus the greatest Progressive victory was realized in the political sphere instead of in the built environment.

A fresh look at U.S. Census data clarifies how social divisions played out in both old and new San Francisco neighborhoods, confirming William Issel and Robert Cherny's observation that "patterns of residence, work, ethnicity, and family not only continued but also in some instances intensified" in the post-disaster city.[6] Despite obvious demographic change, civic leaders, for the most part, ignored social disparities. Their myopic goal of economic recovery included hosting the Panama Pacific International Exposition in 1915, an international event that showcased the new San Francisco. When visitors arrived in San Francisco to see the impressive exposition, they may not have noticed how the exposition's stylized buildings and intriguing exhibits masked the city's widened social divide.

REBUILDING OPPORTUNITIES: THE PROGRESSIVE AGENDA

The catastrophe literally cleared the way for the "City Beautiful" urban design championed by Progressive women and men. This was a tremendous opportunity for local Progressives, who sorely missed James Phelan's influential tenure as city mayor (1897–1901). After years of resistance from a pro-labor mayor, Phelan used his newfound power over disaster relief to support his work with the Association for the Improvement and Adornment of San Francisco. Phelan endorsed the Progressive view that San Francisco's destruction presented an invaluable opportunity to build an ideal city and citizen. Local clubwomen supported Phelan's redesign campaign. They needed time to alter the urban landscape, however, and they butted heads with an uncooperative mayor, anxious downtown property owners, and laborers who were all eager to rebuild. Progressive efforts ultimately achieved political reform and, in the process, further solidified women's place in the public realm.

City Beautiful was a national movement that proposed solving urban problems by creating beautiful, rationalized cities. The "crusade against ugliness," as one City Beautiful proponent termed it, included new park and boulevard systems, paved streets, and monumental public buildings placed in a harmonious relationship with one another.[7] California's clubwomen had supported these efforts even before the disaster; in 1902, California Club president Laura White founded the California Outdoor Art League "to preserve the natural attractions of localities . . . [and] to promote all work relating to the artistic and industrial development of California." When James Phelan formed the Association for the Improvement and Adornment of San Francisco in 1904, he found ready allies in the Outdoor Art League.[8] Phelan had learned of City Beautiful possibilities at the 1893 Columbian Exposition in Chicago, for which architect Daniel H. Burnham designed the perfect city (called "White City").[9] With a goal of redesigning San Francisco, the Improvement Association brought Burnham west in 1904 and gave him a hilltop studio (perched on Twin Peaks, the geographic center of the city), from which he drew elaborate plans for a Parisian-style San Francisco.[10] The 1905 report outlined a radically overhauled city by recommending seventy major alterations, from the extension of Golden Gate Park to the removal of Chinatown.[11] The 1906 disaster could not have been better timed for City Beautiful enthusiasts.

In the eyes of City Beautiful believers, the destruction of Chinatown and the working-class South of Market area cleared the way for a healthier city. "Fire has reclaimed to civilization and cleanliness the Chinese ghetto," read the review in the *Overland Monthly*. "Intact upon the hill stands the Fairmont [Hotel] and from this center will radiate the wonderful new city of the Western seas, the city beautiful."[12] This sentiment was echoed by another news account of the working-class district: "Thousands and thousands of old shacks 'south of Market' are gone. The burning of this district was no loss to the city. It can now be built up properly."[13] James Phelan started the ball rolling immediately. Within days of the disaster, Phelan's private correspondence read: "San Francisco's calamity will enable us now to proceed to rebuild the city on the lines of the Burnham Plan."[14] By early May, Phelan requested that Burnham visit the disaster zone. "Glad to hear you are coming. Sooner the better for us," read Phelan's telegram to Burnham. "Please advise immediately by letter . . . [w]hat new laws we need, long leases and other ideas."[15] Phelan quickly distributed copies of Burnham's plan to the relief committee, noting, "There is, of course, a very strong feeling here in favor of improving the city, now that the ground has been bared, but on the other hand, there is an element that desires no delay in rebuilding the city and new street planning involves some delay."[16] Campaigning hard for the design changes, Phelan in his report to the municipal government argued, "A rare opportunity has been presented to the citizens by the fire to carry out plans which once seemed remote, but which are now within the grasp of immediate execution."[17]

Burnham streamlined his 1905 report to spotlight the disaster zone. He simplified his original recommendations and proposed widening several streets in the downtown district, scaling Nob Hill, and adding diagonals that cut across Market Street. San Francisco engineer Marsden Manson supplied statistical support for the changes, arguing that street improvements would add $75 million to city property values by 1916.[18] New avenues and wider streets, however, were easier to draw on paper than to pave on land. Phelan understood that "property owners, anxious to get some return from their property as it is, are also reluctant to take the larger view to improve their property and city alike by effecting street widening and street opening."[19]

City Beautiful plans ultimately failed despite—or perhaps because of— the efforts of Progressive reformers.[20] One of the biggest impediments was local government. Mayor Eugene Schmitz's close political ally, Abraham Ruef, pressed for a reconstruction amendment that granted the mayor and the Board of Supervisors the right to dispose of or acquire city land.[21] Some scholars have speculated that Progressives pulled back from their ambitious rebuilding plans to prevent the expansion of civic power under the Schmitz administration.[22] Post-disaster civic improvements, as Christine Rosen's study of the 1904 Baltimore Fire indicates, required an alignment of Progressive interests and the executive branch of the city government, and that proved impossible in San Francisco.[23] Thus civic improvements played out on a smaller scale under the watchful eye of local clubwomen. Laura White, for example, successfully spotlighted park enhancements during the summer of 1906. "I have recently visited Dolores Street and must confess that the scene of our desolate parks is not very encouraging," White wrote to the city engineer. She lobbied the park commissioners to "take care of them [the parks] now" and thus initiated one small piece of Progressive beautification.[24]

Progressives pursued another route toward urban purification as well: clean government. As the unanimous praise that Mayor Schmitz earned during the emergency period faded, the federal investigation of his office was back on track. The local press hailed the pursuit of "good government" as equal in importance to reconstruction, with the *San Francisco Call* proclaiming, "Now the campaign of regeneration is on and the day of bribers and bribe takers is over."[25] A determined Phelan agreed, writing, "Nothing but vigorous action and perhaps a new administration will be necessary to accomplish the changes for which we have labored so long."[26] Progressives celebrated their dismantling of the mayor's office after the graft prosecution led to convictions of Schmitz (in June 1907) and Ruef (in December 1908) for extortion.[27] But the dramatic political trial took both time and attention away from urban redesign. By the time Mayor Schmitz's Progressive replacement took office, rebuilding was well under way.

San Francisco Progressives enjoyed a brief surge in political power with the downfall of the Union Labor Party. A well-known Progressive, Dr. Edward Robeson Taylor, accepted a temporary appointment as mayor after Schmitz's conviction. Taylor went on to win the 1907 election, shunning the Labor Union Party all the while. Indeed, one notable feature of Taylor's Board of Supervisors was the "scarcity of Labor Union Supervisors."[28] Instead, Mayor Taylor's good government turned to the political involvement of clubwomen. Taylor credited the support of local clubwomen, who had not yet won the right to vote for him, with his successful campaign. "Back of the forces of good government in the campaign," wrote the new mayor, "were for the first time in the history of the city arrayed a great majority of the women of the city." Taylor further explained that women "seemed to realize, in great measure even more than did the men, the real significance of the contest, and to them must be attributed in great measure the victory achieved."[29] The new mayor backed up his political rhetoric with action. He appointed Laura White to the Playground Commission in 1908. The institutionalization of women's volunteer work continued as women gained additional positions in city services. Their early contributions to relief work may have helped them to secure their place in San Francisco politics.[30]

Progressives did not control local politics for long. They lost support after the graft prosecution targeted San Francisco capitalists, who allegedly bribed labor politicians. A new alliance between business and labor shifted the political balance by the 1909 election, and Building Trades Council president, P. H. McCarthy, won the mayoral election. This alliance weakened under McCarthy, making his single term in office the end, rather than the resurgence, of the Union Labor Party.[31] A political compromise of sorts came about in the 1911 election when James Rolph, Jr., a non-partisan politician, began his nineteen-year mayoral career. The son of immigrants and a resident of the Mission District, the self-made millionaire embodied both Progressive values and a commitment to the city's working class.[32] In fact, the disaster had added luster to Rolph's image since he organized early relief efforts (the Mission Relief Committee) in his own neighborhood.[33] As Issel and Cherny point out, "Rolph smothered partisanship with his hearty conviviality and effusive love for his city."[34]

Mayor Rolph struck an important balance between Progressive and labor interests. On the one hand, he pleased local Progressives with his campaign promise to clean up the Barbary Coast, that infamous strip of dance halls and bars that was rebuilt in downtown San Francisco. On the other hand, Rolph refused to make the city a "closed town" and instead closely supervised entertainment establishments.[35] Under Mayor Rolph's tenure, the city expanded its public works programs, which ranged from a new water supply to a city-owned transportation system. In accomplishing these improvements, Rolph was both Progressive, in that he based his decisions on expert advice, and conventional, in that he continued to play "traditional politics of personal relationships."[36] Mayor Rolph's Progressive leanings showed when he supported the bond measure to build Daniel Burnham's City Hall. In doing so, the astute Rolph assuaged labor interests by guaranteeing local workers jobs building the massive structure. As San Franciscans later bragged, their new City Hall was "built without any scandal and without any graft."[37]

The failure to overhaul San Francisco according to City Beautiful standards should not overshadow other important Progressive gains. The 1906 catastrophe gave Progressives a new opportunity to enter public debate. To be sure, San Francisco did not see political change as dramatic as that following Galveston's 1900 storm or Baltimore's 1904 fire. With its "instant city" origins and pro-union leanings, San Francisco was in no position to accept wholesale Progressive restructuring. The disaster also spurred a major Progressive victory in terms of women's political involvement in the public sphere. Viewed from the perspective of incremental gains rather than that of sweeping victories, the disaster provoked a surge in Progressive discourse, followed by a more gradual adaptation of a Progressive agenda during the long career of Mayor Rolph.

REBUILDING: HOME AND WORK

The obstacles to rapid rebuilding—lost land titles, insurance companies struggling to differentiate between earthquake and fire losses, and revisions of building permit guidelines—were removed relatively quickly. In the end, residential and commercial rebuilding demarcated San Francisco's social divide in the physical landscape.

Commercial property holders found a friend in Mayor Eugene Schmitz, who approved non-permit rebuilding without question. As early as April 28, 1906, Schmitz "announced that one story wooden or corrugated iron structures could be built without a permit."[38] The mayor ignored Progressive arguments for strict permits, which would have guaranteed public improvements. Instead, he made a convincing case that building temporary wooden structures encouraged property owners to clear earthquake and fire rubble.[39] Downtown landlords cleared debris and built quickly in order to return the retail shopping district from its temporary location at Polk Street and Van Ness Avenue. Rapid rebuilding brought at least nineteen thousand wood-frame buildings to the disaster zone.[40] Unfortunately, nothing proved more permanent than temporary wooden buildings.

Progressive reformers found few supporters for a ban on wooden structures. San Francisco's fire limit restrictions, like those in other American cities, prohibited wood-frame construction within a particular area in order to minimize potential fire damage. The first fire limit proposal used the 1906 disaster zone as the boundary, increasing the fire limit by 50 percent (or ninety city blocks). The call to expand urban fire limits after a major conflagration was a familiar one. After Chicago's 1871 Great Fire, the extension of the city's fire limits was hotly contested and eventually curtailed by opposition from working-class residents.[41] In San Francisco, the debate ended before it started as business interests were too strong to be swayed by the good intentions of Progressives. In the interests of speeding rebuilding and reducing construction costs, property owners opposed new fire limits. M. H. de Young's Down Town Property Owners' Association, for example, lobbied the California Senate for "quick rebuilding" to restore "San Francisco's commercial supremacy."[42]

The loss of land titles presented another obstacle to rapid rebuilding. Relief committee member Garrett W. McEnerney argued before the California Superior Court that "permitting the title of millions of dollars worth of the most valuable land in the state to remain without public proof of their validity, and practically withdrawn from commerce" was "manifest evil."[43] He proposed the "Quiet Title" Act (or the McEnerney Act) to prevent inordinate delays in restoring land titles. The *Merchants' Association Review* called the act "one of the most important measures passed" after the disaster.[44] By June 1908, property owners had filed more than nine thousand title cases, which were granted to all uncontested claims.[45] Interestingly, "quiet titles" advantaged property owners across the city. As private owners filed new titles, they shifted property lines, and $254,610 worth of city property fell into private hands.[46] San Francisco's post-disaster land grab differed from Baltimore's 1904 post-fire rebuilding. In Baltimore, a powerful Progressive municipal government took almost seven hundred private lots for civic improvements and strong-armed property owners into ceding their personal property for the public good.[47] Not so in San Francisco. Rudolph Spreckels, San Francisco's millionaire newspaper owner and relief administrator, waged a legal battle with the city over a nine-inch-wide strip of land at the front of his downtown lot.[48] As this example demonstrates, financial interest could trump Progressive beliefs when it came to rebuilding.

Insurance claims were in disarray. As the San Francisco Chamber of Commerce summarized, the catastrophe was the "most difficult in the whole history of fire insurance. In the first place, the conflagration itself had been the largest that there had ever been; secondly, it was not an ordinary conflagration but had been preceded by an earthquake for whose direct effects the companies had not been liable and yet the evidence of which had been largely obliterated by the fire."[49] Insurance representatives formed the Bureau of Adjustment in Oakland to calculate a standard insurance formula.[50] The first negotiated settlements ranged from 40 percent to 75 percent of total insurance values.[51] Those companies that honored policies in full delayed payment in order to raise additional funds. "The earthquake complication, embarrassing as it has been from many standpoints, has yet been the saving of a number of [insurance] Companies," wrote one insurance manager, "as they have been able to stave off payments and criticisms."[52] Such delays put additional pressure on property owners, who were anxious to recover their losses.

Some cash-strapped property owners settled for meager insurance payments, agreeing to settlements that "in general, were on less favorable terms." As the Chamber of Commerce reported, "The first payments were largely to poor people who were in no position to insist upon anything better."[53] Further, bargaining for payments was cumbersome. Zoeth Eldredge, the president of the National Bank of the Pacific, wrote that insurance adjusters made it as difficult as possible for individual policyholders: "Many insurance managers became very exclusive; they were hard to get at; they removed their offices to Oakland." Once in Oakland, adjusters used "every possible reduction of values" and "every argument and threat" to reduce insurance payments. "This bore heavily on the poor man," wrote Eldredge, "the man with little insurance and nothing but that insurance to begin life again with."[54]

As property owners cleared permit and insurance hurdles, their projects brought new jobs to San Francisco. Thousands of men found work on civic and private reconstruction projects. They worked around the clock, some starting by loading trains and horse-drawn wagons with broken bricks and masonry, while others salvaged bricks for reuse.[55] One historian estimated that the massive cleanup effort cost more than $20 million.[56] The jobs seemed endless for able-bodied men, as salvage work created space for new construction. Between July 1, 1908, and 1909, $8.5 million in municipal contracts (for new sewer and water systems, street improvements, and buildings) created at least two thousand additional jobs.[57] A state-of-the-art fire-suppression water-supply system and a city sewer system revamped urban infrastructure. Then a special tax levied in 1908 and 1909 funded street repair and paving.[58] Even small contractors benefited from the building boom. Lilas Mugg remembered

Some of the 5,610 earthquake cottages under construction for a Richmond District relief camp, 1906. San Francisco's impossibly high rents made the cottages a necessity for many working-class and poor refugees. In late 1907 and 1908, the cottages were plucked off the campgrounds and pulled by horse cart to private property. (Courtesy of the California Historical Society, Luke Fay Collection, FN-30199/ CHS2010.382.tif.)

how her father, a painting contractor, "made money hand over fist" after losing their South of Market home: "On Friday nights when my father was making out the payroll, I would build bridges and houses and whatnot with the gold pieces!"[59]

Private reconstruction and municipal contracts abounded, and skilled laborers found themselves in high demand. Further, the temporary suspension of union work rules opened reconstruction work to all men.[60] San Francisco unions ballooned with "earthquake mechanics," the popular name for reconstruction workers. By the fall of 1906, fifty-two Building Trades Council locals increased their membership by 45 percent, with wages for skilled artisans topping $20 per day.[61] The abundance of rebuilding work drew men from around the country. The city engineer acted as the gatekeeper for civil service jobs, rejecting requests for employment from men who were not residents of San Francisco.[62] However, many working men and women did not benefit from the post-disaster job boom; thus, rebuilding further increased the economic divide between the city's working class and elite.

For the male laborers, the array of new jobs did not necessarily restore their pre-disaster living standards; common laborers found that their regular wages were no match for escalating rental rates. Thus the relief camps remained home to many workingmen despite the fact that 89 percent of them found employment through private construction and relief work projects. Male refugees worked as laborers, carpenters, and patrolmen inside the camps, and hauled debris, cleaned bricks, and worked on new construction outside the camps. The relief committee created special projects to provide refugee men with "moderate wages," such as the July 18, 1906, decision to grade the land between Golden Gate Park and the Presidio.[63] With patience and planning, rebuilding work helped some working-class families recover their place in San Francisco. The Harman family, for example, lived in makeshift housing while saving money to rebuild. "Being a carpenter, after everything got started he [Father] made money, he made plenty," recalled Walter Harman, who was ten years old at the time of the earthquake. But the Harmans spent almost one year camping outdoors before saving enough to build a home of their own.[64]

Single working-class women, meanwhile, faced the prevailing assumption that they did not need assistance because they could easily find domestic work or turn to their extended families for support. Relief officials endorsed such employment by supplying washtubs and sewing machines for laundry workers and seamstresses; by doing so they made refugee women dependent on disaster relief to acquire the necessary tools for work. In one case, an unemployed, Irish washerwoman lived in two relief camps before she was issued a washboard and tub. In the meantime, her children walked about without shoes and bathed without soap.[65]

Irregular post-disaster wages for women often intensified the need for child labor. One quarter of children in the relief camps worked, but for child workers wages were low and job opportunities few. One relief camp mother sent her oldest child to work in Oakland, despite the fact that more than

A woman at a relief camp washbasin, 1906. Some women managed to resume domestic work in the relief camps by taking in laundry or sewing, but the assumption that they could easily find such work was unfounded. (Courtesy of the Bancroft Library, University of California, Berkeley.)

one-third of his four-dollar weekly wage went to carfare and boat trips.[66] Even so, children's incomes, however minuscule, might be critical to their family's survival. One mother relied on her son's help to feed her family after her husband failed to return from his search for employment. "Husband left 3 months ago to try his luck at work in the country, since which time he has not been heard from," read her relief file. "Her boy of 13 has been providing the food for all since the [camp] Kitchen closed, by picking up junk, and earning $1. to $1.50 per week."[67] Mary McAllister, an elderly widow with a middle-aged daughter, "had a hard struggle to get along" after they both lost their jobs sewing for factories and department stores. McAllister's daughter continued to sew by day but could not earn enough to make ends meet. As a result, they spent four years relying on a patchwork of funds from relatives and the Associated Charities.[68]

Post-disaster employment patterns followed pre-disaster class and gender norms. In perhaps the clearest example, a heightened concern over female domestic servants who abandoned their jobs (see Chapter 2) fueled widespread fears of social disorder. The remedy was to return such women to their work, which would at once restore domestic order and reestablish social hierarchies. Moreover, employment opportunities after the disaster remained clearly defined by gender. For working-class women, relief funding did not break down workplace gender barriers; rather, it supported their return to female-identified work in which low wages and limited opportunities prevailed. Plentiful rebuilding jobs for working-class men expanded the economic divide between working men and women at the same time as the gap between the city's social classes widened. The hidden advantages to the middle and upper classes, already set in motion by the disaster itself, burst into view during rebuilding and remained a feature of the city's physical landscape.

POST-DISASTER NEIGHBORHOODS

A new comparison of 1900, 1910, and 1920 U.S. Census data reveals how post-disaster population mobility solidified class, gender, and racial neighborhood boundaries in the recovering city. Rebuilding brought financial institutions into the city's center (growing by 44 percent), leaving less space for residents and manufacturing firms. Rapid decentralization and residential expansion stretched San Francisco's geographical perimeter, which, in turn, increased segregation by class and economic function.[69] Reconstruction created a "second instant city."[70] Rapid suburbanization, or "disaster suburbanization," pushed city boundaries west and south. In 1911, 75 percent of San Franciscans lived outside the 1906 disaster zone. Looking three to four and a half miles from downtown, the population jumped by 50 percent (50,000 residents), while the area beyond the four-and-a-half mile marker added another 50,000.[71] "Tracts were thrown open to home builders, where a few months before cattle had been pastured, and many of these are now covered with modest dwellings," reported the *San Francisco Chronicle* in 1909. "There is no place within the boundaries of the city and county of San Francisco that has not taken on the aspect of a city."[72]

Laborers were busy hammering nails into residential homes, replacing one-third of the city's lost housing (approximately eight thousand new housing units) by October, 1907.[73] But new housing was not open to everyone. A sample of two thousand residents from the city directories shows that between 1907 and 1908, 92 percent of San Franciscans with white-collar employment returned to their pre-disaster addresses. In contrast, few unskilled workers maintained consistent residences between 1907 and 1911.[74] New refugee relocation data gleaned from a relief camp directory illuminates this post-disaster trajectory.

Records from one relief camp paint a clear picture of how social class constrained post-disaster residential mobility. Lafayette Square, situated just a few blocks west of the disaster zone (bounded by Washington, Laguna, Sacramento, and Gough Streets), sheltered residents who had been burned out of the Downtown and South of Market Districts. Refugees at the camp tallied 786 at the end of April and, at one point, numbered as many as 1,400.[75] The majority of camp residents were whites (630), followed by Asians (142), and African Americans (14). The temporary camp segregated Asian refugees, which was a precursor to the official camp policy that soon followed. The

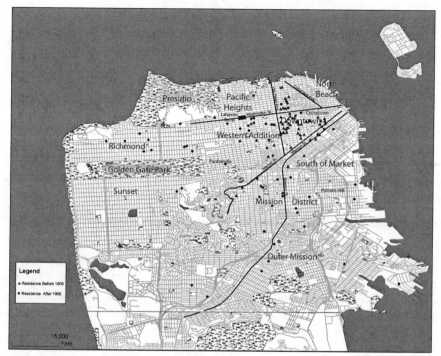

Lafayette Square Camp refugee relocation map. The camp housed working-class residents burned out of the Downtown and South of Market Districts. This map, based on an 18 percent sample of Lafayette Camp refugees, shows how many refugees did not return to their pre-disaster homes. (Courtesy of Stephanie Rozek.)

Lafayette Camp Directory, dated May 1, 1906, is one of the few surviving records of relief camp occupants. On that date, camp officials listed a total of 591 residents (all non-Asian names, with only one refugee identified as "colored").[76] The camp directory recorded important data for most residents: address, occupation, and current financial resources. The majority of Lafayette's residents were employed in working-class occupations (plasterer, tinsmith, laborer, maid, dressmaker, and the like) and stated that they lacked financial resources.

Where did these refugees go after Lafayette Camp? The answer to this question, found in the pages of the San Francisco City Directories, suggests that a working-class suburbanization followed the fires. An 18 percent sample of Lafayette Camp refugees (107 individual names, or 70 households) shows that by 1915 most were living in the Mission District, Outer Mission (south of the Mission District), Western Addition, and the western suburban districts called Richmond and Sunset.[77] Early U.S. suburbs, as Richard Harris argues, were not solely a middle-class domain. Lower-class suburbanization was common in the early twentieth century, when reduced land costs allowed members of the working class to buy land and build homes within reasonable commuting distance to their places of work.[78] This process seems to have been accelerated by the earthquake and fires. In the case of Lafayette Camp relocation, not a single refugee returned to his or her pre-disaster home.

Post-disaster suburbanization altered the city. Census data from 1900, 1910, and 1920 show how the calamity pushed residents out of the heart of the city and pulled them into the new suburban areas south and west of the disaster zone. Disaster suburbanization brought rapid growth to some neighborhoods. The estimated population size in the Outer Mission increased almost sevenfold between 1900 and 1910 and fivefold between 1910 and 1920. In the Sunset District, the population tripled between 1900 and 1910 and more than doubled between 1910 and 1920. Richmond's population doubled between 1900 and 1910 and almost doubled again in the next decade. (See Table 1 in the Appendix.) What do these numbers mean? Breaking down census data by social class status helps to illuminate post-disaster neighborhood transformations.

By 1910, most neighborhoods outside the disaster zone housed an increased proportion of working-class residents. Not surprisingly, the proportion of "not working" (unemployed, not in the labor force, or retired) residents decreased overall during this period. The South of Market District experienced an influx of single, working-class men (and an overall decrease in population share), boosting the proportion of working-class residents from 41 percent to 61 percent. This was also true for the downtown area, which dropped in non-working occupants and, in 1910 only, found half of its residents representing the working classes.[79] Outside the disaster zone, two neighborhoods stand out as opening their doors to working-class residents: Potrero Hill shot up from 24 percent to 34 percent, while the Richmond District jumped from 20 percent to 30 percent. Potrero Hill may have attracted working-class refugees because of its close proximity to the working-class inhabitants of the South of Market District (the 1900 Census did not record any professional/white-collar residents in Potrero Hill). The McKittrick family, who walked with their two young daughters from their burning flat in South of Market to their relatives in Potrero Hill, exemplify the easy access provided by the small neighborhood to those escaping South of Market. Working-class residents may well have been drawn to the Richmond District because of its proximity to the Presidio and Golden Gate Park, two prime locations for relief camps. In addition, the Richmond presented a fairly flat walking route toward downtown (the Sunset required traversing Twin Peaks). Working-class suburbanization was tied to the ease of commuting to work in the post-disaster city.

However, not all of these working-class demographic shifts held up between 1910 and 1920. The proportion of non-working residents, for example, increased in many neighborhoods by 1920. It is possible that reconstruction jobs did not permanently alter the city's share of unemployed and other non-working residents. In addition, the number of working-class residents in San Francisco's suburbs waned by 1920. This was especially true in the Richmond and Sunset neighborhoods, where the number of working-class

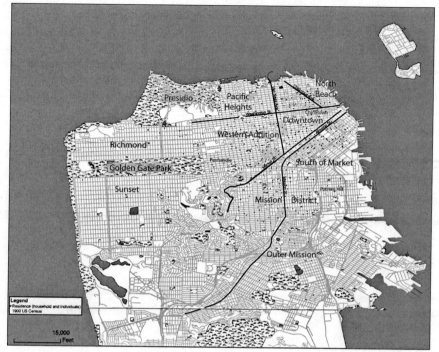

Population of San Francisco, 1900. Census data from 1900, 1910, and 1920 show that the calamity pushed residents out of the heart of the city into the new suburban areas south and west of the disaster zone. (Source: One percent IPUMS U.S. census, 1900. Courtesy of Stephanie Rozek.)

residents dropped from nearly one-third (30 percent) to 18 percent and 14 percent, respectively. San Francisco's suburbs became increasingly professional/white-collar by 1920, when white-collar residents (26 percent in the Richmond and 25 percent in the Sunset) outnumbered working-class residents for the first time. Interestingly, the Outer Mission consistently attracted professional white-collar residents. Yet despite these increases in the white-collar workforce, few neighborhoods had more professional than working-class residents after the catastrophe.

The rise in the professional workforce living in San Francisco did not always translate to a decline in working-class residents. For example, the number of professional/white-collar residents in Potrero Hill jumped from 0 percent to 15 percent of the total population, but at the same time, the proportion of working-class residents leapt from 24 percent to 47 percent of the total. (See Table 2 in the Appendix.) However, the Outer Mission stands out as a neighborhood that attracted white-collar and professional workers, who did not reside in this neighborhood in 1900. By 1910, 5 percent of Outer Mission residents were white-collar, while working-class residents dropped

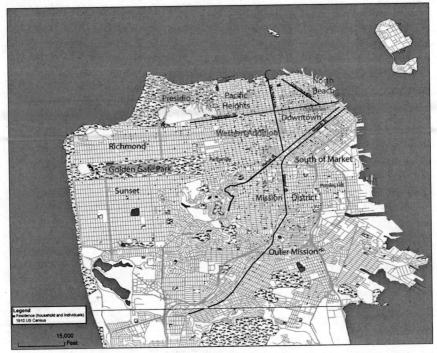

Population of San Francisco, 1910. Neighborhoods faced permanent change after San Franciscans offered temporary shelter to friends and family who fled the disaster zone. The Outer Mission, just south of the Mission District, nearly exploded with new inhabitants. (Source: One percent IPUMS U.S. Census, 1910. Courtesy of Stephanie Rozek.)

from 71 percent to 59 percent of the whole. This trend continued in 1920, when 10 percent of Outer Mission residents were professional/white-collar and working-class residents fell to 30 percent. (See Table 2 in the Appendix.) Even though the Outer Mission attracted white-collar workers, they still did not outnumber their working-class neighbors in either 1910 or 1920.

How did the disaster affect San Francisco's families? Census household data, which are available for only 1900 and 1910, reveal a significant shift in the percentage of distribution of household types in San Francisco neighborhoods after the disaster. (See Table 3 in the Appendix.) For disaster zone neighborhoods, a significant drop in the percentage of married households is clearly evident. In South of Market, for example, the percentage of married households dropped from 66 percent to 38 percent of all households. A reduction in married households appeared in other disaster zone neighborhoods as well: in Chinatown (33 percent to 26 percent); Downtown (34 percent to 22 percent); and the Western Addition/Pacific Heights (65 percent to 55 percent). Interestingly, the percentage of married households held steady in the Italian enclave of North Beach. This difference may be attributed to North Beach's internal financial infrastructure and strong connections to Italy for reconstruction support. Thus North Beach may have had more control than other neighborhoods in determining the type and function of new construction. Yet some Italians who had been burned out of North Beach left the neighborhood for the Mission District and Outer Mission. An Italian settlement in the Outer Mission was a logical choice because Italian truck and dairy farmers worked in this area before the catastrophe. A new Mission District branch of Bank of Italy (opened in 1907) was most likely a response to this demographic shift.

As married households decreased, the percentage of households without families increased in most disaster zone neighborhoods. The most dramatic change was South of Market, which soared from 15 percent in 1900 to 44 percent in 1910. Further, Chinatown's non-household population more than quadrupled (6 percent to 28 percent), and Downtown demonstrated an increase as well (38 percent to 65 percent). Brian Godfrey notes that the South

Population of San Francisco, 1920. South of Market stands out as the only San Francisco neighborhood that consistently declined in population share from 1900 (18 percent) to 1910 (10 percent) to 1920 (8 percent) and was almost immediately transformed into an industrial area. (Source: One percent IPUMS U.S. Census, 1920. Courtesy of Stephanie Rozek.)

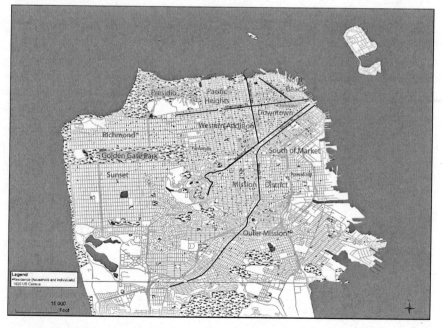

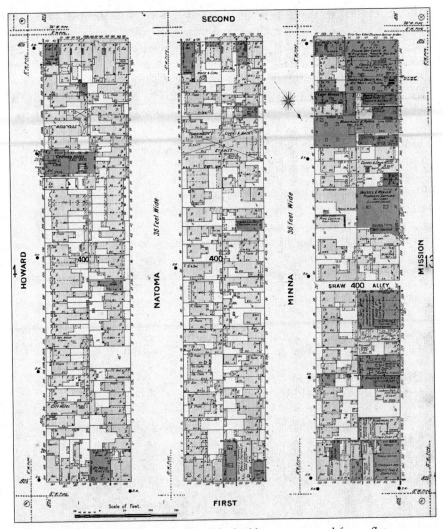

South of Market, 1899. The majority of the buildings were wood-frame flats or dwellings (shown in light gray). (Source: Sanborn Fire Insurance Map, 1899.)

of Market neighborhood "persisted as a point of entry for newly-arrived immigrants in San Francisco, particularly for unattached male laborers."[80] One probable reason for the reduction in married households shortly after the calamity is the loss of housing stock.

Many disaster survivors fled to family, friends, and land outside both the disaster zone and the city. The founding of a working-class town, Daly City, by South of Market refugees is one important example of post-disaster suburbanization. "I still remember the people—some with a cat, a dog, or a canary in a cage—walking out Mission Road," wrote Edmund Cavagnaro, "turning to look at the flames and smoke over their shoulders every now and then but not actually coming to a stop. It just seemed they couldn't get far enough away."[81] Many South of Market refugees kept walking out Mission Road to the edge of the city, where they camped on Daly's Hill. Owned by San Francisco's milk magnate John Daly, the hill was close enough to Mission Road streetcars that they could commute to work inside the city and far enough away from the disaster zone that they felt safe. "It scared them

South of Market, 1913. The majority of the buildings were brick constructions: manufacturing facilities or other businesses (shown in dark gray). (Source: Sanborn Fire Insurance Map, 1913.)

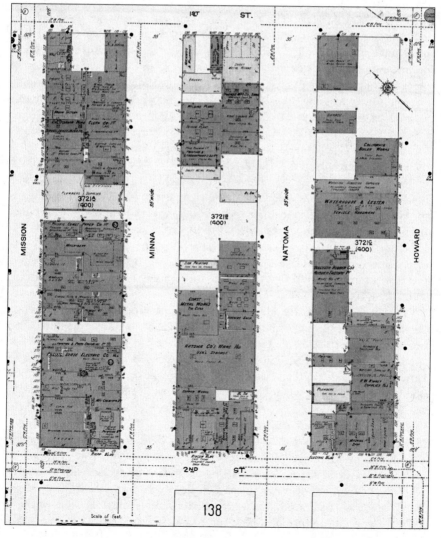

enough to move," recalled the granddaughter of South of Market refugees who camped on Daly's Hill and remained to build in the area.[82] Within a matter of years, the refugee campground turned into a town. Like Daly City, many refugees took up permanent residence in the Bay Area cities and towns to which they fled. On the whole, the 1906 calamity acted as an accelerant for the ongoing process of San Francisco and Bay Area suburbanization.[83]

Although the 1920 Census failed to record household data, a closer look at the status of single men (never married, divorced, or widowed) offers an important perspective on household changes. (See Table 4 in the Appendix.) The total percentage of single men rose slightly between 1900 and 1910 (from 35 percent to 38 percent), then fell to pre-disaster levels by 1920 (34 percent).[84] Indeed, South of Market and Downtown account for half of the neighborhoods where there was an increase in the number of single men between 1900 and 1910. The decline in the total percentage of single men living in San Francisco by 1920 may well reflect an overall increase in the percentage of households. For example, the Outer Mission demonstrated a decline in the number of single men between 1900 and 1910 (57 percent to 29 percent) coupled with an increase in married households during that period.[85]

The Outer Mission stands out as the neighborhood with the most substantial changes in household type between 1900 and 1910. Unlike other neighborhoods, it seemed to attract families. Married households accounted for one-third of the Outer Mission in 1900 (33 percent), but more than three-quarters (77 percent) of the neighborhood in 1910. The remaining households in 1910 (22 percent) were single-headed households (10 percent single-male households; 12 percent single-female households). By 1910, anyone living in the Outer Mission did so in some type of household (non-households declined from 67 percent of the whole in 1900 to 0 percent in 1910). Groups like the Excelsior Homestead Progressive Association may have encouraged this type of growth. At the founding of a new elementary school in 1910, members of the association predicted that the undeveloped area around the school would soon "be built up solid with fine mansions."[86]

U.S. Census data are also useful for understanding racial differences between Asian and non-Asian residents. (See Table 5 in the Appendix.) Few non-Asian minorities resided in San Francisco before World War II. African Americans made up less than 1 percent of the city population (0.4 percent) between 1900 and 1920 and they did not congregate in a particular neighborhood until the 1920s, when black families settled in the northwest corner of the Western Addition. This transition may have been the result of the 1906 calamity, when African Americans lost their homes in the city's downtown locale.[87] According to 1900, 1910, and 1920 Census data, San Francisco's neighborhoods were predominantly white except for Chinatown. In fact, of the three years considered here, 1920 is the only year during which virtually all of the Chinatown residents in the Census sample were Asian.

Asian residents found refuge in neighborhoods outside Chinatown by 1920 as well. In South of Market, the few Asian residents (1 percent) who lived there before the disaster disappeared by 1910 (0 percent), but by 1920 Asians living in South of Market tallied 4 percent. In addition, both the Western Addition/Pacific Heights and Richmond areas saw higher percentages of Asian residents in 1910 and 1920 than in 1900. The overall increase in the Asian population of the Western Addition (2 percent in 1900 to 3 percent in 1920) and the Richmond District (<1 percent in 1900 to 3 percent in 1920) foreshadowed the creation of Japan Town in that area.

Some San Francisco neighborhoods may have provided a temporary residence for Asian refugees. Both Potrero Hill and Outer Mission recorded an increase in 1910, which dropped off to 1 percent Asian by 1920. A rise in reported assault cases against Japanese residents may have been a result of such post-disaster relocations. When President Roosevelt sent his commerce secretary to San Francisco, the secretary recorded nineteen assault cases resulting from "a feeling of racial hostility."[88] San Francisco's new Japanese and Korean Exclusion League, a response to Japan's growing global military presence, sponsored a boycott of Japanese-owned restaurants by white unions. The short-lived strike gave way to a school crisis when white citizens became alarmed at post-disaster desegregation. The Exclusion League lobbied hard for school segregation, which the school board passed on October 11, 1906.[89] The school board's decision escalated to the White House and a San Francisco delegation met with President Roosevelt in February 1907. The president altered the school board's ruling, leaving only Chinese and Korean students subject to segregation. This led to the infamous gentlemen's agreement between the United States and Japan, the informal agreement that both limited Japanese immigration and alleviated overt discrimination against Japanese residing in the United States. President Roosevelt's decisions in Washington, however, did not end racial tensions in San Francisco. Another round of anti-Japanese violence transpired in May 1907 when a mob destroyed a Japanese restaurant and bathhouse.[90] Indeed, San Francisco's social dislocations continued to be felt in the years following the calamity.

The 1906 disaster accelerated the process by which industrial development and residential suburbanization worked in tandem to drive "the outward flow of urban growth."[91] Brian Godfrey's study of San Francisco's neighborhoods explains how, between 1860 and World War I, "the relatively fluid and mobile communities of the instant city were replaced by an orderly series of socially sorted neighborhoods."[92] The 1906 disaster hastened this transition. As rapid reconstruction favored commercial and elite interests, financial institutions consumed the city's center. Then residential construction, supported by insurance and relief payments, allowed wealthier homeowners to rebuild at their pre-disaster locations. U.S. Census data support scholar Richard Walker's finding that the suburbanization of manufacturing in the San Francisco Bay Area took place well before World War II. All of these circumstances meant that working-class and poor refugees, as well as white-collar renters, searched for homes outside the disaster zone. Thus disaster suburbanization sowed the seeds for neighborhood growth south and west of downtown San Francisco. Later post-disaster developments, such as the expansion of municipal transportation services as well as population shifts brought on by World War I, reaffirmed these neighborhood social boundaries.

Rebuilding Chinatown: Race and Social Space

Chinatown epitomizes the way in which reconstruction intensified the social segregation of neighborhoods. By 1900, San Francisco's Chinatown was widely regarded as the economic and social hub for Chinese living in the United States, and its residents were determined to re-create their neighborhood. "Any Chinese group in the rest of the United States when facing insult from white citizens, or when planning to set up public services . . . looked up to San Francisco's Chinatown for support," confirmed a post-disaster editorial in the *Chung Sai Yat Po*. "The feelings of the San Francisco Chinese towards their former residence were understandably beyond expression. They would not want to desert it, not at any rate."[93] U.S. Census data show that the percentage of Chinese living in the neighborhood rose to nearly 70 percent by 1910 and to a full 100 percent by 1920, a higher proportion of Chinese residents than before the calamity (93 percent). Remarkably, this growth was achieved at the same time as San Francisco's political and business leaders attempted to exclude Chinatown from the city limits.

The city's Chinese population grew as a result of an unprecedented opportunity afforded by the calamity—the destruction of reams of civic records. Seizing the moment, local Chinese reapplied for their certificates of residence, adding "sons" born in China to these official documents.[94] If a U.S.-born Chinese man with a certificate of residence or merchant papers claimed to have fathered a son while on a trip to China, the son could legally immigrate to the United States. "Paper son" immigration soared. As Adam McKeown notes, by 1907, a "chain of citizenship claims had been established that was impossible to break." Hay Ming Lee, whose father was a laborer in San Francisco, remembered how the calamity was a life-changing event for their community: "This was a big chance for a lot of Chinese. They forged themselves certificates saying that they were born in this country, and then when the time came, they could go back to China and bring back four or five sons, just like that!"[95] Indeed, Chinatown exhibited significant changes in single-headed households. Following the disaster, Chinatown's percentage of single-male-headed households declined from 61 percent to 38 percent, leading to a drop in the overall percentage of single-headed households.[96] (See Table 3 in the Appendix.) After 1910, Census data reveal a dramatic rise in Chinatown's percentage of single men (31 percent to 54 percent). (See Table 4 in the Appendix.) This increase in single men may well reflect the new, post-disaster paper son immigration. Entering the United States became increasingly difficult, however, with the opening of the Angel Island Immigration Station in 1910 and tightening immigration inspections.[97]

Rapid rebuilding created a space from which the Chinese community combated prevailing racial biases. As one journalist noted at the time, "The Chinese knew what property rights were theirs. . . . The Chinese are everywhere coming to a knowledge of the fact that they have rights, and are preparing to assert themselves to see that they actually get them."[98] As business and civic leaders staked a verbal claim on Chinatown's fifteen blocks of prime real estate, San Francisco's Chinese-language daily newspaper encouraged immediate non-permit rebuilding. During the first week of May, *Chung Sai Yat Po* editors announced: "Chinese leaders had contacted famous lawyers who . . . said that anyone who owned or leased properties could legally build new buildings there without any interference from local authorities."[99] By May 1906, the Chinese Merchant Exchange Association returned to San Francisco and by June, Chinese businesses were using temporary wooden structures. Chinese business leaders challenged city leaders who opposed their return by threatening to take Chinatown's lucrative tourist trade to another city. Their strategy worked and Chinese businesses obtained forty-three building permits by October 1906. By the following Chinese New Year, the neighborhood was coming back to life: "Even though Chinatown was not completely rebuilt," reported the *Chung Sai Yat Po*, "several dozens of buildings were already erected. There are a lot of returned residents."[100]

Chinatown leaders maintained a strong economic and political grip on their neighborhood. The Chinese consul, for example, loaned merchants $30,000 for reconstruction.[101] The Canton Bank, founded in 1907, also helped guarantee Chinese economic independence. As historian L. Eve Armentrout Ma argues, the Canton Bank aided Chinese merchants and promoted the international interests of China: "Only Chinese were allowed to own shares, and the bank was to show by example how a Western-style bank, using Chinese capital, could flourish in the modern world."[102] Thus the destruction created an opening for Chinatown's leadership to shore up its political power.

After staking their claim through rapid rebuilding, Chinese merchants worked closely with white landlords and city officials to bolster Chinatown's tourist industry.[103] When bubonic plague struck the city in 1907, Chinatown fared better than it had during the 1900 outbreak of the plague. At that time Chinatown was blamed for San Francisco's epidemic after the discovery of deaths from the plague in the neighborhood. The ensuing panic associated disease with race, exacerbating racial tensions in the city. Chinatown's new design, which included wider streets, fewer blind alleys, and new connections to the city sewer and waste disposal infrastructure, sanitized the dangerous alleys and dark dens associated with pre-disaster Chinatown. "Let it be a compound for Asiatics, let it be as oriental as may be," wrote the *San Francisco Newsletter* publishers, "and yet sanitary in every respect and under absolute control of the authorities."[104] While the racialization of Chinatown did not fade away, the new Chinatown was not a locus for plague, or blame, the second time around.

Chinatown looked different from the ground up. As Nayan Shah argues, the "'sanitary' exoticism" of the hybrid architectural style gave physical substance to racialized differences.[105] The *Merchant's Association Review* noted how many of Chinatown's new buildings were designed with an "oriental type of architecture."[106] The tiered pagoda towers, fringe-tile roofs, and dragon decorations on building façades solidified Chinatown's role as a lucrative tourist attraction. However, this focus on the tourist trade created a neighborhood that was disconnected from the surrounding city.[107] The "pseudo-oriental" architecture of post-disaster Chinatown simultaneously perpetuated racialized differences and promoted Chinese autonomy. The architectural boundaries of Chinatown created an important space for the community's economic, political, and social development.

RELIEF AND DISASTER SUBURBANIZATION

In the aftermath of the disaster, relief and rebuilding policies stimulated regional suburbanization. The destruction drove a quarter of a million San Franciscans out of the city, though most remained in the Bay Area. Local civic leaders used disaster relief grants to entice middle-class and elite San Franciscans to stay and used relief camps to discourage poor refugees from taking up permanent residence, pushing them to relocate outside of their cities and towns. As Linda McDowell points out, geographical boundaries are at once social and spatial; "they define who belongs to a place and who may be excluded, as well as the location or site of experience."[108]

A general fear of San Francisco's refugees unified Bay Area cities and towns. Class-, race-, and ethnic-based rumors about dangerous urban refugees traveled as far south as Los Angeles, where relief committee leaders believed "that a horde of undesirable characters would descend upon their city."[109] Mimicking San Francisco's official relief practices, civic leaders increased law enforcement, created civic relief committees, and established camps to contain refugees without means. To the north in San Rafael, for example, the sheriff ensured "good order" by deputizing 6 percent of the population and arming 250 men with guns and rifles.[110] Across the bay in Oakland, military personnel segregated refugees in their relief camps. Even the relief committee in the southern town of Palo Alto, whose members were eager to help any refugees arriving at the local depot, cautioned that "citizens must not take strangers home."[111] Throughout Bay Area cities and towns, civic leaders used disaster relief to shield their residents and encourage suburban growth.

Oakland

Oakland was an easy destination for thousands of refugees. Not surprisingly, San Francisco civic and relief leaders maintained close ties with Oakland because they needed a ready supply of able-bodied workers to help with rebuilding. As early as April 21, 1906, San Francisco relief organizers canvassed potential Bay Area relocation sites.[112] James Phelan reminded the relief committee "that some provision should be made in order that the skilled workmen and manufacturers should be ordered to stay within easy reach of the city, as their services would undoubtedly be required within the next few days."[113] The group endorsed East Bay relocation because they believed that Alameda County's well-developed transportation networks would "better insure their [refugees] return" to San Francisco.[114] Unlike other Bay Area locations, Oakland stood out in that San Francisco provided both money and military support to monitor refugees.[115] As an editorial in the *San Francisco Call* explained, "God Bless Oakland: Our neighbor Oakland has been to the people of San Francisco a city of refuge, and more."[116]

Oakland's ferry service and rail terminus made the city an easy destination for hundreds of thousands of refugees without extended family ties in the Bay Area.[117] The city adopted San Francisco relief policy standards to cope with the torrent of incoming disaster migrants. It built relief camps, under U.S. military supervision, to care for refugees while monitoring refugee behavior and protecting Oakland's citizens. According to the state health officer, Oakland camps "would be of great advantage, first, because the objectionable individuals in the camps could be more easily watched by the police; next, because they could be conducted at less expense and finally, for the most important of all reasons, the health of the inmates could be more carefully guarded, as could also the health of the residents of Oakland."[118] Thus relief camps clarified the boundaries of Oakland's healthy civic body by containing the perceived social problems embodied by poor and Chinese refugees.

For those who could afford it, new housing sprang up along Oakland's eastern foothills. "The advantages of the lower foothills of Oakland as sites for homes," wrote a booster in 1911, "became fully appreciated when the people from the other side of the Bay came to Oakland in April, 1906." Local ferries and trains made the move more attractive by simplifying daily commutes. On the hills of Oakland, residents "found themselves as far removed from the dirt and turmoil of the work-a-day world as though they had traveled fifty miles into the mountains."[119] Oakland indeed experienced phenomenal population growth after San Francisco's misfortune, increasing 123 percent from the 1900 census.

Oakland's Progressive mayor Frank K. Mott encouraged the city's growth by backing new civic policies and commercial expansion. The city welcomed the temporary relocation of San Francisco businesses, many of which became permanent. The calamity helped city leaders finish the Oakland port, which had been mired in litigation since the 1850s. The disaster aided Mayor Mott's negotiations with Southern Pacific Company in 1907 to build a new system of municipal docks, quays, wharves, and beltline railways that extended city limits west toward San Francisco.[120] Mayor Mott, who governed the city from 1905 to 1915, used the disaster to push for civic reform as well. During his tenure, he ushered in a new city charter, the reorganization of civil service, and civic improvements such as the rebuilding of the City Hall as Oakland's first skyscraper. It all started with San Francisco's calamity and the mayor's skill in maintaining social order after Oakland absorbed thousands of new citizens.

Marin County

Citizens of San Rafael were less concerned about the early arrival of the summer city crowd than they were about the onslaught of poor refugees. The largest city in Marin County, San Rafael, was founded as an auxiliary mission (*asistencia*) in 1817. Distant from the city's fog and wind, mission fathers used Marin's agreeable climate to heal the ailing California Indians they confined to San Francisco's Mission Dolores. Nearly a century later, however, incorporated San Rafael steeled itself against San Francisco's needy. Fear of the city's lower classes spread after the local paper published reports that "drunken, hungry and famine stricken crowds from San Francisco" were "defying officers" in the southern Marin town of Sausalito.[121] Civic leaders increased their police force to guard against the expected influx of poor refugees. They swore in men as deputies, collected guns, and organized a relief committee to ensure that San Francisco's homeless registered at their relief camp. California Red Cross president and San Rafael resident William W. Morrow modeled the relief camp after those in San Francisco, proudly admiring the orderly rows of tents on a "beautiful block of land."[122] This block of land highlighted class differences among refugees. San Rafael's relief tents were lined up near Hotel Rafael, where San Francisco's elite enjoyed luxurious, European-style accommodations.

For the wealthy, Marin County was the place to buy a summer cottage or spend an afternoon in the country. San Rafael's luxury hotel was a prime location from which guests could tour the countryside in comfort. With the addition of the California Pacific line between San Rafael and Point San Quentin in 1870, Marin County held the potential of becoming what Kenneth Jackson refers to as an "upper-class railroad suburb."[123] It is not surprising, then, that Marin's summer residents and visitors rushed back in April. After the catastrophe, newspaper ads encouraged wealthy San Franciscans to stay at the Hotel Rafael for the summer, a place where their credit would be accepted and a place that offered "splendid cuisine, comfort and fine service . . . coupled with a fine train service to the metropolis."[124] Indeed, San Rafael reassured these San Franciscans that the earthquake had not shaken their class status. Helen de Young, for example, was not hindered by lack of food or money after she stepped off the train in San Rafael. Instead, the daughter of *San Francisco Chronicle* owner and editor M. H. de Young found that her "credit was good" at the local stores.[125] Helen de Young's post-disaster hardship amounted to spending the summer without servants. She enjoyed the freedom from parental supervision so much so that she even found the gendered tasks of the domestic sphere delightful: "We had to wait on ourselves for the first time in our lives. . . . We cooked our own meals and made clothes for ourselves, and I must say we had an awfully good time."[126]

The proximity of nearby Sausalito to the bay intensified class-based fears. The bayside town responded much like Oakland did, although on a smaller scale. As one resident wrote, "The citizens of Sausalito organized and kept watch in fear of the crowds escaping from San Francisco."[127] The San Francisco ferry docked at Sausalito, as did North Beach fishing boats. A total of four thousand refugees found their way to the small port, where they quickly outnumbered the town's residents. Sausalito leaders wasted no time in closing their saloons and deputizing 113 male citizens to protect town property and citizens.[128] While the townspeople anxiously eyed their refugee neighbors, they enthusiastically welcomed new home owners. "We have been discovered!" proclaimed one *Sausalito News* editorial, "Lots and home sales in those parts of Marin lightly hit by the quake suddenly skyrocketed. To the delight of civic leaders and real estate speculators, many of those who fled San Francisco decided to make Marin their new home."[129]

Berkeley

Berkeley experimented with an ambitious program to board refugees in local homes. Shrugging off San Francisco military supervision, the Berkeley Relief Committee (BRC) enticed refugees with domestic comforts: "All who come here are quickly cared for, given food and shelter and made to feel once more the peace of a home."[130] While Berkeley's organized relief effort included the basic elements of civic relief—the mayor endorsed increased law enforcement, supervised relief camps, and relief claim investigation—Berkeley was the only city to place the majority of its refugees in residential housing.[131] By introducing more than six thousand refugees to Berkeley homes, officials hoped that they would absorb the city's hospitality and remain as model citizens.[132] Thus gender and family were the linchpin of BRC policy, which relied on the domestic sphere to execute relief and development plans.

The BRC's housing program was part of the city's larger relief effort. The University of California campus was used as a relief center, with campus buildings segregating refugees by gender, race, and ethnicity. University buildings housed kitchens and a temporary hospital, while separate outdoor camping areas were designated for Chinese (at a site off campus), Italians, single men, and families.[133] As in San Francisco, the segregated Chinese camp was more ideological than practical. While few Chinatown refugees resided at the Berkeley camp, it nonetheless marked a clear reinforcement of racial differences.[134]

The BRC plan worked out civic goals in the domestic sphere. Thirteen hundred volunteers, who were predominantly middle-class, home-owning families, opened their doors to San Francisco refugees with no compensation for their effort.[135] As one volunteer explained, these residents believed they should "do all possible" to "see that they [refugees] do not suffer."[136]

In nearly half of the recorded cases, married women took responsibility for organizing relief in their households. Home owners specified the desired gender, age, and marital status of prospective refugees and most assumed that the BRC would send "respectable people" their way.[137] On only a few occasions did volunteers remind the relief committee that "if the people whom you send are nice and very quiet—I think we will be able to keep them longer than a few days."[138] Although some asked the relief committee to "send those especially in need," the disaster did not eliminate class- and race-based considerations.[139] The number of Chinatown refugees in Berkeley prompted one volunteer to insist on "no Chinamen."[140] Another volunteer used relief as an opportunity to acquire domestic help and asked for "a good girl for general housework."[141] Overall, the BRC's initial attempt to place refugees was surprisingly successful and nearly two-thirds of the volunteer home owners welcomed refugees who matched their criteria.[142] Just one week after the disaster, the BRC made plans to request San Francisco relief funding for their project and investigated more than 1,100 homes, gathering data "to enable Berkeley to get its share of relief funds."[143]

Relief leaders and real estate developers alike hoped that introducing desirable refugees to the intimacy of Berkeley's domestic sphere would entice them to stay. The appeal of new, affordable housing for San Franciscans was enhanced by the new transit system opened in 1903, which reduced the commute time to San Francisco to a mere thirty-six minutes. The Key Route was the brainchild of East Bay entrepreneur and real estate promoter Francis Marion Smith. Electric-railway promoters like Smith envisioned the Bay Area as a single territory, linked by new technology.[144] Massive refugee relocation was a boon to real estate speculators. "Cheap Homes . . . For the People," read an ad for the Magee Tract. "Buy while you can get a handsome building site."[145] By December 1906, the *Berkeley Reporter*'s Robert Duponey wrote: "Berkeley is increasing everyday! . . . Everywhere you smell timber, every street is obstructed with barrels of plaster, the hammers fill the air with noise."[146] Indeed, the success of post-disaster development was easily measured by Berkeley's record-setting post-disaster growth rate of 200 percent, the population swelling from 13,200 in 1900 to 40,400 by 1910.[147]

THE TRIUMPHANT CITY:
THE 1915 PANAMA PACIFIC INTERNATIONAL EXPOSITION

As the city raced toward urban recovery, civic and business leaders balked at memorializing the catastrophe. Rather than highlight the earthquake or fires, they focused on commemorating the city's revival with the 1915 Panama Pacific International Exposition. The first official Exposition handbook recapitulated the instant history narrative: "And in that black, deserted zone / They built a city, stone on stone; / A city that, on history's page, / Is crowned the marvel of its age."[148] Mayor James Rolph proudly invited the world to witness San Francisco's recovery when he announced: "No sooner had the fire stopped smoking than San Francisco began to build again. Evidence of what she has done are [sic] visible on every hand, and we are glad to show the city to our guests from all over the world."[149] City Beautiful advocates realized their vision of reform by designing the fairground buildings along San Francisco's northern waterfront. As Mel Scott suggests, the exposition "was in every respect the product of the 'City Beautiful' movement and could be regarded as a partial fulfillment of the city plan."[150] Notable architects designed eleven palaces, bringing a splendid array of muted colors and red tile roofs to the shoreline. The buildings offered physical proof of San Francisco's full recovery from disaster. Indeed, the rebuilt city and the exposition became interchangeable. As a 1934 San Francisco tourist brochure historicized the event: "Following the catastrophe of 1906 their only thought was for the building of the city upon an even grander scale. When nine years later they invited the world to the Panama Pacific International Exposition it was to one of that world's most striking cities."[151] However, Progressive ambitions and idealized descriptions of the exposition masked the reality of post-disaster social stratification. Thus the exposition can be read in two ways: as a symbol of Progressive vision and as a symbol of intensified social differences.

The idea for an exposition was first proposed by Reuben Hale, an influential member of San Francisco's business elite, in 1904. Hale found a sympathetic ear after the disaster when other prominent businessmen agreed that creating a "city of palaces" would bolster investor confidence.[152] As Issel and Cherny point out, the Exposition "epitomized many of the dominant values of the city's business community at that time," values that were embedded in city government as well.[153] These Progressive values included civic unity, opposition to patronage in hiring, reliance on research and analysis for event planning, and a search for experts (architects, artists, experienced exposition planners).[154] Local clubwomen played an important role in the drive to win the exposition and accompanied a San Francisco delegation that lobbied Congress for the exposition bid in 1910. A small women's committee met with California's representatives and "secured a list of the men who favored San Francisco and those whose votes should be secured. With this information the women enlisted every possible influence" to win congressional approval for the fair.[155] As a result of their diligence, San Francisco won the exposition, on January 31, 1911.

Although local Progressives lost out to business interests during reconstruction, they gained new ground with the exposition. Plans for the Civic Center Plaza, comprising four city blocks, to be surrounded by magisterial government buildings, finally gained approval. The impressive City Hall with its 308-foot dome was finished just before the exposition opened in 1915. The Exposition Auditorium was completed as well, providing seating for up to fifteen thousand for the city's public events. The exposition helped James Rolph's mayoral campaign as well; his support for the fair symbolized his commitment to civic unity and progress. Middle-class women applied the lessons learned from disaster relief to their work in planning the fair. In 1912, they formed the Woman's Board, which took charge of reception and entertainment duties at the fair's California Building.[156] As one woman involved in both events wrote, "In the 'calamity days,' women used to comforts always and conveniences at every hand, worked without a murmur to aid the men upon whom rested the responsibilities of reconstruction. It was then that they learned something not expressible in words that made them ready to help carry some of the burdens that must come with the building of an exposition city."[157]

While the celebration of civic improvement and disaster recovery was a boon to Progressive San Franciscans, the event incongruously threatened the health of the city. In 1912, event planners selected two and a half miles of waterfront property between Fort Mason and the Presidio as the site for the monumental event. Despite the harrowing lesson on landfill's earthquake vulnerability, they poured 300,000 cubic yards of fill into 100 acres of submerged land. Thus the very event celebrating earthquake recovery rested on hazardous landfill.[158] Building the exposition's "dream city" brought an end to some forms of disaster relief when event construction displaced more than one thousand refugee cottages.[159] Private interests aligned with public health as the San Francisco Real Estate Board encouraged the removal of refugee cottages from the area.[160] The San Francisco Board of Health pressured "property owners in the Harbor View District [to] remov[e] the unsanitary refugee shacks that are on their property."[161] Between 1911 and 1915, the local health board and the U.S. Public Health Service condemned and destroyed 1,272 refugee cottages, which accounted for 77 percent of all condemned buildings in this period.[162] This must have been a painful lesson in urban design for residents who lost their relief cottages so that San Francisco could celebrate its full recovery from disaster.

Even as event planners demolished relief housing, they also offered full-time employment to some three thousand workers. To do so, exposition leaders utilized disaster relief notions of deserving and undeserving citizens. Exposition employment, although temporary, offered a brief respite to San Francisco's economic depression in 1913 and 1914.[163] Exposition jobs, though mostly menial tasks such as street and lot cleaning, were in great demand. In a sense, this construction project mirrored disaster relief because it supported two-parent families with funds from private donations. First, a forty-eight-hour registration period sorted "the honest workers from the idlers and so that those who do not really desire work will drift out of the city."[164] Even the appeal for donations reinforced the two-parent, male-headed household: "Men and Women of San Francisco: Five thousand men are asking you for a livelihood. They have tried in vain to get regular employment. These men have families. Our duty is to help them."[165]

The event, from construction to opening day, cloaked the city in Progressive ideals of gender and family. The elaborate fairgrounds entwined both progress and a homelike atmosphere as evidence of urban recovery.

Once again, local clubwomen reaffirmed their domesticating presence in the public realm. "In plan, the Exposition was compact, almost homelike in its intimate snugness, so that psychically it promoted the whole-human-family feeling," recorded Frank Todd in the official history of the exposition.[166] The "whole-human-family feeling" included moral protection, yet another Progressive hallmark. Thus the exposition reinforced women's role in the public sphere, a process that had been gaining momentum since the catastrophe.

Female moral influence over the exposition was most clearly demonstrated by women's staffing of Travelers' Aid stations. The Woman's Board expanded the mission of Travelers' Aid, a national agency founded to protect traveling women and children, to guard visitors from around the world. A special gold star badge, "emblematic of honor, light and purity" signified Travelers' Aid volunteers as safe, moral guardians to visiting women.[167] Recalling the effectiveness of the Red Cross badge after the disaster, the women selected the gold star to "stand for moral protection always, as the Red Cross does for aid in times of stress."[168] Clubwomen were especially concerned with the possibility of increased prostitution during the yearlong event. Their goal of "a clean bill of moral health for its Exposition" extended to the city as well.[169] Clubwomen's efforts during the exposition intensified the campaign against brothels, and the city later enforced a police blockade of the red-light district in 1917.[170]

The exposition won international acclaim as a wildly successful world's fair and, at the same time, the fairgrounds highlighted class and gender differences. Middle-class white women volunteers played a key role in this success by ensuring that visiting dignitaries and organizations from around the world encountered a prosperous, cultured image of San Francisco.[171] At the same time, most working-class women could not afford to volunteer, pay the price of admission, or take the time to attend the historic event. Katharine Felton worried that "many hard working women, especially mothers of families" would never see the fair. She negotiated four days of free passes for 4,000 women and children. In a city of more than 400,000, however, one wonders how many working-class and poor San Franciscans experienced the celebration firsthand.

The Panama Pacific International Exposition displayed San Francisco's successful recovery from disaster and revealed the widening social divide in the post-disaster city. A monument created for the event symbolized these social differences. Visitors to one of the exposition's most popular sites, the Palace of Fine Arts designed by Bernard Maybeck, were greeted by the outstretched arms and benevolent face of *The Pioneer Mother*.[172] The statue of a white female pioneer glossed over the more recent heroic work of San Francisco's women and, instead, harked back to the U.S. settlement of California. "The statue is heroic in proportion. This world-mother typifies majesty, dignity, intellect, efficiency, sympathy and love," wrote Woman's Board historian Anna Pratt Simpson. "She is presenting her two beautiful children to the future with full faith, but protecting them all the while."[173] The bronzed mother was the perfect addition to Maybeck's architecture, which he designed as an expression of "the life of the people of California."[174] At the statue's ceremonial unveiling on June 30, 1915, University of California president Benjamin Ide Wheeler declared, "This woman who draws her children about her creates the sacred shelter of the home and lays thereby the deep and sacred foundations of human society."[175] The city that emerged after the disaster glorified industrial progress, but that progress was framed within traditional and idealized notions of race, gender, and family.

San Francisco's earthquake and fires exposed existing social inequalities but did not eliminate them. Although the massive disruption to public and private space created opportunities for local residents and communities, the catastrophe never created a tabula rasa for social change. Rebuilding advantaged wealthier property and business owners when new insurance, rebuilding, and relief policies facilitated their prompt return to the urban landscape. The catastrophe accelerated San Francisco and Bay Area suburbanization by pushing residents farther away from the city center. Reconstruction prompted significant demographic shifts that solidified the boundaries between San Francisco's socially stratified neighborhoods. Ethnic differences became more pronounced after rebuilding, as Issel and Cherny point out, where "the Mission became more Irish . . . the Geary-Fillmore area of the Western Addition became more Jewish . . . [and] North Beach became more Italian."[176] U.S. Census data also show larger numbers of Chinese living in Chinatown and more single working-class men South of Market. Thus disaster relief, and the rebuilding that followed, intensified San Francisco's social stratification by re-creating order based on earlier definitions of difference. In the drive to restore the city's losses, the new San Francisco reconstructed the social divisions it claimed to eschew.

Epilogue

Disaster Remnants

This book begins with a brief description of disaster narratives, those vital accounts that make sense out of wide-scale destruction. San Francisco, of course, had its own disaster narrative that defined the catastrophe for both the city and the nation. But that story was not entirely truthful. Rather it was a fictive yarn spun by business and political leaders, who wanted to rebuild an economically prosperous city. To understand why this was so, it is useful to turn to Carl Smith's thoughtful exploration of a calamity's "imaginative reverberations." Smith contends that disaster narratives are the attempt to make sense of how catastrophic events challenge what we believe is "right" or "normal," and as a result, they are not necessarily accurate reflections of reality.[1] San Francisco's master disaster narrative carefully engineered its own set of erroneous claims that overshadowed the collective and individual stories emerging from the city's diverse families and neighborhoods. If we consider that which the master narrative conceals, we gain a much more expansive view of the disaster's impact.

News of San Francisco's earthquake and fires splashed across almost every newspaper front page in the country. Before the fires ended, business and political leaders crafted their own tale of San Francisco's demise. On the Chicago train bound for the burning city, future American National Red Cross president Ernest Bicknell listened to businessmen discussing how the "widespread impression that the city was subject to destructive earthquake" would be detrimental to economic resurgence. The rumbling train car filled with loud cheers as the businessmen agreed to spread the word "that the disaster in San Francisco was due solely to fire . . . as might occur in any well-ordered city."[2] That was their story, and they were sticking to it.

Earthquakes evoked the unfamiliar and could make even seasoned investors skittish; thus those with a financial stake in San Francisco closely monitored disaster publicity. The fire story was told from the top down, starting with California's governor and Southern Pacific Railroad owners. As early as June 1906, Governor George Pardee told the state senate, "The earthquake, severe and destructive as it was, did not do, as has been so wildly heralded, much damage, in comparison with the following fire. . . . It was the fire, and not the earthquake, that laid half of San Francisco low."[3] Southern Pacific executives then instructed civic and business leaders in the art of describing the disaster: "We do not believe in advertising the earthquake. The real calamity was undoubtedly the fire," explained a Southern Pacific representative to the Stockton Chamber of Commerce. "In press matter, I would call attention to the small area of the State which was affected by the earthquake and the relatively small results in the way of destruction."[4] Even published photographs substantiated this one-sided view. The ever popular hand-tinted disaster post-cards depicting raging flames and billowing smoke were frequently altered by local artists. In a panoramic shot taken from the roof of the Fairmont San Francisco hotel, for example, an artist redrew the Hall of Justice tower and added texture to the clouds of smoke.[5] The press, in general, repeated the narrative, but if they happened to print the "wrong" story, then influential San Franciscans were quick to respond. A telegram sent by a "prominent gentleman in San Francisco" corrected the *American Monthly*'s report that "overstated the earthquake damage." "None of the large buildings shown in your pictures, except the City Hall, was damaged by the earthquake," read the telegram. "Outside of the City Hall, 99 per cent of San Francisco's damage was from fire."[6] Building confidence in urban recovery was serious business.

Gendered images of San Francisco's noble survivors bolstered the tale of the city's resilience. In particular, examples of women's behavior became evidence of the peaceful and nurturing nature of survivors and their city. "Woman, ever the balm of distress, outdid her history of heroism," wrote Bailey Millard for *Cosmopolitan* magazine. "I saw a beautiful girl of former social rank driving a great white motor car, piled high with the poor bedding and household goods of squalid refugees."[7] Such gendered generosity signified that the city was speeding toward full recovery. Masculine imagery, redolent of the mythic California pioneer or forty-niner, was likewise used to instill confidence in post-disaster San Francisco. "Much of this readiness was American, much of it Californian," wrote renowned scholar William James. "The commonest men, simply because they *are* men, will keep on singly and collectively showing this admirable fortitude of temper."[8] Frank Putnam, writing for the *National Magazine*, described Californians as "Americans of the best sort." "We may well be proud of their swift courage, their fortitude, their generosity," continued Putnam, and "their stubborn determination to pluck victory out of defeat."[9] Proof of resiliency was plucked from San Francisco's instant-city past. "San Francisco will have to rely on the same force which created her former beauty and activity," read an article in *Harper's Weekly*, "to wit, the toil, the energy, and the spirit of her citizens."[10] Thus narratives that recapitulated popular conceptions of gender, race, and class further inspired confidence in the city's resilience.

But the obsession with the 1906 catastrophe as a "fire only" event masked highly individualized experiences of the calamity. As Lawrence Vale and Thomas Campanella explain, "All disasters, not only earthquakes, have epicenters. Those who are victimized by traumatic episodes experience resilience differently, based on their distance from the epicenter."[11] These varied disaster narratives can be found in a wide variety of nonverbal remains, or disaster remnants.[12]

As residents evacuated their homes, they instinctively reached for belongings that held the greatest personal meaning. Those with the finances and good fortune to find a wagon or car to transport their belongings could salvage almost their entire household. But many refugees could save only those objects that they could carry away in their own hands. Disaster remnants point to this symbiotic relationship between geography and identity. For many working-class women, for example, their personal identity was entwined with the objects they owned as well as the places they lived. Laurel Thatcher Ulrich shows how women during the colonial era "used property to assert identities, build alliances, and reweave family bonds torn by marriage, death, or migration."[13] The death and destruction wrought by the 1906 disaster threatened the family bonds of thousands of women and families as it forced their migration both inside and outside the city. For those hit hardest by the catastrophe, the bits and pieces of property saved made it possible to both reassert individual identities and reweave family ties.

Records of what household artifacts were saved illustrate how emergency conditions forced disaster survivors to make unfamiliar choices.[14] What objects were their most valuable possessions? Family heirlooms? Valuables purchased in their own lifetime? Objects required for work? During a moment of crisis, economic value was not the sole measurement of worth. As one disaster survivor recalled, "We took with us in the Park the least important things, such as mama's Brass Candlesticks, some lovely things we highly cherished."[15] The choices they made can be viewed as a physical manifestation of social identity. A middle-aged woman observed pushing her sewing machine along the city's uneven terrain is one such example. "Oh no, she wouldn't' [sic] let the machine out of her sight. It was her livelihood," recalled one witness who had suggested that she discard the sewing machine and walk unfettered. "She went on up [the hill] and you couldn't stop her."[16] In Chinatown, residents of the Oriental Home for Chinese Women and Girls were directed to run back into the mission home "between shakes" to retrieve their valuables. According to the mission secretary, "Every girl tried to get her Bible first of all."[17] By keeping their Bibles, they preserved their identification with the home's gendered mission. The disaster tested the priorities of the wealthy as well. The wife of a San Francisco millionaire, afraid that the encroaching fires would engulf their mansion, ordered her maid to cut the tapestries from the frames of the chairs.[18] Each of these chosen objects simultaneously revealed, and continued to construct, its owner's social identity during a time of crisis. The sewing machine ensured the single working-class woman's capacity for self-support, the Bibles sustained the religious identity and claim to respectability of the Christian Chinese girls, and the rare tapestries preserved a measure of social standing for the elite San Francisco woman.

At 5:12 A.M. on April 18, 1906, place made all the difference. The earthquake was most devastating to the South of Market District, where warehouses, hotels, and flats were built on landfill. This neighborhood was the first to crumble and burn, leaving little for residents to salvage. As we know, this was also a neighborhood to which few working-class families returned. But a disaster artifact from the South of Market District helps reconstruct the past and recover the meaning of the loss by telling the story of both family and neighborhood.

A young working-class couple, Joseph and Lenora Moore, slept soundly in their small South of Market flat until the earthquake struck. Having only recently married and moved to San Francisco, Lenora found the tremors terrifying and unfamiliar. As the couple ran for safety, Joseph Moore clutched only one household object in his hand: a beer glass, an artifact of not only Irish working-class life but also a unique family story.[19] Measuring nearly eight inches in height, the quarter-inch-thick glass holds a pint of liquid. The glass was neither distinctive nor well made; its stem and bowl show no craft of artisan skill. No emblems announce, as was common during this period, an affiliation with a particular brewery. Indeed, the value of the weight of its thick glass and stem derives from its being resistant to breaking and chipping as it made its rounds in one of the hundreds of saloons in San Francisco.

The masculine social world of the saloon exemplified workingmen's public culture. The saloon created, as Kathy Peiss explains, an "interlocking network of leisure activities [that] strengthened an ethos of masculinity among workingmen."[20] There were more saloons than churches in the predominantly Catholic working-class district (the 1900 census lists thirty-two saloons in a one-block area).[21] The exclusion of women from this male social world is further demonstrated by the glass itself. The size, shape, and weight of the vessel make it heavier and more cumbersome than glassware typically found in a working-class household.

While this beer glass belonged in a saloon, on April 18, 1906, it was inside the flat of Joseph and Lenora Moore. For reasons unknown to his new wife, Joseph Moore walked out of the saloon with the glass and brought it home to stay. Was it an intentional souvenir or an oversight? Was it a favorite glass carried to the saloon and stored at home? Or was it a marital compromise, a way to drink within the private sphere? Whatever the reason that this newly wed, Irish working-class man chose his beer glass over his wedding photograph, his choice certainly reveals the strong ethnic attachments to the masculine social world of the saloon. But after it was rescued from the catastrophe, the beer glass became an artifact of multiple experiences: the social world of the saloon, the construction of gender in the home, and the individual experience of disaster.

As a disaster remnant, the story of the beer glass became a woman's story. For the past century, Lenora Busby Moore, her daughter, and now her granddaughter have displayed the glass high on their kitchen shelves. As time passes, the stories handed down to explain the beer glass have loosened the artifact's attachment to South of Market's masculine social world, and the glass has come to symbolize cultural and religious differences and the persistence of family bonds. Just one month before the April disaster, Lenora Busby, born in Park City, Utah, to Mormon parents in 1881, married San Francisco–born Irish laborer Joseph Henry Moore.[22] It was not a simple matter as to how Lenora Busby came to be born in Utah. Her mother was born in Calcutta, India, and immigrated to Salt Lake City after her British officer father and Indian mother were converted to Mormonism by missionaries in England.[23] Busby's marriage and move to San Francisco severed her ties to family, religion, and the place that embodied both. Then the destruction of their flat destroyed the few remaining connections to her previous life. Photographs, linens, or other keepsakes that she undoubtedly carried with her to California were gone. The glass marked this absence, signifying both the life she led before her marriage and her marital attachment to her husband's social world. The stories she told her daughter and granddaughter were ones of multiple social dislocations: India to Utah, Utah to San Francisco, San Francisco to suburb.

As refugees fled San Francisco during the disaster, the objects they carried brought social continuity to their post-disaster migration. For refugees like the Moores, disaster artifacts were the sole physical representation of their pre-disaster lives. The connection to their working-class neighborhood remained central to the Moores as they camped with other refugees on Daly's Hill, just south of San Francisco. This chance encampment of working-class refugees later became the permanent working-class town of Daly City. As the beer glass suggests, social identity was intimately connected with urban geography: *where* they were explained *who* they were. And the few objects, along with the families who owned them, helped to rebuild their lost community.

The repeated telling of San Francisco's master disaster narrative left no time to grieve and no room for misery. But the loss experienced by many survivors was not so easily forgotten. A working-class mother who lost her South of Market home to fire and her neighborhood to rebuilding refused to forget the place she loved. She memorialized the disaster with a simple ritual. Every April 18, she returned to the place where her family had once lived and selected a single rock to take to her new home. For nearly half a century, she never missed an anniversary of the catastrophe. Her son could not forget the forty-seven rocks arranged on the mantelpiece in their home.[24] That she gathered a rock on each disaster anniversary suggests that this working-class mother was unable to save anything of value from her pre-disaster home. At first, the rocks symbolized the physical loss of home and perhaps the deaths of friends and neighbors who disappeared on April 18, 1906. But the meaning of these rocks changed over time. As the number of stones increased, they marked the many years of remembering that fateful April day. The sizable collection of rocks weighed the mantelpiece down with the memories of the home and neighborhood that had been erased by both the calamity and the master disaster narrative. Her ritual of remembering loss created its own reality.

What do catastrophes mean to those who survive them? The stories evoked by disaster artifacts reveal how a single catastrophe generates multiple meanings. The common saloon beer glass calls our attention to the complex relationship between place and social identity because this single object tells stories of both neighborhood and family. The earthquake and fires were frightening and life-changing events for the Moores. The earthquake took their home and the fires obliterated their neighborhood, forcing them to migrate out of San Francisco. Their personal struggle to rebuild their lives, and to build a new community out of what once was a cow pasture, was masked by a master disaster narrative that celebrated San Francisco's phoenix-like rise from the ashes of fire. Although city leaders refused to memorialize the suffering and despair that accompanied the 1906 disaster, many survivors did exactly that. The disaster objects that San Franciscans saved, and the stories they told, preserved the past they knew as they adapted to an uncertain future.

Appendix

Tables

The data employed for Tables 1–5 were drawn from the 1 percent Integrated Public Use Microdata Series (IPUMS) samples of the 1900, 1910, and 1920 U.S. Census, provided by the Minnesota Population Center. Data pertain to the households included in the 1 percent samples whose members resided in San Francisco as designated by the city codes in the censuses of those years. Given the focus of this study on a small geographic area, a detailed household weight—a sampling weight provided by IPUMS—was used to estimate more accurate and nationally representative statistics. Analysis in this study examines six variables of interest: population sizes of neighborhoods in San Francisco, and distributions of social (occupational) class, household type, individuals' marital status, home ownership, and race by neighborhood. Neighborhoods are defined using boundaries noted in William Issel and Robert W. Cherny's *San Francisco, 1865–1932: Politics, Power, and Urban Development*; enumeration districts are used to categorize household addresses into the twelve neighborhoods examined in this study. Social class here reflects occupational class, which was first categorized into seven groups (unskilled and skilled labor, professional and white-collar work, agriculture, military employment, homemaking, retirement/unemployment, outside of labor force) and then aggregated into three groups for analysis (not working, professional and white-collar, working-class). Household type reflects composition in terms of the sex of the householder and the marital status of the householder; non-households are further labeled as either male or female to infer the percentage of a neighborhood that is single male or single female. Additionally, marital status—non-married (i.e., never married/single, divorced, widowed) or married—is used to examine neighborhood differences in demographics. The categories of race are aggregated into Asian (Chinese, Japanese, other Asian, or Pacific Islander) and non-Asian (white, black, American Indian/Alaskan Native), because there were relatively few black and American Indian/Alaskan Native residents in the city during those years (sixteen in 1900, fourteen in 1910, and fifty in 1920) and because Asian groups constituted a significant minority in the city at that time. Likelihood ratio chi-square tests were used to assess statistical significance of neighborhood differences in these attributes.

TABLE 1. POPULATION SHARES AND ESTIMATED POPULATION SIZES BY NEIGHBORHOOD, 1900, 1910, AND 1920

Neighborhood	Population share (%)			Estimated population size		
	1900	1910	1920	1900	1910	1920
South of Market	18	10	8	61,000	45,000	75,000
Mission District	24	26	22	78,000	120,000	210,000
Potrero Hill	1	2	3	2,502	11,000	25,000
Outer Mission	1	4	10	2,100	19,000	96,000
Western Addition/ Pacific Heights	26	28	26	86,000	130,000	250,000
North Beach	6	3	4	21,000	14,000	40,000
Chinatown	2	3	1	8,211	14,000	12,000
Downtown	11	4	9	36,000	18,000	88,000
Panhandle Area	2	4	2	5,017	19,000	16,000
Sunset	2	5	6	7,211	23,000	60,000
Richmond	6	10	8	21,000	45,000	78,000
Military	<1	<1	2	1,404	2,102	19,000

Source: One percent Integrated Public Use Microdata Series (IPUMS) U.S. Census, 1900, 1910, and 1920.
Sample sizes: 3,293 in 1900, 4,540 in 1910, 9,568 in 1920.
Note: Percentages may not add up to 100 percent because of rounding.

TABLE 2. SOCIAL CLASS BY NEIGHBORHOOD, 1900, 1910, AND 1920

Distribution by neighborhood (%)

Neighborhood	1900			1910			1920		
	Not working	Working-class	Professional/ white-collar	Not working	Working-class	Professional/ white-collar	Not working	Working-class	Professional/ white-collar
South of Market	49	41	10	27	61	13	39	50	11
Mission District	54	33	13	54	32	14	53	27	20
Potrero Hill	76	24	0	57	34	10	39	47	15
Outer Mission	29	71	0	59	36	5	60	30	10
Western Addition/ Pacific Heights	53	27	20	42	33	25	46	28	26
North Beach	59	33	8	57	36	7	52	39	9
Chinatown	21	49	30	28	34	39	44	46	10
Downtown	35	42	22	22	50	28	32	29	39
Panhandle Area	68	20	12	51	20	29	67	13	20
Sunset	61	33	6	55	30	15	61	14	25
Richmond	56	20	24	48	30	22	56	18	26
Military	29	71	0	38	52	10	5	93	2
All neighborhoods	51	34	16	46	35	19	48	31	21

Source: One percent IPUMS U.S. Census, 1900, 1910, and 1920.

Sample sizes: South of Market, 606–444–746; Mission District, 782–1,167–2,062; Potrero Hill, 25–113–248; Outer Mission, 21–185–948; Western Addition/Pacific Heights, 861–1,277–2,470; North Beach, 210–140–396; Chinatown, 82–137–122; Downtown, 359–181–868; Panhandle Area, 50–192–158; Sunset, 72–232–594; Richmond, 211–451–768; Military, 14–21–188.

Note: "Not working" denotes anyone who was unemployed, not in the labor force, retired, or "keeping house" (a category in the 1900 Census). Changes in percentage distribution between 1900 and 1910 are statistically significant ($p < 0.05$) except in Mission District, North Beach, Chinatown, and Sunset. Changes in percentage distribution between 1910 and 1920 are statistically significant ($p < 0.05$) except in North Beach. Overall, changes in percentage distribution between 1900 and 1920 are statistically significant in all neighborhoods except North Beach.

TABLE 3. HOUSEHOLD TYPE BY NEIGHBORHOOD, 1900 AND 1910

Distribution by neighborhood (%)

	1900					1910				
Neighborhood	Non-household, male	Non-household, female	Married household	Single male household	Single female household	Non-household, male	Non-household, female	Married household	Single male household	Single female household
South of Market	11	3	66	8	12	41	3	38	7	11
Mission District	1	1	77	10	11	2	2	73	6	18
Potrero Hill	20	0	80	0	0	22	5	55	11	7
Outer Mission	67	0	33	0	0	0	0	77	10	12
Western Addition/Pacific Heights	2	2	65	8	23	9	6	55	11	20
North Beach	2	0	72	11	14	4	0	81	8	8
Chinatown	6	0	33	61	0	19	9	26	38	9
Downtown	23	15	34	7	21	52	13	22	6	7
Panhandle Area	10	0	78	0	12	2	1	72	10	15
Sunset	7	0	72	8	13	13	6	69	4	8
Richmond	2	0	66	<1	31	7	2	69	8	14
Military	71	0	29	0	0	81	19	0	0	0
All neighborhoods	7	3	65	9	17	12	4	60	9	15

Source: One percent Integrated Public Use Microdata Series (IPUMS) U.S. Census, 1900 and 1910.
Sample sizes: South of Market, 606–444–746; Mission District, 782–1,167–2,062; Potrero Hill, 25–113–248; Outer Mission, 21–185–948; Western Addition/Pacific Heights, 861–1,277–2,470; North Beach, 210–140–396; Chinatown, 82–137–122; Downtown, 359–181–868; Panhandle Area, 50–192–158; Sunset, 72–232–594; Richmond, 211–451–768; Military, 14–21–188.
Note: Changes in percentage distribution between 1900 and 1910 are statistically significant ($p < 0.05$) except in North Beach.

TABLE 4. PERCENTAGE OF NON-MARRIED MEN BY NEIGHBORHOOD AND YEAR

Neighborhood	Non-married men (%)		
	1900	1910	1920
South of Market	42	61	48
Mission District	34	33	31
Potrero Hill	44	42	39
Outer Mission	57	32	29
Western Addition/Pacific Heights	29	36	28
North Beach	33	39	38
Chinatown	38	31	54
Downtown	39	52	41
Panhandle Area	30	33	32
Sunset	38	35	29
Richmond	29	35	26
Military	71	71	91
All neighborhoods	35	38	34

Source: One percent IPUMS U.S. Census, 1900, 1910, and 1920.

Sample sizes: South of Market, 606–444–746; Mission District, 782–1,167–2,062; Potrero Hill, 25–113–248; Outer Mission, 21–185–948; Western Addition/Pacific Heights, 861–1,277–2,470; North Beach, 210–140–396; Chinatown, 82–137–122; Downtown, 359–181–868; Panhandle Area, 50–192–158; Sunset, 72–232–594; Richmond, 211–451–768; Military, 14–21–188.

Note: "Non-married" can mean never married/single, divorced, or widowed.

TABLE 5. RACE BY NEIGHBORHOOD, NON-ASIAN AND ASIAN, 1900, 1910, AND 1920

Neighborhood	Distribution by neighborhood (%)					
	1900		1910		1920	
	Non-Asian	Asian	Non-Asian	Asian	Non-Asian	Asian
South of Market	99	1	100	0	96	4
Mission District	99	<1	99	<1	99	<1
Potrero Hill	96	4	94	6	99	1
Outer Mission	100	0	96	4	99	1
Western Addition/Pacific Heights	98	2	95	5	97	3
North Beach	100	0	100	0	99	1
Chinatown	7	93	31	69	0	100
Downtown	96	4	100	0	96	4
Panhandle Area	100	0	99	1	100	0
Sunset	100	0	100	0	100	0
Richmond	99	<1	97	3	97	3
Military	100	0	100	0	99	1
All neighborhoods	96	4	96	4	97	3

Source: One percent IPUMS U.S. Census, 1900, 1910, and 1920.

Sample sizes: South of Market, 606–444–746; Mission District, 782–1,167–2,062; Potrero Hill, 25–113–248; Outer Mission, 21–185–948; Western Addition/Pacific Heights, 861–1,277–2,470; North Beach, 210–140–396; Chinatown, 82–137–122; Downtown, 359–181–868; Panhandle Area, 50–192–158; Sunset, 72–232–594; Richmond, 211–451–768; Military, 14–21–188.

Note: "Non-Asian" includes white, black, and American Indian or Alaskan Native.

Notes

INTRODUCTION

1. Steven Biel, ed., *American Disasters* (New York: New York University Press, 2001), 5.

2. *San Francisco Newsletter*, May 12, 1906.

3. Rosalie Meyer Stern Papers, Judas Magnes Museum, Berkeley.

4. Elizabeth Hayes Turner, *Women, Culture, and Community: Religion and Reform in Galveston, 1800–1920* (New York: Oxford University Press, 1997), 11.

5. Ted Steinberg, "Smoke and Mirrors: The San Francisco Earthquake and Seismic Denial," in *American Disasters*, ed. Steven Biel (New York: New York University Press, 2001), 104. Instant histories, such as Charles Morris's *The San Francisco Calamity by Earthquake and Fire* (Philadelphia: J. C. Winston, 1906) and Sydney Tyler's *San Francisco's Great Disaster: A Full Account of the Recent Terrible Destruction of Life and Property by Earthquake, Fire and Volcano in California and at Vesuvius* (Philadelphia: P. W. Ziegler, 1906), focused on only the three days of disaster. Other instant histories published in 1906 include Charles Eugene Banks, *The History of the San Francisco Disaster and Mount Vesuvius Horror* (San Francisco: C. E. Thomas, 1906); Will Irwin, *The City That Was: A Requiem of Old San Francisco* (New York: Huebosch, 1906); Richard Linthicum and Trumbull White, *Complete Story of the San Francisco Horror* (Chicago: Hubert Russel, 1906); Alexander Livingstone, *Complete Story of San Francisco's Terrible Calamity of Earthquake and Fire* (San Francisco: Continental, 1907); Frank Searight, *The Doomed City: A Thrilling Tale* (Chicago: Laird and Lee, 1906); and James Wilson, *San Francisco's Horror of Earthquake and Fire: Terrible Devastation and Heart-Rending Scenes* (Philadelphia: Percival Supply, 1906).

6. See, e.g., Karen Sawislak, *Smoldering City: Chicagoans and the Great Fire, 1871–1874* (Chicago: University of Chicago Press, 1995); and Carl Smith, *Urban Disorder and the Shape of Belief: The Great Chicago Fire, the Haymarket Bomb, and the Model Town of Pullman* (Chicago: University of Chicago Press, 1995).

7. Souvenir photography books typically included captions under each photograph and sometimes added brief eyewitness accounts to bolster their appeal. Occasionally a souvenir book's title used more words than the pages inside did, such as *The "Old Frisco" Souvenir Book: The Saddest Story Ever Told in Pictures* (Oakland: Progressive Novelty, 1906). Other examples include *The Picture Story of the San Francisco Earthquake, Wednesday, April 18, 1906* (Los Angeles: George Rice and Sons, 1906); *The San Francisco Disaster Photographed: Fifty Glimpses of Havoc by Earthquake and Fire* (New York: C. S. Hammond, 1906); *Views: Ruins of San Francisco, April 18, 1906* (Watsonville, CA: Meddaugh and Chapman, 1906).

8. Kevin Rozario, *The Culture of Calamity: Disaster and the Making of Modern America* (Chicago: University of Chicago Press, 2007).

9. Morris, *The San Francisco Calamity*, 175.

10. William Bronson, *The Earth Shook, the Sky Burned* (New York: Doubleday, 1959); John Castillo Kennedy, *The Great Earthquake and Fire: San Francisco, 1906* (New York: Morrow, 1963); Eric Saul and Don DeNevi, *The Great San Francisco Earthquake and Fire, 1906* (Millbrae, CA: Celestial Arts, 1981); Gordon Thomas and Max Morgan Witts, *The San Francisco Earthquake* (New York: Stein and Day, 1971).

11. Rebecca Solnit offers a new perspective on the 1906 disaster when she argues that disasters create a utopic moment of community building. Rebecca Solnit, *A Paradise Built in Hell: The Extraordinary Communities That Arise in Disaster* (New York: Viking, 2009). The centennial commemoration produced two new accounts: Philip L. Fradkin's *The Great Earthquake and Firestorms of 1906: How San Francisco Nearly Destroyed Itself* (Berkeley: University of California Press, 2005); and Simon Winchester's *A Crack in the Edge of the World: America and the Great California Earthquake of 1906* (New York: HarperCollins, 2005). A full academic historical account of the 1906 catastrophe has yet to be published. Historian Erica Pan's published master's thesis examines Chinatown: Erica Y. Z. Pan, *The Impact of the 1906 Earthquake on San Francisco's Chinatown* (New York: Peter Lang, 1995). For a discussion of city planning after the disaster, see Judd Kahn, *Imperial San Francisco: Politics and Planning in an American City, 1897–1906* (Lincoln: University of Nebraska Press, 1979). See also Kevin Rozario's treatment of economic recovery in San Francisco in *The Culture of Calamity*.

12. Historian Ted Steinberg builds on Gladys Hansen's "seismic denial" thesis to argue that emphasis on the fire was made by and for San Francisco's business class. Steinberg, "Smoke and Mirrors"; Gladys Hansen and Emmet Condon, *Denial of Disaster: The Untold Story and Photographs of the San Francisco Earthquake and Fire of 1906*, ed. David Fowler (San Francisco: Cameron, 1989).

13. See Christine Misner Rosen, *The Limits of Power: Great Fires and the Process of City Growth in America* (Cambridge: Cambridge University Press, 1986).

14. Hansen and Condon, *Denial of Disaster*; Steinberg, "Smoke and Mirrors."

15. "San Francisco," *Harper's Weekly*, May 5, 1906, 619.

16. Scholars Lawrence Vale and Thomas Campanella describe the construction of disaster narratives as a process during which "key figures in the dominant culture claim (or are accorded) authorship, while marginalized groups or peoples are generally ignored." Lawrence J. Vale and Thomas J. Campanella, eds., *The Resilient City: How Modern Cities Recover from Disaster* (Oxford: Oxford University Press, 2005), 341.

17. Russell Sage Foundation, ed., *San Francisco Relief Survey* (New York: Survey Associates, 1913).

18. Unfortunately, thousands of these historical accounts disappeared during the 1920s. H. Morse Stephens, a professor at the University of California, collected an estimated three thousand stories of disaster survivors. Although the collection was lost

after Stephens's death in 1919, a partial account was reprinted in a local newspaper series in 1926. For a full account, see Fradkin, *The Great Earthquake*, 248–254.

19. William Randolph Hearst's *San Francisco Examiner*, M. H. de Young's *San Francisco Chronicle*, Fremont Older's *San Francisco Bulletin*, and Claus Spreckels's *San Francisco Call* all ran stories on the catastrophe, disaster relief, and reconstruction. Hearst, consistent with his reputation for sensationalism and his quest for public office, used the disaster to further his own political career. Spreckels and Older supported Progressive interests, while de Young favored profits for the business elite. My interpretation of these sources is based on the consideration of each editor's political agenda and, whenever possible, a reading of multiple sources for each particular event. For an excellent interpretation of San Francisco's newspaper publishers, see Gray Brechin, *Imperial San Francisco: Urban Power, Earthly Ruin* (Berkeley: University of California Press, 1999).

20. Samuel Henry Prince, "Catastrophe and Social Change, Based on a Sociological Study of the Halifax Disaster" (Ph.D. diss., Columbia University, 1920).

21. Mike Davis, *Ecology of Fear: Los Angeles and the Imagination of Disaster* (New York: Metropolitan Books, 1998).

22. Prominent disaster scholar E. L. Quarantelli encourages us "to disentangle disasters from being solely linked to physical agents or physical environments." E. L. Quarantelli, ed., *What Is a Disaster? Perspectives on the Question* (London: Routledge, 1988), 244. See also E. L. Quarantelli, ed., *Disasters: Theory and Research* (London: Sage Publications, 1978). Robert Kates provides one of the earliest foundations for this perspective. See Robert W. Kates, "Natural Hazard in Human Ecological Perspective: Hypotheses and Models," *Economic Geography* 47, no. 3 (July 1971): 439–451.

23. See historian Daniel T. Rodgers's influential essay "In Search of Progressivism," *Reviews in American History* 10, no. 4 (December 1982): 113–132; and Peter G. Filene's "An Obituary for 'The Progressive Movement,'" *American Quarterly* 22 (1970): 22–34. Historians debate the beginning and end of the Progressive Era. Maureen A. Flanagan uses a broad periodization in order to show how U.S. reform movements changed over time. For an overview of the Progressive Era, see Steven J. Diner, *A Very Different Age: Americans of the Progressive Era* (New York: Hill and Wang, 1998); Maureen A. Flanagan, *America Reformed: Progressives and Progressivism, 1890s–1920s* (New York: Oxford University Press, 2007); and Daniel T. Rodgers, *Atlantic Crossings: Social Politics in a Progressive Age* (Cambridge, MA: Harvard University Press, 1998). The rich historiography of Progressivism is well documented by others. The debate over who the Progressives were is neatly divided up and labeled as particular schools of thought. Many of the Progressives involved in 1906 disaster relief most closely resemble those described by Robert H. Wiebe: members of the new middle class that prized organization. "The heart of progressivism," Wiebe concluded, "was the ambition of the new middle class to fulfill its destiny through bureaucratic means." Robert H. Wiebe, *The Search for Order, 1877–1920* (New York: Hill and Wang, 1967), 166.

24. Paul Boyer, *Urban Masses and Moral Order in America, 1820–1920* (Cambridge, MA: Harvard University Press, 1978), 221.

25. Linda Gordon, "Putting Children First: Women, Maternalism, and Welfare in the Early Twentieth Century," in *U.S. History as Women's History: New Feminist Essays*, ed. Alice Kessler-Harris, Linda K. Kerber, and Kathryn Kish Sklar (Chapel Hill: University of North Carolina Press, 1995), 71–72.

26. For more on this scholarly approach, see Linda Gordon, *Heroes of Their Own Lives: The Politics and History of Family Violence* (London: Virago, 1989); Thomas A. Krainz, *Delivering Aid: Implementing Progressive Era Welfare in the American West* (Albuquerque: University of New Mexico Press, 2005); Michael Katz, *Poverty and Policy in American History* (New York: Academic Press, 1983).

27. *The Associated Charities of San Francisco: Annual Reports, 1904–1910* (San Francisco: Blair-Murdock, 1911), 21.

28. Robyn Muncy, *Creating a Female Dominion in American Reform, 1890–1935* (New York: Oxford University Press, 1991), xiv–xv.

29. Robert M. Crunden, *Ministers of Reform: The Progressives' Achievement in American Civilization, 1889–1920* (New York: Basic Books, 1982).

30. In the case of San Francisco, disaster relief played a major role during the restoration period. Robert W. Kates and David Pijawka, "From Rubble to Monument: The Pace of Reconstruction," in *Reconstruction following Disaster*, ed. J. Eugene Haas, Robert W. Kates, and Martyn J. Bowden (Cambridge, MA: MIT Press, 1977).

31. Vale and Campanella propose studying variations, not similarities, among catastrophes in order to ask "*who* recovers *which* aspects of the city, and by what mechanisms." Vale and Campanella, *The Resilient City*, 337.

32. Vale and Campanella argue that governments utilize emergency response "as a means of saving face and retaining public office." Ibid., 340.

33. William Issel and Robert W. Cherny, *San Francisco, 1865–1932: Politics, Power, and Urban Development* (Berkeley: University of California Press, 1986), 78.

34. Robert O. Self, *American Babylon: Race and the Struggle for Postwar Oakland* (Princeton, NJ: Princeton University Press, 2003), 17.

CHAPTER 1

1. Roland M. Roche, "The Great Earthquake and Fire," *Argonaut*, January 1, 1927. Mr. Roche lived at 527 Castro Street.

2. Helen Hillyer Brown, *The Great San Francisco Fire* (San Francisco: Hillside Press, 1906).

3. *San Francisco Newsletter*, May 12, 1906.

4. Brian J. Godfrey, "Inner-City Neighborhoods in Transition: The Morphogenesis of San Francisco's Ethnic and Nonconformist Communities" (Ph.D. diss., University of California–Berkeley, 1984), 96.

5. William Issel and Robert W. Cherny, *San Francisco, 1865–1932: Politics, Power, and Urban Development* (Berkeley: University of California Press, 1986), 24, 26, 54, table 1.

6. William Issel and Robert Cherny demonstrate that by 1906 "San Francisco's residential areas differed from one another in ethnicity, sex, marital status, occupations, and income." Ibid., 58. For a history of social differences in early San Francisco, see Barbara Berglund, *Making San Francisco American: Cultural Frontiers in the Urban West, 1846–1906* (Lawrence: University Press of Kansas, 2007).

7. James E. Vance, Jr., *Geography and Urban Evolution in the San Francisco Bay Area* (Berkeley: Institute for Government Studies, 1964), 3.

8. Malcolm Margolin, *The Ohlone Way: Indian Life in the San Francisco–Monterey Bay Area* (Berkeley: Heyday Books, 1978). See also Ramon A. Gutierrez and Richard J. Orsi, eds., *Contested Eden: California before the Gold Rush* (Berkeley: University of California Press, 1998).

9. Mel Scott, *The San Francisco Bay Area: A Metropolis in Perspective* (Berkeley: University of California Press, 1959), 10.

10. Ibid., 18. For early histories of San Francisco, see Hubert Howe Bancroft, *History of California*, vol. 6, *1848–1859* (San Francisco: History Company, 1888); John S. Hittell, *A History of the City of San Francisco and Incidentally of the State of California* (San Francisco: A. L. Bancroft, 1878); and Frank Soule, John H. Gihon, and James Nisbet, *The Annals of San Francisco* (New York: D. Appleton, 1855).

11. James K. Polk, quoted in Scott, *The San Francisco Bay Area*, 26.

12. Bancroft, *History of California*, 159; Charles Lockwood, *Suddenly San Francisco: The Early Years of an Instant City* (San Francisco: California Living, 1978), 164.

13. Richard White, *"It's Your Misfortune and None of My Own": A New History of the American West* (Norman: University of Oklahoma Press, 1991), 191.

14. William Ingraham Kip, *The Early Days of My Episcopate* (New York: Thomas Whittaker, 1892), 72.

15. Gunther Barth, *Instant Cities: Urbanization and the Rise of San Francisco and Denver* (New York: Oxford University Press, 1975), 131. For historical accounts of urbanization in the American West, see also Carl Abbott, *The Metropolitan Frontier: Cities in the Modern American West* (Tucson: University of Arizona Press, 1993); Richard C. Wade, *The Urban Frontier: The Rise of Western Cities, 1790–1830* (Cambridge, MA: Harvard University Press, 1959); and White, *"It's Your Misfortune."*

16. Italics in original. Martha Hitchcock, letter, quoted in White, *"It's Your Misfortune,"* 192.

17. Berglund, *Making San Francisco American*, 29.

18. Judy Yung, *Unbound Feet: A Social History of Chinese Women in San Francisco* (Berkeley: University of California Press, 1995), 29. For the history of U.S. prostitution after 1900, see Ruth Rosen, *The Lost Sisterhood: Prostitution in America, 1900–1918* (Baltimore: Johns Hopkins University Press, 1982).

19. See Peggy Pascoe, *Relations of Rescue: The Search for Female Moral Authority in the American West, 1874–1939* (New York: Oxford University Press, 1990).

20. Robert Griswold argues that the American West "legitimated women's efforts to 'civilize' the West and provided a vocabulary with which to redefine the nature of manhood." Robert L. Griswold, "Anglo Women and Domestic Ideology in the American West in the Nineteenth and Early Twentieth Centuries," in *Western Women: Their Land, Their Lives*, ed. Lillian Schlissel, Vicki L. Ruiz, and Janice Monk (Albuquerque: University of New Mexico Press, 1988), 18.

21. Kip, *The Early Days of My Episcopate*, 72–73.

22. As Philip Ethington points out, "San Francisco took shape in the 1850s at a point midway along the long process of class formation in the United States, after classes had begun to form but long before they constituted major divisions in society." Philip J. Ethington, *The Public City: The Political Construction of Urban Life in San Francisco, 1850–1900* (New York: Cambridge University Press, 1994), 53. Influential works on nineteenth-century middle-class formation include Stuart M. Blumin, *The Emergence of the Middle Class: Social Experience in the American City, 1760–1900* (New York: Cambridge University Press, 1989); and Mary P. Ryan, *Cradle of the Middle Class: The Family in Oneida County, New York, 1790–1865* (New York: Cambridge University Press, 1981).

23. William Issel and Robert Cherney describe a "business elite" in San Francisco, which they measure by the number of board of director memberships in incorporated companies. There were two hundred male members of the business elite between 1890 and 1930. The two most important were James D. Phelan and William Henry Crocker. Issel and Cherny, *San Francisco*, 16, 34.

24. White, *"It's Your Misfortune,"* 287.

25. Michael Kazin, *Barons of Labor: The San Francisco Building Trades and Union Power in the Progressive Era* (Urbana: University of Illinois Press, 1987), 14–15.

26. Ethington, *The Public City*, 265–268. See also Gwendolyn Mink, *Old Labor and New Immigrants in American Political Development: Union, Party, and State, 1875–1920* (Ithaca, NY: Cornell University Press, 1986).

27. Ethington, *The Public City*. Barbara Berglund also finds that "social divisions rooted in class and ethnic differences became more acute and racial hostilities more severe" during this time. Berglund, *Making San Francisco American*, 13.

28. These social groups were not hardened identities at the turn of the century. Ethington's "public sphere" is derived from Jürgen Habermas and Hannah Arendt. For Ethington, public sphere is neither the public sector ("that portion of the economy controlled by the government") nor public space ("simply a geographic area like a park or a street in which persons may meet"). Like Habermas, Ethington finds that "the substance of the public sphere is communication." Ethington, *The Public City*, 319–320. See also Jürgen Habermas, *The Structural Transformation of the Public Sphere: An Inquiry into a Category of Bourgeois Society*, ed. Thomas Berger and Frederick Lawrence (Cambridge, MA: MIT Press, 1989).

29. Erika Lee, *At America's Gates: Chinese Immigration during the Exclusion Era, 1882–1943* (Chapel Hill: University of North Carolina Press, 2003), 7. See also Lucy Salyer, *Laws Harsh as Tigers: Chinese Immigrants and the Shaping of Modern Immigration Laws, 1891–1905* (Chapel Hill: University of North Carolina Press, 1995); Sucheng Chan, ed., *Entry Denied: Exclusion and the Chinese Community in America, 1882–1943* (Philadelphia: Temple University Press, 1991); Daniel Rogers, *Asian America: Chinese and Japanese in the United States since 1850* (Seattle: University of Washington Press, 1988).

30. Lee, *At America's Gates*, 79.

31. Ibid., 29.

32. The Exclusion Act did not address the issue of Chinese women, but subsequent federal court cases enacted their exclusion. For example, the exclusion of Chinese laborers was extended to include their wives. In addition, legislation predating the Exclusion Act barred Chinese women from entry. Estelle T. Lau, *Paper Families: Identity, Immigration Administration, and Chinese Exclusion* (Durham, NC: Duke University Press, 2006), 17.

33. Sucheta Mazumdar, "Through Western Eyes: Discovering Chinese Women in America," in *A New Significance: Re-envisioning the History of the American West*, ed. Clyde Milner. (New York: Oxford University Press, 1996).

34. Lee, *At America's Gates*, 27.

35. Ibid., 93.

36. U.S. Census data indicate that Chinese residents accounted for 4.1 percent of the population in San Francisco. They far outnumbered Japanese residents, who made up 0.5 percent of city residents. There were only 1,654 African Americans in San Francisco (0.4 percent). The U.S. Census, however, underestimated the number of Chinese living in San Francisco. Brian J. Godfrey, *Neighborhoods in Transition: The Making of San Francisco's Nonconformist Communities* (Berkeley: University of California Press, 1988), 68, table 4.

37. Shah argues, "The creation of 'knowledge' of Chinatown relied upon three key spatial elements: dens, density, and the labyrinth. The enclosed and inhuman spaces of dens were where the Chinese lived. High density was the condition in which they lived. And the labyrinth was the unnavigable maze that characterized both the subterranean passageways within the buildings and streets and alleys above ground." Nayan Shah, *Contagious Divides: Epidemics and Race in San Francisco's Chinatown* (Berkeley: University of California Press, 2001), 18. See also Lau, *Paper Families*.

38. Shah, *Contagious Divides*, 11.

39. Eleanor Watkins, "The 1906 San Francisco Earthquake: A Personal Account by Mrs. James T. Watkins," in *Eyewitness to Disaster: Five Women (Each in Her Own Words) Tell Their Stories of the 1906 Earthquake and Fire in San Francisco* (San Francisco: National Society of the Colonial Dames of America in California, 1987), 4.

40. Sarah Deutsch, *Women and the City: Gender, Space, and Power in Boston, 1870–1940* (Oxford: Oxford University Press, 2000), 286.

41. Winds during April, for example, averaged 14.1 to 22 miles per hour. "Report of City Engineer," *San Francisco Municipal Reports for the Fiscal Years 1905–1906 and 1906–1907* (San Francisco: Neal Publishing, 1908), 680–681.

42. Gerald Dow, "Bay Fill in San Francisco" (master's thesis, California State University, 1973).

43. J. D. Whitney, quoted in Ted Steinberg, "Smoke and Mirrors: The San Francisco Earthquake and Seismic Denial," in *American Disasters*, ed. Steven Biel (New York: New York University Press, 2001), 106. Documentation of earthquakes in San Francisco began in the nineteenth century, the largest recorded being the Great Hayward Earthquake of October 21, 1868.

44. Andrew C. Lawson, "Preliminary Report of the State Earthquake Investigation Commission" (Berkeley: State Earthquake Investigation Commission, 1906). This seismic activity was defined as "liquefaction" during the 1960s.

45. Reinforced concrete buildings would have provided the best earthquake resistance for buildings higher than six stories. Ordinary brick structures, on the other hand, showed the most damage from earthquake. Interest in fireproof construction emerged during the nineteenth century, which recorded one major conflagration every year. During the mid-nineteenth century, brick and cast iron were considered fireproof. The 1871 Chicago Fire, however, proved that building materials must resist heat as well as combustion. Sara Wermiel, *The Fireproof Building: Technology and Public Safety in the Nineteenth-Century American City* (Baltimore: Johns Hopkins University Press, 2000).

46. "Proceedings of the 39th Annual Meeting of the National Board of Fire Underwriters," 1905.

47. Arthur Welch, Captain, Engine 7, Sixteenth and Albion Streets, San Francisco Virtual Museum (http://www.sfmuseum.org/conflag/e7.html, accessed July 15, 2009).

48. There were hundreds of ruptures to the city's main pipe distributing system, "especially where the streets crossed filled ground and, particularly, where such filled ground covered former deep swamps." San Francisco relied on three reservoirs—Pilarcitos, Crystal Springs, and San Andres—which were all located south of the city, in San Mateo County. Three pumping plants pushed 16 million gallons of water into San Francisco each day. After the earthquake, it would take sixteen hours to pump 7 million gallons of water per day into the city. Within sixty-two hours this was increased to 15 million gallons. Hermann Schussler, *The Water Supply of San Francisco, California: Before, during, and after the Earthquake of April 18th, 1906, and the Subsequent Conflagration* (New York: Martin B. Brown Press, 1906), 7.

49. Report of the city engineer, cited in Gladys Hansen and Emmet Condon, *Denial of Disaster: The Untold Story and Photographs of the San Francisco Earthquake and Fire of 1906*, ed. David Fowler (San Francisco: Cameron, 1989), 31.

50. Bonds totaling $5.2 million funded the project, making San Francisco the only city at that time to construct a fire suppression water supply separate from domestic water. In addition, two new fireboats protected the waterfront, and a hundred cisterns were placed in the center of city streets, adding 75,000 gallons of water to residential districts. *Public Work of San Francisco since 1906: Supplement to Municipal Reports 1908–9* (San Francisco, 1909).

51. They operated thirty-eight engines, twelve ladder companies, and eight chemical units. "Report of the Fire Department," *Municipal Reports for the Fiscal Years 1905–1906 and 1906–1907* (San Francisco: Neal Publishing, 1908), 680–681.

52. Frederick N. Freeman, "Report" (Mare Island, CA: U.S. Navy, 1906), no. 8.

53. J. J. Conlon, Battalion Chief District No. 9, San Francisco Virtual Museum (http://www.sfmuseum.org/1906/ew10.html, accessed July 15, 2009). Battalion Chief

Fred J. Bowlen also agreed that the use of dynamite without experience caused more fires. Fred J. Bowlen Papers, Bancroft Library, University of California, Berkeley.

54. Patrick H. Shaughnessy, "Chief Engineer Report," San Francisco Fire Department, September 13, 1906, San Francisco Virtual Museum (http://www.sfmuseum.org/conflag/cod.html, accessed July 15, 2009).

55. Frederick Funston, "How the Army Worked to Save San Francisco," *Cosmopolitan* 41, no. 3 (July 1906): 246.

56. "The Misuse of Explosives," *Mining and Scientific Press*, April 28, 1906.

57. This account was told to Mrs. Wilson, a friend of the boardinghouse owner, and Carrie Mangels. Carrie A. Mangels, letter to Jewel Smaus, n.d., San Francisco Earthquake and Fire Collection, California Historical Society, San Francisco.

58. Gladys Hansen, "Who Perished?" (San Francisco: San Francisco Archives, 1980); Hansen and Condon, *Denial of Disaster*.

59. According to Kazin, "From the neighborhoods where they lived to the newspapers they read, most San Franciscans in the early twentieth century defined themselves as member of a social class." Kazin, *Barons of Labor*, 21–23. Godfrey's study documents how social mobility shifted ethnic alliances: "As selected Germans, Irish, and others moved up in social status, they very often left their ethnic neighborhoods behind with the cultural trappings of their ethnicity." Godfrey, "Inner-City Neighborhoods," 82.

60. Berglund, *Making San Francisco American*, 10. Scholars have explored the complex process of immigration and the construction of whiteness in the United States. See David Roedigers's influential work *The Wages of Whiteness: Race and the Making of the American Working Class* (London: Verso, 1991); and Matthew Frye Jacobson, *Whiteness of a Different Color: European Immigrants and the Alchemy of Race* (Cambridge, MA: Harvard University Press, 1998). Neil Foley's study of agricultural life in Central Texas reveals the complex interaction of race, class, and gender in an environment that lacks binary racial divisions. Neil Foley, *The White Scourge: Mexicans, Blacks, and Poor Whites in Texas Cotton Culture* (Berkeley: University of California Press, 1998).

61. Issel and Cherny use the 1900 U.S. Census to examine Tehama Street. Several blocks from the waterfront and Market Street, Tehama ran parallel to Market, bounded by Howard and Folsom Streets. The block that Issel and Cherny analyzed ran from Second to Third Streets. Issel and Cherny, *San Francisco*, 61–63.

62. Roger R. Olmsted and Nancy L. Olmsted, *San Francisco Waterfront: Report on Historical Cultural Resources for the North Shore and Channel Outfalls Consolidation Projects* (San Francisco: San Francisco Wastewater Management Program, 1977), 22.

63. Ibid., 181.

64. Bernadette A. McKittrick and Tessie Dowd, "Remembrances of the San Francisco Earthquake April 18, 1906" (dictated 1966), San Francisco Earthquake and Fire Collection, California Historical Society.

65. Harry F. Walsh, "The Great Fire of 1906," *Argonaut*, May 15, 1926.

66. Andrew C. Lawson and Harry Fielding Reid, "The California Earthquake of April 18, 1906: Report of the State Earthquake Investigation Commission" (Washington, DC: Carnegie Institution of Washington, 1908), 239.

67. James Madison Jacobs, Room 56, Brunswick House, quoted in Hansen and Condon, *Denial of Disaster*, 23–24.

68. E. J. Wiskotchill, "The Great Fire of 1906," *Argonaut*, June 5, 1926.

69. Carrie A. Mangels, letter to Jewel Smaus, n.d., California Historical Society.

70. Schussler, *The Water Supply of San Francisco*, 7.

71. Edward C. Jones to Pacific Coast Gas Association, 1908, quoted in Hansen and Condon, *Denial of Disaster*, 31.

72. Lawrence J. Kennedy, "The Progress of the Fire in San Francisco April 18th–21st, 1906: As Shown by an Analysis of Original Documents" (master's thesis, University of California–Berkeley, 1906).

73. Funston, "How the Army Worked to Save San Francisco," 248.

74. William M. Ross, "The Great Fire of 1906," *Argonaut*, May 22, 1926.

75. Freeman, "Report," no. 10, no. 6.

76. The naval ship *Leslie* pumped water to Eighth and Townsend Streets until the fire came under control on April 19 at 2:30 A.M. Freeman, "Report," no. 5.

77. Maurice S. Behan, "The Great Fire of 1906," *Argonaut*, June 19, 1926.

78. Thornwell Mullally, "The Great Fire of 1906," *Argonaut*, September 3, 1926.

79. McKittrick and Dowd, "Remembrances of the San Francisco Earthquake."

80. Thomas A. Burns, "The Great Fire of 1906," *Argonaut*, May 29, 1926.

81. John J. Conlon, in Patricia Turner, ed., *1906 Remembered* (San Francisco: Friends of the San Francisco Public Library, 1981), 35–36.

82. Seneca Gale, letter to Charles Gale, April 20, 1906, Berkeley Historical Society.

83. Bessie Shum, quoted in Jonathan Curiel, "'06 Survivor: First Chinatown Resident to Join S.F. Quake Memorial," *San Francisco Chronicle*, April 14, 2000.

84. Chalsa M. Loo, *Chinatown: Most Time, Hard Time* (New York: Praeger, 1991), 43.

85. At the time of the earthquake, Japanese immigrants had yet to develop a distinctive neighborhood; they lived in Chinatown as well as South of Market. The impact of Japanese immigration on San Francisco differed significantly from that of the Chinese. Although the number of Japanese immigrants remained far fewer than that of Chinese immigrants, Japanese immigration continued while anti-Chinese immigration legislation was enforced. The Asiatic Exclusion League, formed in 1905, specifically targeted Japanese immigration and school segregation.

86. Erica Y. Z. Pan, *The Impact of the 1906 Earthquake on San Francisco's Chinatown* (New York: Peter Lang, 1995), 105–106.

87. San Francisco's Chinese Consolidated Benevolent Association, or Jinshan Zhonghua Huiguan, was first formed in 1882 in response to anti-Chinese legislation. The new association united district organization leaders, who were titled scholars from China, to represent Chinese interests. The "Chinese Six Companies" nomenclature refers to an association size of six districts representing the six geographic areas in Guangdong, although the association ranged from four to eight districts. Before the formation of the Chinese Consolidated Benevolent Association, Chinese immigrants found district organizations and clan associations in San Francisco. Clan associations reflected the Confucian extended family system, while district organizations promoted regional economic interests. The association assumed the responsibilities of both groups, serving the political, economic, and social needs of the American Chinese community. Shehong Chen, *Being Chinese, Becoming Chinese American* (Urbana: University of Illinois Press, 2002); Willard T. Chow, *The Reemergence of an Inner City: The Pivot of Chinese Settlement in the East Bay Region of the San Francisco Bay Area* (San Francisco: R&E Research Associates, 1977).

88. Shah, *Contagious Divides*, 18.

89. Freeman, "Report," no. 7.

90. Kennedy, "The Progress of the Fire."

91. T. J. Murphy, Captain, Engine No. 29, San Francisco Virtual Museum (http://www.sfmuseum.org/conflag/e29.html, accessed July 15, 2009).

92. Hansen and Condon, *Denial of Disaster*, 73.

93. Charles C. Lanferweiler, quoted in "Survivors Unable to Give Aid," *Chicago Record Herald*, April 23, 1906.

94. Captain Stephen V. Bunner, "The Great Fire of 1906," *Argonaut*, August 14, 1926.

95. Tom, letter to Jessie, April 26, 1906, San Francisco Earthquake and Fire Collection, California Historical Society.

96. Lanferweiler, *Chicago Record Herald*.

97. Chinatown's "bachelor society" has been the focus of most historical discussion. The predominantly male Chinatown population was validated by the 1900 census, which found the Chinese in San Francisco to be 85 percent male. Two-parent families were an important resource for single male refugees after the disaster. Yung, *Unbound Feet*, 293–300, tables 1, 3, and 6.

98. Leland Chin, in Victor G. Nee and Brett de Bary Nee, *Longtime Californ': A Documentary Study of an American Chinatown* (Stanford, CA: Stanford University Press, 1972), 76–77.

99. Alice Sue Fun in Judy Yung, *Unbound Voices: A Documentary History of Chinese Women in San Francisco* (Berkeley: University of California Press, 1999), 268.

100. Charles F. Reddy, "The Great Fire of 1906," *Argonaut*, July 31, 1926.

101. Edith H. Rosenshine, "The San Francisco Earthquake of 1906," Bancroft Library, University of California, Berkeley, 13.

102. Katherine Hooker, "Fire and Earthquake Days" unpublished memoir, 8, Katherine Hooker Papers, San Francisco Virtual Museum Archives, San Francisco.

103. Pascoe, *Relations of Rescue*, 16.

104. For a complete account of the Presbyterian Chinese Mission Home missionary effort in San Francisco, see Pascoe, *Relations of Rescue*. Earlier accounts of Donaldina Cameron's work include Mildred Crowl Martin, *Chinatown's Angry Angel: The Story of Donaldina Cameron* (Palo Alto: Pacific Books, 1986); Carol Green Wilson, *Chinatown Quest: One Hundred Years of Donaldina Cameron House* (San Francisco: California Historical Society, 1974).

105. Donaldina Cameron, "Donaldina Cameron's Account of the Flight from Chinatown," San Francisco Virtual Museum Archives (http://www.sfmuseum.org/1906/ew15.html, accessed July 15, 2009)

106. Ibid.

107. Although Methodist missionary work in Chinatown dated back to 1870, an independent mission home was not built until 1901. Located in a remodeled house and cigar factory just two blocks from Cameron's Presbyterian mission home, the Oriental Home, at 912 Washington Street, was administered by Carrie G. Davis.

108. Emma S. Allen, "After the Earthquake and Fire," *Women's Home Missionary Society* (New York, n.d.), San Francisco Disaster Papers, California State Archives.

109. "Girls in Danger," *Oakland Tribune*, April 27, 1906.

110. Dr. Reverend Edward A. Wicher, "The San Francisco Theological Seminary," San Francisco Earthquake and Fire Collection, San Francisco Theological Seminary Archives, 2.

111. Ibid.

112. Pascoe, *Relations of Rescue*, 121.

113. Allen, "After the Earthquake and Fire."

114. Carrie G. Davis, "The Latest from Our Chinese Home," *Woman's Home Missions* 24 (April 1907): 63.

115. Ah Wing, handwritten transcript, San Francisco Earthquake and Fire Collection, Stanford Special Collections, Stanford University.

116. Lawson, "Preliminary Report."

117. Amelia Ransome Neville, *The Fantastic City* (Cambridge, MA: Riverside Press, 1932), 179.

118. Eugene Schmitz, "The Great Fire of 1906," *Argonaut*, January 15, 1927.

119. Emma Maxwell Burke, "A Woman's Experience of Earthquake and Fire," *Overlook Magazine*, June 1906, 276.

120. Issel and Cherny, *San Francisco*, 66.

121. Mary Ann Irwin, "'The Air Is Becoming Full of War': Jewish San Francisco and World War I," *Pacific Historical Review* 74, no. 3 (August 2005): 335.

122. Issel and Cherny selected the 1700 block of Bush Street. Issel and Cherny, *San Francisco*, 66–68.

123. Otille Vandermaydn Taylor, quoted in Turner, *1906 Remembered*, 14.

124. Hansen and Condon, *Denial of Disaster*, 55.

125. Ernest and Bella Lilienthal Papers, quoted in Irena Narell, *Our City: The Jews of San Francisco* (San Diego: Howell-North Books, 1981), 279–280.

126. Brown, *The Great San Francisco Fire*, 13.

127. Charles De Y. Elkus, "Memories" (1956 dictated), San Francisco Earthquake and Fire Collection, San Francisco Public Library.

128. Brown, *The Great San Francisco Fire*, 13.

129. Elkus, "Memories."

130. Navy records also show the successful protection of a block of buildings on Montgomery and Jackson Streets, including the Bank of Italy, Hotaling and Company, and the Appraisers' building. Funston, "How the Army Worked to Save San Francisco," 246–247.

131. Hooker, "Fire and Earthquake Days," 29.

132. Robert Cunningham Hall, letter to Alice (sister), May 1906, reprinted in Beverly Bastian, "Belvedere—A True Refugee From 1906 Quake," Oral Histories, Kent Room, Marin County Library, San Rafael, California.

133. Florence Sylvester, letter, May 3, 1906, printed in Nancy A. Mavrogenes, "Experiencing the '06 Earthquake—with a Female Physician Who Was There," *California Historical Courier* 32, no. 2 (1980): 3.

134. The Laguna de Manatial, which measured five blocks in width, was crossed by Valencia, Mission, and Capp Streets. Made ground over a tidal inlet from Mission Creek further contributed to the Mission District's seismic vulnerability. Hansen and Condon, *Denial of Disaster*, 24–25, 93; Charles E. Leithead, "Account of the 1906 San Francisco Earthquake and Fire," San Francisco Earthquake and Fire Collection, California Historical Society, 2.

135. James D. Phelan, "Personal Notes Taken at the Time of the San Francisco Earthquake and Fire," James D. Phelan Papers, Bancroft Library, University of California, Berkeley, 1.

136. Ibid., 9.

137. Roland M. Roche, "The Great Fire of 1906," *Argonaut*, January 8, 1927.

138. Issel and Cherny used 1900 census data to examine the 400 block of Bartlett Street, a residential street found between Mission and Valencia Streets. Three other German-speaking churches, Calvinist, Lutheran, and Methodist, were accompanied by Baptist, Methodist, Presbyterian, and Unitarian churches. Both schools and social institutions were easily accessible. The local Masonic Hall housed meetings for the Mission Masonic Lodge, the Order of the Eastern Star, Knights of Pythias, Native Sons of the Golden West, Order of Chosen Friends, and Woodmen of the World. Three blocks away, a Fraternal Hall housed the Odd Fellows and Workmen meetings. Issel and Cherny, *San Francisco*, 63–66.

139. F. Ernest Edwards, "Statement of F. Ernest Edwards," James D. Phelan Papers, Bancroft Library.

140. F. Ernest Edwards, "The Great Fire of 1906," *Argonaut*, October 30, 1926.

141. "1906 San Francisco Fire Department Operations Overview," San Francisco, August 1, 1906, San Francisco Virtual Museum (http://www.sfmuseum.org/conflag/06overview.html, accessed July 15, 2009).

142. Kennedy, "The Progress of the Fire." Buttressing South of Market and the Mission was the Potrero District. This heavy-industry sector housed the Union Iron Works, Pacific Rolling Mills, and the Spreckels' California Sugar Refinery. Fire extension into the Potrero District was prevented by the resources of heavy industry; the United Railroads building had not only a water well and tank but also a supply of salt water drawn from the bay. The water supply held the fire in check at Folsom and Howard Streets.

143. Minnie Coleman, letter to her sister, April 24, 1906, reprinted in *Noe Valley Voice*, June 2006 (http://www.noevalleyvoice.com/2006/June/Letr.html, accessed March 13, 2009).

144. Kennedy, "The Progress of the Fire."

145. Dino Cinel, *From Italy to San Francisco* (Stanford, CA: Stanford University Press, 1982), 112.

146. Hansen and Condon, *Denial of Disaster*, 83.

147. For more on the Latin Quarter, see Godfrey, "Inner-City Neighborhoods"; Godfrey, *Neighborhoods in Transition*; and Cinel, *From Italy to San Francisco*.

148. This figure began to rise at the end of the century. An 1892 survey calculated the percentage of Italian immigrant women at 17 percent. Cinel, *From Italy to San Francisco*, 197.

149. Raymond Stevenson Dondero, *The Italian Settlement of San Francisco* (San Francisco: R&E Research Associates, 1974). Dino Cinel defines *campanilismo* as a sub-regionalism, arguing that it encompassed a "sense of loyalty and attachment to the traditions of one's commune (literally to the local belltower), rather than to the entire region." Cinel argues that *campanilismo* was the basis for personal interaction, while regionalism was the foundation for social and economic activity in early San Francisco. Cinel, *From Italy to San Francisco*, 197.

150. See Jacobson, *Whiteness of a Different Color*. Thomas Guglielmo's study of Italian immigration in Chicago shows how their identification as whites did not eclipse their identification as Italians until World War II. Thomas A. Guglielmo, *White on Arrival: Italians, Race, Color, and Power in Chicago, 1890–1945* (New York: Oxford University Press, 2003).

151. Henry Anderson Lafler, "How the Army Worked to Save San Francisco, Personal Narrative of the Acute and Acting Commander," 1906, Bancroft Library, University of California, Berkeley, 5.

152. Henry Anderson Lafler, cited in Hansen and Condon, *Denial of Disaster*, 84; Henry Anderson Lafler, "The Great Fire of 1906," *Argonaut*, March 19, 1927.

153. Most Italian refugees lived near their boats on the waterfront. One Sausalito resident recalled housing "two or three families, fishing people" for a period of six months, an arrangement most likely the result of a pre-disaster relationship. James V. Coulter, Oral History Interview, February 10, 1982, Marin County Library.

154. Eleanor Warner Rawlings to Stuart Rawlings, April 22, 1906, reprinted in "'Mamma's Earthquake Letter," *Mill Valley Historical Review* (Spring 1991): 2.

155. Grace McCombie Wolfe in James Heig and Shirley Mitchell, eds., *Both Sides of the Track: A Collection of Oral Histories from Belvedere and Tiburon* (San Francisco: Scottwall Associates, 1985), 12.

156. "Good Work of the Sausalito Board of Health," *Sausalito News*, April 28, 1906; "Saloons in Sausalito Must Remain Closed," *Sausalito News*, April 28, 1906; Phil Frank, "Witness to Disaster," *Moments in Time: Sausalito Historical Society Newsletter* (Spring 2002): 2.

157. "Vacant Houses for Homeless," *San Francisco Chronicle*, April 24, 1906.

158. Tina Pastori, Oral History Interview, Marin County Library, 5.

159. For more on Giannini, see Felice A. Bonadio, *A. P. Giannini: Banker of America* (Berkeley: University of California Press, 1994); and Gerald D. Nash, *A. P. Giannini and the Bank of America* (Norman: University of Oklahoma Press, 1992).

160. Burke, "A Woman's Experience," 277.

161. Carl Smith and Karen Sawislak both analyzed 1871 Great Chicago Fire instant histories and fire literature and found frequent depictions of the fire as an event that enhanced the bonds of Christian faith and democratic sentiment. Carl Smith, *Urban Disorder and the Shape of Belief: The Great Chicago Fire, the Haymarket Bomb, and the Model Town of Pullman* (Chicago: University of Chicago Press, 1995); Karen Sawislak, *Smoldering City: Chicagoans and the Great Fire, 1871–1874* (Chicago: University of Chicago Press, 1995).

162. Lillian Ferguson, "Bravery of the Women," *San Francisco Examiner*, April 25, 1906, 12.

CHAPTER 2

1. Rutherford H. Platt, *Disasters and Democracy: The Politics of Extreme Natural Events* (Washington, DC: Island Press, 1999), 1.

2. On congressional appropriations for local disasters during the nineteenth and early twentieth centuries, see Michele Landis Dauber, "The Sympathetic State," *Law and History Review* 23, no. 2 (Summer 2005): 387–442; Christopher Morris Douty, "The Economics of Localized Disasters: An Empirical Analysis of the 1906 Earthquake and Fire in San Francisco" (Ph.D. diss., Stanford University, 1969), 38.

3. For an overview of these issues, see Daniel T. Rodgers, "In Search of Progressivism," *Reviews in American History* 10, no. 4 (December 1982): 113–132. A more detailed discussion of the Progressive Era is outlined in the Introduction.

4. Daniel T. Rodgers, *Atlantic Crossings: Social Politics in a Progressive Age* (Cambridge, MA: Harvard University Press, 1998), 6–7.

5. Fredrickson offers the following definition of the Sanitary Commission's scientific philanthropy: "The commission's concept of 'scientific' philanthropy with its tough-minded 'realism' and its emphasis on discipline and efficiency could lead to a genuinely hardhearted approach to the problems of the unfortunate—an approach which could be readily justified in terms of 'scientific' theories.'" George M. Fredrickson, *The Inner Civil War: Northern Intellectuals and the Crisis of the Union* (Urbana: University of Illinois Press, 1965), 112.

6. See Paul Boyer, *Urban Masses and Moral Order in America, 1820–1920* (Cambridge, MA: Harvard University Press, 1978); Walter I. Trattner, *From Poor Law to Welfare State: A History of Social Welfare in America* (New York: Free Press, 1974); Robert H. Bremner, *From the Depths: The Discovery of Poverty in the United States* (New York: New York University Press, 1956).

7. Robyn Muncy, *Creating a Female Dominion in American Reform, 1890–1935* (New York: Oxford University Press, 1991), 67–68. For more on the settlement house movement, see Kathryn Kish Sklar, *Hull House in the 1890s: A Community of Women Reformers* (Chicago: University of Chicago Press, 2005); Ruth Hutchinson Crocker, *Social Work and Social Order: The Settlement Movement in Two Industrial Cities, 1889–1930* (Urbana: University of Illinois Press, 1991); Mina Carson, *Settlement Folk: Social Thought and the American Settlement Movement, 1885–1930* (Chicago: University of Chicago Press, 1990); Rivka Shpak Lissak, *Pluralism and Progressives: Hull House and the New Immigrants, 1890–1919* (Chicago: University of Chicago Press, 1989); and Ellen Fitzpatrick, *Endless Crusade: Women Social Scientists and Progressive Reform* (New York: Oxford University Press, 1990).

8. Robert M. Crunden, *Ministers of Reform: The Progressives' Achievement in American Civilization, 1889–1920* (New York: Basic Books, 1982).

9. William James, *Memories and Studies* (New York: Longmans, Green, 1911), 221.

10. The "Proclamation by the Mayor" read as follows: "The Federal Troops, the members of the Regular Police Force and all Special Police Officers have been authorized

by me to KILL any and all persons found engaged in Looting or in the Commission of Any Other Crime. I have directed all the Gas and Lighting Co.'s not to turn on Gas or Electricity until I order them to do so. You may therefore expect the city to remain in darkness for an indefinite period of time. I request all citizens to remain at home from darkness until daylight until order is restored. I WARN all Citizens of the danger of fire from Damaged or Destroyed Chimneys, Broken or Leaking Gas Pipes or Fixtures, or any like cause. E. E. Schmitz, Mayor." A Mission District job-printing shop churned out five thousand copies by hand, and the document was posted throughout the city. While the proclamation did not constitute marital law, it was perceived as such by most San Franciscans. A precedent for the declaration of martial law was set during the emergency period following the Great Chicago Fire in 1871. Eugene Schmitz, "Proclamation by the Mayor," San Francisco Virtual Museum Archives (http://www .sfmuseum.org/1906.2/killproc.html, accessed June 12, 2011).

11. *San Francisco Chronicle*, April 29, 1906; *San Francisco Call*, April 29, 1906; *San Francisco Bulletin*, April 20, 1906.

12. E. E. Schmitz, quoted in Gladys Hansen and Emmet Condon, *Denial of Disaster: The Untold Story and Photographs of the San Francisco Earthquake and Fire of 1906*, ed. David Fowler (San Francisco: Cameron, 1989), 46.

13. Erica Y. Z. Pan, *The Impact of the 1906 Earthquake on San Francisco's Chinatown* (New York: Peter Lang, 1995), 64–66.

14. Brigadier-General Funston, General Orders No. 12, April 22, 1906.

15. Katherine Hooker, "Fire and Earthquake Days," unpublished memoir, 51–52, Katherine Hooker Papers, San Francisco Virtual Museum Archives, San Francisco.

16. Ibid., 54–55.

17. Elmer Enewold, letter to Lawrence Enewold, n.d., San Francisco Earthquake and Fire Collection, California Historical Society.

18. The Committee of 50 meetings literally coincided with the fire's progress. The group first met at the Hall of Justice, then moved across the street to Portsmouth Square, where it met "in the shadow of the monument to Robert Louis Stevenson." Within hours, the group moved another five blocks to the Fairmont Hotel. The following day, it moved another eight blocks, to the North End Police Station, then wound up at Franklin Hall, on the corner of Fillmore and Bush Streets. "Organization of Relief Work," in *San Francisco Relief Survey*, ed. Russell Sage Foundation (New York: Survey Associates, 1913), xxv, 9.

19. On the Great Chicago Fire, see Karen Sawislak, *Smoldering City: Chicagoans and the Great Fire, 1871–1874* (Chicago: University of Chicago Press, 1995); for the Galveston Flood, see Elizabeth Hayes Turner, *Women, Culture, and Community: Religion and Reform in Galveston, 1800–1920* (New York: Oxford University Press, 1997).

20. Only one woman, San Francisco Associated Charities general secretary Katharine Felton, was appointed. Felton chaired the "Relief of Sick and Wounded" subcommittee and was a member of the "Roofing the Homeless" subcommittee. By April 26, the Committee of 50's twenty-one subcommittees were as follows: Resumption of Civil Government; Resumption of the Judiciary; Transportation of Refugees; Restoration of Water; Restoration of Light and Telephone; Relief of Hungry; Housing the Homeless; Restoration of Fires in Dwellings; Finance Committee of the Relief and Red Cross Funds; Press Agent; Roofing the Homeless; Drugs and Medical Supplies; Relief of Sick and Wounded; Relief of Chinese; Permanent Location of Chinatown; Restoration and Resumption of Retail Trade; Citizens' Police Committee; Auxiliary Fire Committee; Restoration of Abattoirs; History and Statistics; Organization of the Wholesalers. "Sub-Committees of Citizens' Committee"; Citizens' Committee, April 26, 1906; "Miscellaneous Meeting Minutes," Berkeley Relief Committee Records, Bancroft Library, University of California, Berkeley.

21. "Soldiers Make All Men Work," *San Francisco Chronicle*, April 22, 1906.

22. Catherine, letter to Elise, April 22, 1906, San Francisco Earthquake and Fire Collection, California Historical Society, San Francisco.

23. "Citizens Committee Notice," Ivie Papers, Bancroft Library, University of California, Berkeley.

24. David Greenberg, letter to family, n.d., San Francisco Earthquake and Fire Collection, San Francisco Public Library.

25. Edward T. Devine, "San Francisco Relief and Red Cross Funds Finance Committee Meeting Minutes," May 24, 1906, 60–61, James D. Phelan Papers, Bancroft Library, University of California, Berkeley.

26. As Nayan Shah summarizes, "Public health served as one of the most agile and expansive regulatory mechanisms in nineteenth-century American cities." Nayan Shah, *Contagious Divides: Epidemics and Race in San Francisco's Chinatown* (Berkeley: University of California Press, 2001), 3. On the social construction of public health, see Sheila M. Rothman, *Living in the Shadow of Death: Tuberculosis and the Social Experience of Illness in American History* (Baltimore: Johns Hopkins University Press, 1994).

27. The Board of Health ran advertisements to draw a total of five hundred volunteer physicians to inspection work. *San Francisco Call*, April 22, 1906, quoted in Marie Louise Bine Rodriguez, *The Earthquake of 1906* (San Francisco: privately printed, 1951), 8–9.

28. Charles J. O'Connor, "Organizing the Force and Emergency Methods," in *San Francisco Relief Survey*, ed. Russell Sage Foundation (New York: Survey Associates, 1913), 79.

29. San Francisco Sanitation Reports, San Francisco Earthquake and Fire, 1906, Paperless Archives, 16–21.

30. Ibid., May 16, 1906, 26.

31. Ibid., 36.

32. General Orders no. 18, April 29, 1906, in O. E. Mack, "A Study in Disaster Preparedness," San Francisco, circa 1906, 3.

33. Only the family's four pieces of hardtack remained uncontaminated. James W. Ward, Chief Sanitary Inspector, letter to the Health Commission, Letterman General Hospital Records, National Archives, Burlingame, California.

34. "The Bum-Hill Gazette," San Francisco, May 1906, Bancroft Library, University of California, Berkeley.

35. Catherine, letter to Elise, April 22, 1906, California Historical Society.

36. Gray Brechin uses the term "lace-curtain Irish" to describe Phelan. Phelan inherited Bay Area property holdings and an estimated $11.5 million from his father, who had amassed a fortune in banking, construction, and real estate during California's gold rush. Phelan's own business and real estate practices expanded this fortune. Gray Brechin, *Imperial San Francisco: Urban Power, Earthly Ruin* (Berkeley: University of California Press, 1999).

37. Under Phelan, city indebtedness increased from $186,000 in 1887 to $11,025,000 in 1901. William Issel and Robert W. Cherny, *San Francisco, 1865–1932: Politics, Power, and Urban Development* (Berkeley: University of California Press, 1986), 153–155.

38. Ironically, Schmitz benefited from Phelan's tenure. Phelan pushed for the new San Francisco Charter of 1898 to establish the foundation for reform by centralizing administrative authority in the mayor's office. The 1898 charter, replacing the Consolidation Act Charter of 1856, was part of the national movement for new city charters. Philip J. Ethington, *The Public City: The Political Construction of Urban Life in San Francisco, 1850–1900* (New York: Cambridge University Press, 1994), 387.

39. In January 1906 Older orchestrated a meeting of Phelan, Spreckels, and Francis J. Heney, a special prosecutor for the U.S. Department of Justice. At that meeting, both Phelan and Spreckels "gave informal assurances of their personal financial support" for a graft prosecution. Walton Bean, *Boss Ruef's San Francisco* (Berkeley: University of California Press, 1952), 76–77. The graft prosecution, discussed in Chapter 5, culminated in Schmitz's conviction for extortion on June 13, 1907, and Ruef's on December 10, 1908. The Schmitz conviction, however, was invalidated by the district court of appeals on January 9, 1908, while Ruef served his sentence in San Quentin. Douty, "The Economics of Localized Disasters." For a lively account of the downfall of the Schmitz-Ruef business and political alliances, see Bean, *Boss Ruef's San Francisco*. For a detailed account of the ULP, see *Michael Kazin, Barons of Labor: The San Francisco Building Trades and Union Power in the Progressive Era* (Urbana: University of Illinois Press, 1987).

40. *San Francisco Newsletter*, May 12, 1906.

41. *San Francisco Bulletin*, May 1906, quoted in Bean, *Boss Ruef's San Francisco*, 112.

42. "Citizens Committee Meeting Minutes," no. 5, April 20, 1906, James D. Phelan Papers, Bancroft Library, 2.

43. Bean, *Boss Ruef's San Francisco*, 120.

44. Douty, "The Economics of Localized Disasters," 144. Michael Kazin also agrees that Schmitz's hope "to stall or even halt legal challenge being mounted by their [Schmitz's and Ruef's] political enemies" materialized in the committee appointments. Kazin, *Barons of Labor*, 123.

45. During the 1900 Galveston Flood, for example, total Red Cross aid was estimated at $120,000. If the earthquake and fire were to follow U.S. disaster donation patterns, the fund would be smaller than many of the bribes pocketed by Schmitz and Ruef. Foster Reah Dulles, *The American Red Cross: A History* (New York: Harper and Brothers, 1950), 34.

46. James D. Phelan, "Personal Notes Taken at the Time of the San Francisco Earthquake and Fire," James D. Phelan Papers, Bancroft Library, 15.

47. James D. Phelan, letter to George Duval, June 1, 1906, James D. Phelan Papers, Bancroft Library.

48. Ernest P. Bicknell, *Pioneering with the Red Cross: Recollections of an Old Red Crosser* (New York: Macmillan, 1935), 48.

49. Phelan, "Personal Notes," 26.

50. James Phelan, letter to Mayor E. E. Schmitz, June 6, 1906, James D. Phelan Papers, Bancroft Library.

51. See Christine Misner Rosen, *The Limits of Power: Great Fires and the Process of City Growth in America* (Cambridge: Cambridge University Press, 1986); and Turner, *Women, Culture, and Community*.

52. *San Francisco Newsletter*, May 12, 1906.

53. See Lori Ginzberg, *Women and the Work of Benevolence: Morality, Politics, and Class in the Nineteenth-Century United States* (New Haven, CT: Yale University Press, 1990).

54. Fredrickson, *The Inner Civil War*, 80.

55. The commission itself evolved from women's organized relief work in the Women's Central Association of Relief for the Sick and Wounded of the Army. Ibid., 102.

56. Antebellum humanitarian-influenced charity work, however, still found its way into the war. In Fredrickson's account, the humanitarian work of Dorothea Dix, superintendent of army nurses, posed a counterpoint to the philosophy espoused by the Sanitary Commission. Fredrickson correctly concludes that Dix "had failed because of the very qualities which had produced her prewar triumphs. A 'pathetic sympathy with

suffering' was seemingly out of place in time of war, and it was this knowledge that made the Sanitary Commission effective." Ibid., 110–112.

57. Ibid., 112.

58. Barton wrote, "It may be further made a part of the *raison d'être* of these national relief societies to afford ready succor and assistance to sufferers in time of national or widespread calamities, such as plagues, cholera, yellow fever and the like, devastating fires or floods, railway disasters, mining catastrophes, etc." Clara Barton, "The Red Cross of the Geneva Convention: What It Is," 1878, quoted in Elizabeth Brown Pryor, *Clara Barton: Professional Angel* (Philadelphia: University of Pennsylvania Press, 1987), 195.

59. Ibid., 211.

60. Italics in original. Clara Barton to F. R. Southmayd, November 8, 1882, Clara Barton letterbook, quoted in ibid., 221.

61. Governor Beaver, quoted in David Burton, *Clara Barton: In the Service of Humanity* (Westport, CT: Greenwood Press, 1995), 121.

62. President William McKinley signed the bill on June 6, 1900.

63. Burton, *Clara Barton*, 143.

64. Clara Barton journal, December 12, 1900, quoted in Burton, *Clara Barton*, 144. With a total relief fund of $120,000, Barton stayed in Galveston for two months directing supply distribution, emergency shelter construction, and Red Cross field agents.

65. Biographer David Burton considered Boardman to be "steeped in the spirit of the 'progressive era.'" Ibid., 340.

66. Mable Boardman, quoted in Pryor, *Clara Barton*, 341.

67. Ibid., 349.

68. Mabel T. Boardman, *Under the Red Cross Flag at Home and Abroad* (Philadelphia: J. B. Lippincott, 1915), 98.

69. Ibid., 9.

70. The new Red Cross spent only $2,902 in its first year under the new charter. Dulles, *The American Red Cross*, 85–88.

71. Ibid., 103.

72. Well known for his charity philosophy and work, Edward T. Devine was already traveling to San Francisco when he received a telegram from the president asking for his assistance.

73. Clara Barton diary, April 27, 1906, Clara Barton Papers, microfilm, Stanford University Library.

74. Edward T. Devine, *The Principles of Relief* (London: Macmillan, 1905), 461.

75. Clara Barton diary, April 22, 1906.

76. Ibid., April 24, 1906.

77. The San Francisco Relief and Red Cross Funds (SFRRCF) assumed legal control over all aspects of disaster relief after its incorporation on July 20, 1906. Before that date, Phelan's Finance Committee combined both local and Red Cross representatives under the Finance Committee of Relief and Red Cross Funds. "Organization of the Relief Work," *San Francisco Relief Survey*, xxv.

78. Ernest P. Bicknell, "In the Thick of Relief Work at San Francisco," *Charities and the Commons* 16, no. 9 (1906): 297.

79. Calculated by author. Francis H. McLean, "Rehabilitation," *San Francisco Relief Survey*, 154, table 35.

80. James M. Motley, "Housing Rehabilitation," *San Francisco Relief Survey*, 184.

81. Although rehabilitation data do not designate the number of single mothers aided, women caring for children were most likely prioritized. On the basis of the

treatment of refugee women in the relief camps, single mothers received the majority of funds. McLean, "Rehabilitation," table 35.

82. Out of 489 bonus grants, 321 went to married couples, and 5 went to single women. *San Francisco Relief Survey*, 242, table 75. Housing rehabilitation divided refugees into four classes.

83. "Pippy Charges Discrimination," *San Francisco Chronicle*, July 18, 1906.

84. O'Connor, "Organizing the Force and Emergency Methods," 63, 65.

85. Devine reviews the Chicago Fire (1871), the Johnstown Flood (1889), and the Baltimore Fire (1904) in one section of his published work, *The Principles of Relief*.

86. Even Devine admitted that the "principles of relief" still needed "to be formulated," and for this he relied on Katharine Felton. Edward T. Devine, *Efficiency and Relief: A Programme of Social Work* (New York: Columbia University Press, 1906), 36–37.

87. As the city's largest nonsectarian relief organization, the Associated Charities acted as a "distribution center" for the city's multiple charity organizations. Founded in 1889, the new organization created a charity referral service as a means to "raise the needy above the need for relief . . . aid the poor to help themselves . . . [and] prevent indiscriminate and duplicate almsgiving." In 1894, there were already 204 charity organizations in San Francisco. "Articles of Incorporation of the Associated Charities," April 19, 1889, quoted in Lisa Anne Goodrich-Boyd, "Charity Redefined: Katherine [*sic*] Felton and the Associated Charities of San Francisco" (master's thesis, San Francisco State University, 1995), 56–57. For more on women reformers in the Progressive Era, see Fitzpatrick, *Endless Crusade*; Elizabeth N. Agnew, *From Charity to Social Work: Mary E. Richmond and the Creation of an American Profession* (Urbana: University of Illinois Press, 2004); Muncy, *Creating a Female Dominion*.

88. *The Associated Charities of San Francisco: Annual Reports, 1901–1903*.

89. Boyer, *Urban Masses and Moral Order*, 221. Mary Ann Irwin shows how women played an influential role in San Francisco charity work before the founding of San Francisco's Associated Charities. Irwin argues that their work in both public and private charities gave women access to social and political power. "'Going About and Doing Good': The Politics of Benevolence, Welfare, and Gender in San Francisco, 1850–1880," *Pacific Historical Review* 68, no. 3 (August 1999): 367.

90. Italics in original. Katharine Felton, Proceedings of the National Conference of Charities (1905), cited in Jean Burton, *Katharine Felton and Her Social Work in San Francisco* (Stanford, CA: James Ladd Delkin, 1947), 41.

91. *The Associated Charities of San Francisco: Annual Reports, 1904–1910*, 21.

92. Interestingly, Mary E. Richmond also battled with Edward Devine's philosophy as she pushed him to hire practitioners, not "university men," as instructors at his New York School. Although Devine opposed the idea, he ultimately adopted it in 1912. Agnew further argues that the "bifurcation in social work . . . continued to characterize the profession throughout the twentieth century." Agnew, *From Charity to Social Work*, 3, 145–146, 207. See also Robyn Muncy's discussion of Graham Taylor in *Creating a Female Dominion*, 74–92.

93. The primary goal of these investigations was to prevent "pauperization," or indiscriminate charity, since "to prevent any giving and to force the family of individual to depend on its own resources would be the best route." *Associated Charities of San Francisco: Annual Reports, 1901–1903*; *Associated Charities of San Francisco: Annual Reports, 1904–1910*, 5.

94. For an analysis of Chicago Fire disaster relief practices, see Sawislak, *Smoldering City*. For a contemporary account of disaster relief practices after the Great Chicago Fire, see Mary Roberts Smith, "Relief Work in Its Social Bearings," *Charities and the Commons* 16, no. 9 (1906): 310.

95. *San Francisco Relief Survey*, viii; McLean, "Rehabilitation," 117.

96. With the schools closed because of the disaster, 150 schoolteachers were trained as investigators. They were charged with filling out registration cards for relief rations. The teachers would "visit every house or tent or shack, register everybody and learn whether or not they are getting supplies." The charity workers, trained in modern social work methods, who supervised the districts included Mrs. John M. Glenn (Baltimore), Miss Birtwell (Associated Charities of Cambridge), Miss Fischer (New York Association for Improving the Conditions of the Poor), Miss Burrows (New York Charity Organization Society), Miss Seers (Chicago Bureau of Charities), and Miss Osgood (Associated Charities of Minneapolis). Bicknell, "In the Thick of Relief Work at San Francisco," 297; Lilian Brandt, "Rehabilitation Work in San Francisco," *Charities and the Commons* 17, no. 1 (1906): 45; Anna Pratt Simpson, *Story of the Associated Charities since the Fire of 1906* (San Francisco: Associated Charities of San Francisco, 1909), 4.

97. McLean, "Rehabilitation," 117.

98. Linda Gordon calls references to the "deserving" and the "undeserving poor" a "nineteenth-century charity tradition." The fear that aid would foster "pauperism" was palpable until the 1930s, which meant that "welfare called for supervision of a personal nature." Linda Gordon, "Putting Children First: Women, Maternalism, and Welfare in the Early Twentieth Century," in *U.S. History as Women's History: New Feminist Essays*, ed. Alice Kessler-Harris, Linda K. Kerber, and Kathryn Kish Sklar (Chapel Hill: University of North Carolina Press, 1995), 71–72.

99. Katharine Felton, quoted in Burton, *Katharine Felton*, 66.

100. Felton suggested admitting the male cousin to the city's temporary almshouse or transporting him to distant relatives. The "apathetic" young woman, on the other hand, was left to her own devices. Katharine C. Felton, letter to James D. Phelan, December 24, 1907, James D. Phelan Papers, Bancroft Library.

101. Associated Charities Investigator Dietzler, Case No. 8374, October 2, 1906, James D. Phelan Papers, Bancroft Library.

102. Katharine C. Felton, letter to James D. Phelan, October 3, 1906, James D. Phelan Papers, Bancroft Library.

103. Lillian Ferguson, "All Women Can Have Work for the Asking," *San Francisco Examiner*, May 29, 1906.

104. Eleanor Watkins, "The 1906 San Francisco Earthquake: A Personal Account by Mrs. James T. Watkins," in *Eyewitness to Disaster: Five Women (Each in Her Own Words) Tell Their Stories of the 1906 Earthquake and Fire in San Francisco* (San Francisco: National Society of the Colonial Dames of America in California, 1987), 2, 8.

105. Chrysanthemum, letter to Mary Frances, n.d., in *1906 Remembered*, ed. Patricia Turner (San Francisco: Friends of the San Francisco Public Library, 1981), 72.

106. Italics and underlines included in original document. Omira B. Bottum, letter to Mr. Wells Gardner Hodgson or E. R. Barber in Minneapolis, postmarked April 24, 1906, San Francisco Earthquake and Fire Collection, San Francisco Public Library.

107. "Says Servant Girls Must Return to Work," *San Francisco Chronicle*, July 15, 1906.

108. *San Francisco Newsletter*, July 28, 1906. Mabel Boardman, the Red Cross executive working out of Washington, DC, also believed that domestics should be at work and not in the relief camps. Mabel Boardman, letter to Mr. Dohrmann, April 8, 1907, "Extracts from Documents Bearing on the Relations of the American National Red Cross to The San Francisco Relief and Red Cross Funds, a Corporation," James D. Phelan Papers, Bancroft Library, 17.

109. Single women included women who were widowed, divorced, deserted, and unmarried. McLean, "Rehabilitation," 154.

110. Simpson, "Story of the Associated Charities," 11.

111. Linda Gordon, *Pitied but Not Entitled: Single Mothers and the History of Welfare, 1890–1935* (Cambridge, MA: Harvard University Press, 1994), 26. Widows' pensions have received much scholarly attention. See Joanne L. Goodwin, *Gender and the Politics of Welfare Reform: Mothers' Pensions in Chicago, 1911–1929* (Chicago: University of Chicago Press, 1997); Christopher Howard, "Sowing the Seeds of 'Welfare': The Transformation of Mothers' Pensions, 1900–1940," *Journal of Policy History* 4 (1992): 188–227. Molly Ladd-Taylor, *Mother-Work: Women, Child Welfare, and the State, 1890–1930* (Urbana: University of Illinois Press, 1994); and Gwendolyn Mink, *The Wages of Motherhood: Inequality in the Welfare State, 1917–1942* (Ithaca, NY: Cornell University Press, 1995).

112. Felton's work with widows extended to the needs of unmarried mothers. The Associated Charities encouraged unmarried mothers, with the exception of mothers who were "below par mentally," "repeatedly immoral," or threatened by their parents with disownment, to keep their babies. "If a mother loves her baby and wishes to keep it," pledged the Associated Charities in 1912, "she is made to see that she need never give it up simply on account of poverty or because she is friendless." *Report of the Associated Charities of San Francisco: January, 1911 to July, 1912*, 37, 40–41. See also Mary Ann Irwin, "Servant to the Poor: The St. Vincent de Paul Society of San Francisco, 1860–2010" (draft internal document dated January 2010, in possession of author), 30.

113. Frances Joliffe, letter to James D. Phelan, circa 1913, James D. Phelan Papers, Bancroft Library.

114. Ibid.

115. *Associated Charities of San Francisco: Annual Reports, 1912–1913*, 8.

116. McLean, "Rehabilitation," 125.

117. Edward Devine, "Conference Meeting of the Finance Committee," May 4, 1906, James D. Phelan Papers, Bancroft Library, 34.

118. Devine concluded, "It would be a great personal disappointment to me if there will not remain, after all other needs are met, a substantial sum which can be used in this manner, not to compensate people for their losses, but to meet their necessities, and give them a new start in life." Ibid.; "Finance Committee Meeting Minutes," May 24, 1906, 2, James D. Phelan Papers, Bancroft Library.

119. John A. Emery, letter to James D. Phelan, December 27, 1906, James D. Phelan Papers, Bancroft Library.

120. John A. Emery, letter to James D. Phelan, January 10, 1907, James D. Phelan Papers, Bancroft Library.

121. Somewhere between 12.3 percent and 26.1 percent of all rehabilitation applications were refused. Calculated from McLean, "Rehabilitation," 153, 168, tables 33 and 47.

122. Seventy-seven percent of relief applications were for less than $200 and only 4.1 percent were for amounts over $400. Seventy-five percent of Phelan's confidential cases, on the other hand, received between $200 and $500 in aid and 28 percent received over $400. Calculated from ibid., 165, table 45; "Rehabilitation Committee," James D. Phelan Papers, Bancroft Library.

123. Two letters to Phelan clearly stated that the relief checks, four for a total of $1,995 were endorsed to him. While the other letters did not specify endorsement, all but one was sent directly to Phelan. Mrs. Raymond, letter to James D. Phelan, January 4, 1907, James D. Phelan Papers, Bancroft Library; Mrs. Raymond, letter to James D. Phelan, January 11, 1907, James D. Phelan Papers, Bancroft Library.

124. C. J. O'Connor, letter to James D. Phelan, April 15, 1908, James D. Phelan Papers, Bancroft Library.

125. F. W. Dohrmann, "Statement Concerning Relief Work Done by the Associated Charities," August 28, 1909, in Simpson, "Story of the Associated Charities," 34.

126. In the late nineteenth century, the Associated Charities General Fund never exceeded $6,000. After the disaster, the organization was allocated $80,400 from the relief fund. Associated Charities, *Annual Reports*, 1892, 1893, 1895, 1897, 1899; Associated Charities, "Statement of Appropriations as of April 4, 1908," April 6, 1908, James D. Phelan Papers, Bancroft Library.

127. *Associated Charities of San Francisco: Annual Reports, 1912–1913*, 3.

128. Simpson, "Story of the Associated Charities," 40.

129. Katharine Felton, quoted in *Associated Charities of San Francisco: Annual Reports, 1911–1912*, 9.

130. Alexander Johnson, ed., *Proceedings of the National Conference of Charities and Correction* (Philadelphia: Press of Fred J. Heer, 1906), iii.

131. Unknown author, letter to James D. Phelan, June 4, 1909, James D. Phelan Papers, Bancroft Library; Mary Kidder, letter to James D. Phelan, December 12, 1910, James D. Phelan Papers, Bancroft Library; Mary Kidder, letter to James D. Phelan, October 20, 1916, James D. Phelan Papers, Bancroft Library.

132. Red Cross membership, which totaled 3,337 in 1905, increased to 9,262 in 1906. After interest in the disaster subsided, membership dropped to fewer than 6,000. Dulles, *The American Red Cross*, 85.

133. "The Work of the American National Red Cross," *Leslie's Weekly*, May 10, 1906, quoted in Kevin L. Rozario, "Nature's Evil Dreams: Disaster and America, 1871–1906" (Ph.D. diss., Yale University, 1996), 232.

134. James D. Phelan, letter to H. W. Patton, July 19, 1907, James D. Phelan Papers, Bancroft Library. (Patton was a reporter for the *Evening American*, in Bellingham, WA.)

CHAPTER 3

1. Sister M. Thecla in "San Francisco Earthquake and Fire 1906: Destruction of St. Mary's Hospital," unpublished journal, Sisters of Mercy Archives, Burlingame, California, 23.

2. Sister M. Gerard in "San Francisco Earthquake and Fire 1906: Destruction of St. Mary's Hospital," unpublished journal, Sisters of Mercy Archives, 23.

3. Beryl B. Bishop, eyewitness account, Stanford Special Collections, Stanford University.

4. Annie Little Barry, quoted in Sandra L. Henderson, "The *Civitas* of Women's Political Culture," in *California Women and Politics: From the Gold Rush to the Great Depression*, ed. Robert W. Cherny, Mary Ann Irwin, and Ann Marie Wilson (Lincoln: University of Nebraska Press, 2011), 336.

5. Paula Baker, "The Domestication of Politics: Women and American Political Society, 1780–1920," *American Historical Review* 89 (1984). Elizabeth Hayes Turner also found that disaster spurred the political activism of local clubwomen after the 1900 Galveston storm. See Elizabeth Hayes Turner, *Women, Culture, and Community: Religion and Reform in Galveston, 1800–1920* (New York: Oxford University Press, 1997). For more on women's clubs and political activism, see also Robyn Everist, "Women Stretching Outwards: Feminism and the Club Woman Movement in the United States at the Turn of the Twentieth Century," *Lilith* 2 (1985): 30–41; and Anne Ruggles Gere, *Intimate Practices: Literacy and Cultural Work in U.S. Women's Clubs, 1880–1920* (Urbana: University of Illinois Press, 1997).

6. San Francisco Citizen's Committee Meeting Minutes, no. 11, April 25, 1906, James D. Phelan Papers, Bancroft Library, University of California, Berkeley, 2.

7. "Vacant Houses for Homeless," *San Francisco Chronicle*, April 24, 1906.

8. Marion Baldwin Hale, "The 1906 Earthquake and Fire, San Francisco," Oral History Interview, San Francisco Earthquake and Fire Collection, San Francisco Public Library, San Francisco, 9. The president of the California Federation of Women's Clubs confirmed that donations from the Federation of Women's Clubs supplied the Red Cross Headquarters Relief Station. Mrs. Robert P. Hill, "Appeal to State Club to Send Clothing for Nurses," *San Francisco Examiner*, May 1, 1906.

9. Mrs. Roys (chair of the Women's Clubs of Elkhart, Indiana), letter to James D. Phelan, April 27, 1906, Allan Pollock Papers, Bancroft Library, University of California, Berkeley. The work in Elkhart typified the relief efforts from women in the nation's smaller towns. Wives and mothers outside of Modesto, for example, sent children's clothing, while Ashland, Oregon, housewives baked bread and beans to send to the refugees. The Sunshine Club, whose membership consisted of the "wives of hard-working miners" in Nevada, sewed clothes for children. "The Senders," Modesto, California, letter to Relief Committee of San Francisco, May 7, 1906, Allan Pollock Papers, Bancroft Library; "Ashland Housewives Busy," *Portland Oregonian*, April 20, 1906; "Searchlight Women Contribute Clothes," *San Francisco Call*, June 1, 1906, 137.

10. "Willing Hands Are at Work," *Portland Oregonian*, April 22, 1906.

11. Linda Dick, *Palo Alto 1906* (Cupertino: California History Center, 1979), 16.

12. "Gilroy Gives Relief," *Gilroy Advocate*, April 28, 1906.

13. "Hundreds of People Fed," *Fresno Morning Republican*, April 25, 1906.

14. Florence Sylvester, letter, May 3, 1906, printed in Nancy A. Mavrogenes, "Experiencing the '06 Earthquake—with a Female Physician Who Was There," *California Historical Courier* 32, no. 2 (1980): 5.

15. Mrs. C. C. Duniway, quoted in Dick, *Palo Alto 1906*, 17.

16. "Willing Hands Are at Work"; "Half Million to 'Frisco,'" *Portland Oregonian*, April 21, 1906.

17. Emmeline B. Wells, "Earthquake and Fire," *Woman's Exponent* 34 (May 1906): 68.

18. Lillian Ferguson, "Energy of Society Women Is Directed in Relief Work," *San Francisco Examiner*, May 3, 1906.

19. Helen Hillyer Brown, *The Great San Francisco Fire* (San Francisco: Hillside Press, 1906), 11.

20. James D. Phelan, quoted in "Finance Committee Meeting Minutes," May 3, 1906, James D. Phelan Papers, Bancroft Library, 1.

21. Mrs. Helen A. Parker, letter to the Citizen's Relief Committee, May 17, 1906, Allan Pollock Papers, Bancroft Library.

22. Mrs. Emma H. Woodrow, letter to James D. Phelan, n.d., James D. Phelan Papers, Bancroft Library.

23. James P. Walsh, "Peter Yorke and Progressivism in California, 1908," *Eire-Ireland* 10 (1975): 73–81. San Francisco's private Catholic school system, for example, ensured that the children of parish families were educated in a Catholic environment. William Issel and Robert W. Cherny, *San Francisco, 1865–1932: Politics, Power, and Urban Development* (Berkeley: University of California Press, 1986), 102.

24. As Jay Dolan argues in his study of American Catholicism, "For many people the parish became a total community where all religious, social, and recreational needs were met through a host of societies and organizations." Jay P. Dolan, "Catholicism and American Culture: Strategies for Survival," in *American Religious History*, ed. Amanda Porterfield (Oxford: Blackwell Publishers, 2002), 134.

25. Mother Superior Xavier Hayden, "1906 Earthquake Letters," San Francisco Earthquake and Fire Papers, Presentation Archives, San Francisco, 3.

26. Reverend Mother Pia Backes, *Her Days Unfolded*, trans. Mother Bernadina Michel (San Jose: Benedictine Press, 1953), 271–272.

27. Unpublished earthquake account, Sisters of Mercy Archives, 12–13.

28. The Presentation Sisters left their convent near Union Square (Taylor and Ellis Streets) to find safety with their order in Berkeley. A few sisters remained in Berkeley to cook meals for refugees at the convent and school and worked with the Catholic Ladies Aid Society to establish a clothing relief station and sewing room. Six sisters returned to San Francisco and ran a relief station at Montgomery and Alta Streets. Hayden, "1906 Earthquake Letters," 13–15.

29. Sister Genevieve, letter written from relief headquarters at Montgomery and Alta Streets, April 29, 1906, San Francisco Earthquake and Fire Papers, Presentation Archives, 3.

30. "On Telegraph Hill," *Monitor*, July 21, 1906.

31. Sister M. Ignatius Meehan, "Earthquake and Fire of 1906," unpublished account, Sisters of Mercy Archives, 3.

32. Letters were received from eleven convents. Sisters of Mercy, "San Francisco Earthquake and Fire, 1906: Destruction of St. Mary's Hospital," unpublished journal, Sisters of Mercy Archives, 12–45.

33. Meehan, "Earthquake and Fire of 1906," 3; Sisters of Mercy, "San Francisco Earthquake and Fire." After the disaster, Catholic charities modeled a formal charity organization after the SFRRCF. In 1907, Archbishop Riordan organized the Catholic Settlement and Humane Society to match those in need with the society's institutions, programs, and services. Mary Ann Irwin, "Servant to the Poor: The St. Vincent de Paul Society of San Francisco, 1860–2010" (draft internal document dated January 2010, in possession of author), 30.

34. "Chinese Evils Threaten City," *San Francisco Bulletin*, April 21, 1906.

35. Ella Clemens Wong, *Chinatown* (San Francisco: self-published, 1915), 1.

36. "Miss Clemens, Sister of Mrs. Howard Gould Marries Chinese after Custom of His Race," *San Francisco Examiner*, September 28, 1906.

37. General Greely, letter to Mrs. Sun Yue [Ella May] Clemens, November 12, 1906, in Wong, *Chinatown*, 1.

38. "Miss Clemens," 1–2. Peggy Pascoe's study also shows how some white missionary women "developed strong personal fascinations for their 'adopted' cultures." However, Pascoe finds that their fascination did not allow "mission women to overcome all of the racialism inherent in Victorian social thought." Peggy Pascoe, *Relations of Rescue: The Search for Female Moral Authority in the American West, 1874–1939* (New York: Oxford University Press, 1990), 118, 121.

39. Wendy Rouse Jorae, *The Children of Chinatown: Growing Up Chinese American in San Francisco, 1850–1920* (Chapel Hill: University of North Carolina Press, 2009), 199.

40. Fred Wong, oral history interview, in Laura Wong, "Vallejo's Chinese Community, 1860–1960, " *Chinese America: History and Perspectives* 2 (1988): 159.

41. Leland Chin in Victor G. Nee and Bret de Bary Nee, *Longtime Californ': A Documentary Study of an American Chinatown* (Stanford, CA: Stanford University Press, 1972), 77. Local historian Connie Young Yu's grandparents, who lost their home above a shop on Commercial Street, stayed at the Richmond shrimp camp before returning to live in San Francisco's Chinatown. Connie Young Yu, "Chinatown, 1906: The End and the Beginning" (Chinese Chamber of Commerce souvenir booklet, 1968).

42. Chinese immigrants had fished and gathered seafood from San Francisco Bay waters since the 1850s. Marin County's Chinese population fell from 1,827 in 1880 to 915 in 1890 to 489 by 1900. The 1910 county census recorded 555 Chinese, although

that number was cut by more than half by the 1920s. Marin County Census data, cited in L. Eve Armentrout Ma, "Chinese in Marin County, 1850–1950: A Century of Growth and Decline," *Chinese America: History and Perspectives* 5 (1991): 37.

43. On April 23, an estimated two hundred Chinese refugees arrived in Fresno. By April 25, the number of Chinese refugees in Fresno had doubled and the local paper noted, "One fact that has been generally noted is that every train coming into Fresno is bringing with it a horde of Chinese. . . . Fresno has the third largest Chinatown in the state, and it is to be expected that the Chinese who were burned out of their homes would many of them turn their eyes in this direction." "Refugees Fed at the Trains," *Fresno Morning Republican*, April 23, 1906; "Hundreds of People Fed," *Fresno Morning Republican*, April 25, 1906.

44. Hugh Kwong Liang, in Malcom E. Barker, *Three Fearful Days: San Francisco Memoirs of the 1906 Earthquake and Fire* (San Francisco: Londonborn, 1998), 119–122.

45. Few Chinese refugees registered with the Berkeley Relief Committee, accounting for only 1 percent of the committee's registered relief households and 2 percent of the refugees. One-third of the refugees were housed in Chinese businesses, while the majority stayed in American Chinese residences. Only two non-Chinese-surnamed households registered Chinese refugees; one volunteered to house "15 Chinamen" and the other housed a single male, Sam Yuen, who was most likely a servant. In contrast, the remaining Chinatown refugees were not placed by the relief committee but were registered by investigators who canvassed homes and businesses in Berkeley. Calculated by author from 1,396 Berkeley Relief Committee Relief Cards, Berkeley Relief Records, Bancroft Library, University of California, Berkeley.

46. In the Berkeley Relief Committee records, 15 was the average group size of Chinese refugees. The Lee Yaik Company was at 2150 Dwight Way, and Hong Wo was listed at 2152 Dwight Way. The *Berkeley Daily Gazette* reported that at least 350 American Chinese refugees were "confined to the Dwight way district." The report also indicated that single men were separated from women, noting that women were housed at a Chinese grocery store and men at a laundry near Shattuck Avenue. Berkeley Housing Cards; "Caring for Chinese," *Berkeley Daily Gazette*, April 21, 1906.

47. John Dundas Fletcher, "An Account of the Work of Relief Organized in Berkeley in April and May, 1906, for the Refugees from San Francisco," unpublished study, University of California, Berkeley, 1909.

48. Between the 1900 U.S. Census and the 1910 U.S. Census, Berkeley's population grew from 154 to 451. "Chinese Populations in Major Cities," in Erica Y. Z. Pan, *The Impact of the 1906 Earthquake on San Francisco's Chinatown* (New York: Peter Lang, 1995), 145.

49. The meeting was scheduled to take place at Laughlin's home in Oakland. The meeting agenda consisted of four items: "1. Immediate relief, where necessary, in money or goods. 2. Assistance in finding suitable employment. 3. Loan of tools, machines, etc., to competent workers. 4. Other forms of general aid towards self support." "Relief Fund for Chinese Christian Families," Berkeley Relief Committee Records, Bancroft Library.

50. The relief committee visited the family and reported that they were "now living among friends near us [relief committee] at 2604 Durant Avenue. . . . They have hired a house and seem quite comfortably settling down to housekeeping." Mrs. Hannah A. De Voe Wilkins, letter to Rev. E. L. Parsons, Berkeley Relief Committee Records, Bancroft Library; John Fryer (Executive Staff Berkeley Relief Committee), letter to Mrs. Hannah A. De Voe Wilkins, May 2, 1906, Berkeley Relief Committee Records, Bancroft Library.

51. "Chinese Come to the Rescue," *San Francisco Chronicle*, April 22, 1906.

52. Chinese merchants and diplomats raised money for the general relief fund as well as for Chinese refugees. The Chinatown contributions were sent to Chin Fook and Company, 373 Ninth Street, Oakland, where they were controlled by the CCBA. A notice from Consul Chung Pao Hsi was sent to the New York Chinese Merchants Association as well as to Consul Shah Kaifu. Consul Chung Pao Hsi to Consul Shah Kaifu, printed in "Chinese Will Aid Afflicted," *San Francisco Chronicle*, April 25, 1906; Chung Pao Hsi to the Chinese Merchants' Association, New York, printed in "Chinese Raising Fund," *Dallas News*, April 24, 1906.

53. L. Eve Armentrout Ma found that the Chinese political party, the Pao-huang hui, initially offered relief in Oakland. The Pao-huang hui accessed its branch organizations to obtain money and relief supplies. Their efforts were replaced by the CCBA. Ma, *Hometown Chinatown: The History of Oakland's Chinese Community* (New York: Garland Publishing, 2000), 63.

54. *Chung Sai Yat Po*, April 26, 1906, quoted in and translated by Pan, *The Impact of the 1906 Earthquake*, 49.

55. A representative of the CCBA, W. H. Sawtell, reported that West Coast CCBAs were "hurrying cars of provisions to this city [Oakland]," and a Chinese relief committee formed in Los Angeles to send money, supplies, and representatives to Oakland. The supplies were shipped to the CCBA at 478 Tenth Street. "Chinese Come to the Rescue," *Oakland Herald*, April 21, 1906. Los Angeles merchants Ho Lee, Sue Hay, and Wung Quong were part of a group of ten relief committee representatives from Los Angeles. "Chinese Give to Sufferers," *San Francisco Bulletin*, April 23, 1906. Merchants from Sacramento also sent relief supplies. Pan, *The Impact of the 1906 Earthquake*, 99.

56. The editor of the *Chung Sai Yat Po*, Ng Poon Chew, estimated that 6,000 Chinese were in Oakland three months after the disaster. Ng Poon Chew in *Oakland Tribune*, June 1, 1906, quoted in Pan, *The Impact of the 1906 Earthquake*, 42.

57. "Chinese are Shipped Away," *Oakland Herald*, April 21, 1906; "Relief Fund for Chinese Christian Families," Berkeley Relief Committee Records, Bancroft Library.

58. Representatives from the Chinese Red Cross Society were scheduled to meet the invalid refugees and arrange for their living in China. "Aged Chinese Will Be Returning to Native Land," *San Francisco Call*, April 23, 1906, 6.

59. Erica Pan tallied 1,500 departures during the first year after the disaster. The Chinese relief committee negotiated fare reductions to $20 to $30 per person for travel to China. On May 3 several hundred refugees left on the *Mongolia*, and on May 10 an additional 400 refugees purchased tickets for departure. In early June, 750 refugees boarded the *Hong Kong Moru* and the *Korea*, bound for China. The port of Portland also offered free transportation for the elderly, ill, and disabled. *Chung Sai Yat Po*, May 3, 1906; *Chung Ya Sat Po*, May 10, 1906; *San Francisco Examiner*, June 5, 1906; *Chung Sai Yat Po*, July 23, 1906, quoted in and translated by Pan, *The Impact of the 1906 Earthquake*, 49–50. The *San Francisco Call* reported that the Chinese relief committee had transported 800 refugees to China and that it planned to send 1,000 aged and destitute as well. "Finds Chinese Well Cared For," *San Francisco Call*, April 23, 1906; "Aged Chinese Will Be Returning to Native Land."

60. *Chung Sai Yat Po*, May 1, 1906.

61. Between the 1900 U.S. Census and the 1910 U.S. Census, Oakland's Chinese community grew by 46 percent, from 1,950 to 3,609. Erica Pan argues that Oakland's Chinese population grew as much as 60 percent after the disaster. "Chinese Populations in Major Cities," in Pan, *The Impact of the 1906 Earthquake*, 145.

62. Willard T. Chow, *The Reemergence of an Inner City: The Pivot of Chinese Settlement in the East Bay Region of the San Francisco Bay Area* (San Francisco: R&E Research Associates, 1977), 25, 46.

63. William Randolph Hearst, quoted in the "Town Crier," *San Francisco Newsletter*, June 16, 1906, 3.

64. "William Randolph Hearst," *Sausalito News*, April 28, 1906, 1.

65. "Hearst, Our Savior," *Star*, July 21, 1906, 1.

66. The *San Francisco Newsletter* reported that accusations that Hearst regularly misrepresented his relief efforts were "common." "Town Crier," *San Francisco Newsletter*, June 16, 1906, 3.

67. The W. R. Hearst Tent City, Hearst Children and Maternity Hospital, and W. R. Hearst Children's Reunion Camp were all built in Oakland. "W. R. Hearst Camp for Children," *San Francisco Examiner*, April 27, 1906.

68. Mr. J. McShane, letter to Mr. W. R. Hearst, April 21, 1906, San Francisco Virtual Museum Archives.

69. "Hearst's Camp Doing Good," *Oakland Tribune*, April 26; "Good Work Done Hearst City," *Oakland Tribune*, April 26.

70. "Mr. and Mrs. Hearst Visit Relief Camps," *San Francisco Examiner*, May 8, 1906.

71. "W.R. Hearst Eby Is Name Given to Little Lad," *Oakland Examiner*, May 13, 1906.

72. Cited in E. H. Merrill, "The Great Fire of 1906," *Argonaut*, June 25, 1927.

73. E. H. Merrill, "The Great Earthquake and Fire," *Argonaut*, June 18, 1927.

74. Ibid.

75. Ibid.

76. Ibid.

77. Merrill, "The Great Fire of 1906," *Argonaut*, June 25, 1927.

78. Ibid.

79. Refugee protest over relief food began as early as June 1906. "Don't Like Soup Kitchen: Jefferson Square Refugees to Send Their Protest to the Mayor," *San Francisco Chronicle*, June 4, 1906.

80. "Kilian Tells His Side of Story," *San Francisco Chronicle*, July 12, 1906.

81. "Irate Women Mob the Keepers of Relief Stores," *San Francisco Chronicle*, July 7, 1906. Hearst's *Examiner*, like the *Chronicle*, favored the women refugees over the relief corporation. The *Examiner*'s version of the Flour Riot listed slightly fewer female protesters and stolen pounds of flour. "Thirteen Women Refugees Seize 650 Pounds of Relief Flour, Menace Officials with Violence," *San Francisco Examiner*, July 6, 1906; "Mob of Women Make a Demand for Flour," *San Francisco Call*, July 7, 1906.

82. There is a long history of women's food protests. For women's role in other food riots, see Elizabeth Ewen, *Immigrant Women in the Land of Dollars: Life and Culture on the Lower East Side, 1890–1925* (New York: Monthly Review Press, 1985).

83. Ernest P. Bicknell, *Pioneering with the Red Cross: Recollections of an Old Red Crosser* (New York: Macmillan, 1935), 57–58.

84. Ibid.; Mary Kelly, *Shame of the Relief* (1908), 6.

85. Bicknell, *Pioneering with the Red Cross*, 58–60.

86. "The Grand Jury Visits Relief Camps," *San Francisco Chronicle*, July 20, 1906. The *Examiner* also covered the grand jury investigation as front page news. "Grand Jury to Investigate Relief Fund," *San Francisco Examiner*, July 19, 1906.

87. "Captain J. N. Kilian Is Found Guilty of Battery," *San Francisco Chronicle*, July 18, 1906.

88. "Great Heap of Flour That Is Now Ready for Distribution," *San Francisco Chronicle*, May 30, 1906; "Great Stack of Flour at Moulder School Depot," *San Francisco Chronicle*, June 19, 1906.

89. "Will Take Flour Sent for Relief: Milling Companies Form a Pool to Buy Surplus for $200,000," *San Francisco Chronicle*, May 26, 1906; "Refugees Don't Care for Flour," *San Francisco Chronicle*, June 23, 1906.

90. "Finance Committee Meeting Minutes," June 8, 1906, James D. Phelan Papers, Bancroft Library, 17.

91. While the *San Francisco Relief Survey* would later report that flour spoilage was the primary factor, Finance Committee leaders were acutely attuned to local merchant interest. Judd Kahn discusses the correspondence between the Port Costa Milling Company president, S. B. McNear, and the Finance Committee in detail. Judd Kahn, *Imperial San Francisco: Politics and Planning in an American City, 1897–1906* (Lincoln: University of Nebraska Press, 1979), 143.

92. "Relief Flour Is Bought at an Increase of $105,200," *San Francisco Examiner*, June 19, 1906.

93. "Globe Milling Company Gets the Relief Flour," *San Francisco Chronicle*, June 19, 1906. The *Examiner*, whose editorial position was at first opposed to the SFRRCF's sale of flour, later took credit for its sale at a higher price. "The 'Respectable' Flour Looters," *San Francisco Examiner*, June 14, 1906.

94. "Refugees Make Queer Demands," *San Francisco Chronicle*, July 17, 1906. Local San Francisco lawyer and protest leader Alva Udell, for example, obtained 10,000 refugee signatures to block the sale of flour. "10,000 Bring Suit to Recover Relief Flour," *San Francisco Examiner*, June 22, 1906.

95. Committee of Friends of Refugees, "Refugees Attention," July 31, 1906, San Francisco Earthquake and Fire Collection, San Francisco Public Library.

96. A local newspaper estimated 1,500 refugees, while one of the speakers calculated 3,000. "No One Went from the Devine Banquet to Convince the Refugees of Red Cross Sincerity," unknown newspaper source, August 1, 1906, San Francisco Virtual Museum Archives.

97. "2,500 Refugees Demand Bread While Banqueters Feast Dr. E. T. Devine," *San Francisco Examiner*, August 1, 1906.

98. Ibid.

99. Kelly, *Shame of the Relief*, 8.

100. "Dr. Devine Is Honored at Banquet," *San Francisco Bulletin*, August 1, 1906.

101. "Fears Refugees Will Kill Her," *San Francisco Chronicle*, August 5, 1906.

102. United Refugees Notice, October 5, 1906, *Daily News*, in Rene Bine Papers, California Historical Society, San Francisco. "Refugee Leader Gets Her Request Granted," *San Francisco Chronicle*, September 25, 1906.

103. See Karen Sawislak, *Smoldering City: Chicagoans and the Great Fire, 1871–1874* (Chicago: University of Chicago Press, 1995).

104. See Turner, *Women, Culture, and Community*.

105. Udell participated in the "Committee of Friends of the Refugees," as well as under the name the "Committee of the Whole." Alva Udell was most likely a refugee himself; the 1906 San Francisco City Directory lists his home and legal office in downtown San Francisco. *San Francisco City Directory*, 1905.

106. Robert E. L. Knight, *Industrial Relations*, 97, quoted in Michael Kazin, *Barons of Labor: The San Francisco Building Trades and Union Power in the Progressive Era* (Urbana: University of Illinois Press, 1987), 14.

107. Kazin, *Barons of Labor*, 14–15, 28–30.

108. After aligning with the Union Labor Party (ULP) for the 1905 election, for example, the BTC declared election day a holiday for the next three municipal elections to encourage workingmen to "proselytize and vote at their leisure." Ibid., 119.

109. Ibid., 21–23.

110. Ibid., 76–77.

111. *San Francisco Call*, January 8, 1910, quoted in ibid., 77.

112. The mayor's anti-liquor order was printed in the local papers: "To the General Public: The first day of the fire I issued an order that no intoxicating liquors should be sold or given away. It has been brought to my attention in the last few days

that a number of brewers have been attempting to deliver bottled beer to their customers. If this practice is allowed it would mean that bottled beer would be sold not only to the house customers, but also to others on the streets. Those interested in the manufacture and sale of intoxicating liquors are hereby notified that they must refrain from distributing intoxicating liquors of any kind either for sale or for free distribution until further notice." Eugene E. Schmitz, printed in "Sobriety Will Be Enforced," *San Francisco Call*, May 3, 1906.

113. "Father Yorke Says City's Red Tape Is Bad," *San Francisco Examiner*, April 29, 1906.

114. "Starved by Red Tape," *San Francisco Newsletter*, July 28, 1906.

115. Margaret Mahoney, *The Earthquake, the Fire, the Relief* (San Francisco, July 28, 1906), 7. Although Mahoney did not endorse a socialist solution, she remained convinced that class interests were the source of the problem: "Now there are two explanations to the situation: either the trained charity workers are not of big enough caliber for the work or as adjuncts of the merchant class, agents of capitalists, they are guarding the interests of the men who support them." Ibid.

116. *The Associated Charities of San Francisco: Annual Reports, 1904–1910* (San Francisco: Blair-Murdock, 1911), 10.

117. Dr. Margaret Mahoney's name, which appears on 1906 Associated Charities of San Francisco letterhead, was removed from the list of Central Council members in 1907. Her name was removed from the Central Council listing in the Annual Report by 1909. Associated Charities of San Francisco letterhead, 1906–1907, James D. Phelan Papers, Bancroft Library.

118. United Refugees representative, most likely Alva Udell, quoted in "Refugees Incorporate: Fire Sufferers Organize, Select Name and Announce Relief Plans," *San Francisco Call*, August 2, 1906.

119. United Refugee Enrollment Card, Rene Bine Papers, California Historical Society.

120. See Mark Pittenger, *American Socialists and Evolutionary Thought, 1870–1920* (Madison: University of Wisconsin Press, 1993); and Arthur Lipow, *Authoritarian Socialism in America: Edward Bellamy and the Nationalist Movement* (Berkeley: University of California Press, 1982).

121. "Homeseekers [sic] Loan Application," San Francisco Virtual Museum Archives.

122. The three "Rehabilitation Committee" references preprinted on the form, Alva Udell, F. M. Campbell, and Minne Tebow, were all board members of the United Refugees. Refugees who signed the document requested a $250 loan at 3 percent interest secured by United Refugees preferred capital stock. The loan applicant agreed to pay five dollars per month for a period of five years (total of $300) into a "sinking fund" in return for annual stock dividends. Ibid.

123. "Finance Committee Meeting Minutes," December 7, 1906, James D. Phelan Papers, Bancroft Library, 2. Refugees also formed committees inside the relief camps to represent their interests. The United Residents Association, representing refugees residing in a camp in Lafayette Square, for example, appeared before the SFRRCF Finance Committee in late October 1906. The United Residents delegation and the finance committee had "an informal discussion" regarding camp housing policy. Another camp organization, the "Harbor View Refugee Association," took its complaints about lack of access to relief donations directly "to the American Nation." "San Francisco Relief and Red Cross Funds Executive Committee Meeting Minutes," October 30, 1906, James D. Phelan Papers, Bancroft Library, 3; "Harbor View Refugee Association," broadside, Rene Bine Papers, California Historical Society.

124. Mary Kelly presents an accurate picture of the legislative events, but she does not mention Alva Udell in her account. Kelly, *Shame of the Relief*, 14.

125. Assembly Bill 898 outlined the structure of a public relief commission to be staffed by the governor and mayors of cities containing more than 50,000 inhabitants. Justification for the bill was submitted in a resolution two days before, which outlined allegations that the Finance Committee "wrongfully sold a large amount of said food-stuffs, clothing and other supplies" and that relief funds were dispersed by directors "without being responsible to any court or authority for an honest and economically administration of the trust." Resolution, February 14, 1907, Assembly Journal, 18.

126. Alva Udell, letter to George B. Keane, February 15, 1907, San Francisco Virtual Museum Archives.

127. G.W.W. Davis (chairman, Central Committee Red Cross), Memorandum, June 13, 1907, James D. Phelan Papers, Bancroft Library, 4.

128. William D. Sohier and Jacob Furth, "Massachusetts Association for the Relief of California Report," Massachusetts Red Cross, 1906, 10.

129. Mabel Boardman, letter to F. W. Dohrmann, October 20, 1906, reprinted in "Extracts from Documents Bearing on the Relation of the American National Red Cross to the San Francisco Relief and Red Cross Fund," James D. Phelan Papers, Bancroft Library, 13.

130. Davis, Memorandum, 5, 10.

131. Sister Marie Kelly, "Memoirs of Bay Street School," Presentation Archives.

CHAPTER 4

1. Mary P. Ryan, "The Public and the Private Good: Across the Great Divide in Women's History," *Journal of Women's History* 15, no. 2 (Summer 2003): 15–16.

2. In her study of how the Civil War transformed the lives and identities of white, Southern women, Drew Gilpin Faust argues that their "new sense of self was based not in the experience of success but in desperation, in the fundamental need to simply survive." Drew Gilpin Faust, *Mothers of Invention: Women of the Slaveholding South in the American Civil War* (New York: Vintage Books, 1996), 243.

3. A census taken by General Greely on June 1, 1906, estimated 40,000 refugees living in the relief camps. The Southern Pacific Railroad estimated 42,000 refugees in the city, while the *Relief Survey* researchers computed 39,000. Charles J. O'Connor, "Organizing the Force and Emergency Methods," in Russell Sage Foundation, ed., *San Francisco Relief Survey* (New York: Survey Associates, 1913), 77.

4. The estimate for native-born refugees is based on a tally of heads of families, where the nationality of the family was assumed to be identical to that of the father. The estimate for official camp population by sex is based on the period from September 1906 to December 1906. Ibid., 75, table 20.

5. One year after the disaster, for example, more than half of the remaining twelve relief camps were located in or near the pre-disaster Irish and Italian neighborhoods. Calculated by author from "Map of San Francisco Relief," *San Francisco Relief Survey*.

6. General Greely, "Meeting of Citizens' Committee," no. 17, May 2, 1906, James D. Phelan Papers, Bancroft Library, University of California, Berkeley.

7. Similar to Linda Gordon's study of social control in Boston's child welfare agencies, refugees in San Francisco used the agencies of social control to their own ends. On the basis of her findings in Boston, Gordon argues against "anti-social control" historical interpretations that employ an elite domination/plebian victimization paradigm. Linda Gordon, "Family Violence, Feminism, and Social Control," in *Women, the State,*

and Welfare (Madison: University of Wisconsin Press, 1990); Linda Gordon, *Heroes of Their Own Lives: The Politics and History of Family Violence* (London: Virago, 1989).

8. The first citywide refugee registration tallied only 13 percent of San Francisco's refugees within the destroyed area, most living in the four camps established there. Calculated by author from "Map of San Francisco Relief," *San Francisco Relief Survey.*

9. "Some of the Inmates Complain of Lack of Shade at New Location," *San Francisco Chronicle,* July 17, 1906.

10. Mary Roberts Smith, "Relief Work in Its Social Bearings," *Charities and the Commons* 16, no. 9 (1906): 311.

11. Edna Larel Calhan, quoted in Patricia Turner, ed., *1906 Remembered* (San Francisco: Friends of the San Francisco Public Library, 1981), 30–31.

12. Commander Bine's review of the kitchens was made on July 19, 1906. Marie Louise Bine Rodriguez, *The Earthquake of 1906* (San Francisco: Privately printed, 1951), 44–45.

13. W. C. Hassler, "Resume of Work of Sanitation Performed by the Board of Health from April 18th, 1906 to Date," August 14, 1906, in *San Francisco Municipal Reports for the Fiscal Years 1905–1906 and 1906–1907* (San Francisco: Neal Publishing, 1908), 519.

14. Major Gaston, "Order re: Dining Service," Rene Bine Papers, California Historical Society, San Franciscso; Rodriguez, *The Earthquake of 1906,* 62–63.

15. Constance Lawrence Dean, "Call Woman Lives for a Week in a Relief Camp," *San Francisco Call,* July 16, 1906.

16. On the social construction of camps, see Katherine R. Jolluck, *Exile and Identity: Polish Women in the Soviet Union during World War II* (Pittsburgh: University of Pittsburgh Press, 2002), 150. See also Valerie J. Matsumoto, "What Was the Impact of Internment on Japanese American Families and Communities?" in *What Did the Internment of Japanese Americans Mean?* ed. Alice Yang Murray (Boston: Bedford/St. Martin's, 2000).

17. H. R. Richmond to Camp Commanders, Memorandum, circa July 1, 1906, Rene Bine Papers, California Historical Society.

18. A total of 488 evictions were recorded by camp commanders between May 1906 and January 1908. Almost half of these were for drunken and/or disorderly conduct and 15 percent for "immorality." O'Connor, "Organizing the Force," 80, table 24.

19. C. M. Wollenberg, letter to James D. Phelan, December 18, 1907, James D. Phelan Papers, Bancroft Library.

20. Paula Baker, "The Domestication of Politics: Women and American Political Society, 1780–1920," *American Historical Review* 89 (1984).

21. Lucile Eaves, quoted in "Women Organize to Aid the Refugees," *San Francisco Examiner,* July 28, 1906.

22. "Leisure Hours for Relief Work: Philanthropic Women Unite to Look after Welfare of Distressed," *San Francisco Chronicle,* July 28, 1906.

23. Eaves, "Women Organize."

24. Other examples of women's professional and volunteer efforts in other cities include Sarah Deutsch, *Women and the City: Gender, Space, and Power in Boston, 1870–1940* (Oxford: Oxford University Press, 2000); and Maureen Flanagan, *Seeing with Their Hearts: Chicago Women and the Vision of the Good City, 1871–1933* (Princeton, NJ: Princeton University Press, 2002).

25. Mabel T. Boardman, *Under the Red Cross Flag at Home and Abroad* (Philadelphia: J. B. Lippincott, 1915), 165.

26. Lucile Eaves, "Industrial Bureau Report," San Francisco Relief and Red Cross Funds, circa 1906, 7.

27. Ibid., 5.

28. Ibid., 17.

29. Nayan Shah argues that San Francisco Chinese identity was forged exclusively by civic leaders and institutions. This more accurately describes the temporary space of the segregated relief camp than pre- or post-disaster Chinatown. Nayan Shah, *Contagious Divides: Epidemics and Race in San Francisco's Chinatown* (Berkeley: University of California Press, 2001). For an interpretation that finds Chinese agency in San Francisco Chinatown's built environment, see Philip P. Choy, "The Architecture of San Francisco Chinatown," *Chinese America: History and Perspectives, 1990* (1990): 37–65; Philip P. Choy, "San Francisco Chinatown's Historic Development," in *The Chinese American Experience: Papers from the Second National Conference on Chinese American Studies*, ed. Genny Lim (San Francisco: Chinese Historical Society of America and Chinese Culture Foundation of San Francisco, 1984).

30. Just a few months before the catastrophe, Phelan was busy printing and distributing the results of Daniel Burnham's new city beautiful design book, with a conspicuously absent Chinatown. The San Francisco Board of Supervisors had argued for the removal of Chinatown as early as 1885. Meeting Citizens' Committee no. 10, April 24, 1906, James D. Phelan Papers, Bancroft Library; Meeting Citizens' Committee no. 11, April 25, 1906, James D. Phelan Papers, Bancroft Library; Daniel Burnham, *Report on a Plan for San Francisco* (San Francisco: Sunset Press, 1905); Choy, "The Architecture of San Francisco Chinatown," 42–45.

31. The 1900 U.S. Census recorded 1,654 African Americans in San Francisco (0.4 percent of the total population). The total number of blacks living in the relief camps was not recorded. Records from one relief camp, discussed in Chapter 5, clearly show the segregation of Chinese, but not black, refugees. Brian J. Godfrey, "Inner-City Neighborhoods in Transition: The Morphogenesis of San Francisco's Ethnic and Nonconformist Communities" (Ph.D. diss., University of California, Berkeley, 1984), 68, table 4.

32. "Chinese Cared For," *San Francisco Chronicle*, April 26, 1906. The story of the Chinese relief camp's multiple moves is discussed by Erica Pan, who primarily relies on newspaper accounts. Erica Y. Z. Pan, *The Impact of the 1906 Earthquake on San Francisco's Chinatown* (New York: Peter Lang, 1995).

33. "Chinese Colony at the Foot of Van Ness," *San Francisco Chronicle*, April 27, 1906.

34. Citizens' Committee Meeting Minutes, no. 13, April 27, 1906, 5, James D. Phelan Papers, Bancroft Library.

35. Abraham Ruef, quoted in Citizens' Committee Meeting Minutes, no. 16, May 1, 1906, James D. Phelan Papers, Bancroft Library, 3.

36. San Francisco Citizens' Committee Meeting, no. 14, April 28, 1906, James D. Phelan Papers, Bancroft Library, 2.

37. "New Chinatown near Fort Point," *San Francisco Chronicle*, April 28, 1906.

38. "Chinese Camp is Picturesque," *San Francisco Call*, May 13, 1906.

39. Secretary Metcalf of Commerce and Labor, telegram to President Roosevelt, April 26, 1906, Citizens Committee Meeting Minutes, no. 14.

40. Louise Herrick Wall, "Heroic San Francisco," *Century Magazine*, August 1906, 203.

41. Captain Chidester, "Chinese Camp Report," April 28, 1906, National Archives, Burlingame, California.

42. Sanitation Report, n.d., Paperless Archives, 30.

43. Sanitation Report, May 22, 1906, Paperless Archives, 42.

44. M. C. Smith, "Camp Construction," April 28, 1906, National Archives.

45. Sanitation Report, May 14, 1906, Paperless Archives, 24.

46. Sanitation Report, May 15, 1906, Paperless Archives, 24.

47. Alice Sue Fun in Judy Yung, *Unbound Voices: A Documentary History of Chinese Women in San Francisco* (Berkeley: University of California Press, 1999), 268.

48. Acting Secretary of War Oliver, telegram to General Funston, April 23, 1906, San Francisco Virtual Museum Archives.

49. Adam McKeown, "Ritualization of Regulation: The Enforcement of Chinese Exclusion in the United States and China," *American Historical Review* 108, no. 2 (2003): 377–403.

50. Oliver, telegram to Funston.

51. In their April 24, 1906, "long and temperate telegram" to President Roosevelt, signed by political, merchant, relief, and charity leaders, the relief committee offered this generalization: "The committees and even the homeless people themselves are treating the Chinese and all other unfortunates with the consideration and kindness worthy of our civilization and of our country." San Francisco Citizen's Committee Meeting Minutes, no. 10, April 24, 1906, James D. Phelan Papers, Bancroft Library, 5; Relief Committee, telegram to President Roosevelt, April 24, 1906, San Francisco Virtual Museum Archives.

52. Approximately 0.1 percent of the relief fund was allocated to Chinese refugees. Because of the few records saved regarding Chinese relief, secretary of the Board of the Trustees of the San Francisco Relief and Red Cross Funds, Charles J. O'Connor, concluded, "Ten thousand dollars is a liberal estimate of the value of relief given to the Chinese." This amounted to only one-quarter of China's $40,000 fund donation. O'Connor, "Organizing the Force," 95.

53. Relief committee leaders were aware that they relied on the Chinese Consul and the CCBA to care for Chinese refugees. When asked about the closing of Oakland's Chinese Camp, General Greely replied, "That is being taken care of by the Chinese minister." Finance Committee Meeting Minutes, June 8, 1906, James D. Phelan Papers, Bancroft Library, 23.

54. Protesting women could simultaneously accept and deny dominant gender ideology. As Joan Scott's analysis of French feminists demonstrates, "On the one hand, they seemed to accept authoritative definitions of gender; on the other hand, they refused these definitions." Joan Wallach Scott, *Only Paradoxes to Offer: French Feminists and the Rights of Man* (Cambridge, MA: Harvard University Press, 1996), xi. See also Faust, *Mothers of Invention*.

55. Thomas A. Krainz, *Delivering Aid: Implementing Progressive Era Welfare in the American West* (Albuquerque: University of New Mexico Press, 2005); Michael Katz, *Poverty and Policy in American History* (New York: Academic Press, 1983).

56. Paul Boyer, *Urban Masses and Moral Order in America, 1820–1920* (Cambridge, MA: Harvard University Press, 1978), 280.

57. See Linda Gordon's discussion of the deserving poor. Linda Gordon, "Putting Children First: Women, Maternalism, and Welfare in the Early Twentieth Century," in *U.S. History as Women's History: New Feminist Essays*, ed. Alice Kessler-Harris, Linda K. Kerber, and Kathryn Kish Sklar (Chapel Hill: University of North Carolina Press, 1995), 71–72. See also landmark studies on poverty and charity in the United States, including Robert H. Bremner, *From the Depths: The Discovery of Poverty in the United States* (New York: New York University Press, 1956); and Walter I. Trattner, *From Poor Law to Welfare State: A History of Social Welfare in America* (New York: Free Press, 1974).

58. *San Francisco Call*, May 12, 1906, cited in Rodriguez, *The Earthquake of 1906*, 21.

59. Rene Bine, memo to campers, n.d., Rene Bine Papers, California Historical Society.

60. Rene Bine, re: Miss K. Sheehan, Rene Bine Papers, California Historical Society.

61. Rene Bine, re: Mrs. Allie Bailey, Rene Bine Papers, California Historical Society.

62. Emily Kirkwood, letter to Dr. Rene Bine, September 26, 1906, Rene Bine Papers, California Historical Society.

63. Emily Kraus, letter to Dr. Rene Bine, n.d., Rene Bine Papers, California Historical Society.

64. Agness Menzer, letter to James D. Phelan, September 17, 1907, James D. Phelan Papers, Bancroft Library.

65. Miss A. L. Pascoe, letter to chief of police, Rene Bine Papers, California Historical Society.

66. Rene Bine, re: Miss Ida Boyne, August 17, 1906, Rene Bine Papers, California Historical Society.

67. See Linda Gordon, *Heroes of Their Own Lives: The Politics and History of Family Violence* (London: Virago, 1989).

68. "Refugee Forces Her Admittance," *San Francisco Chronicle*, December 8, 1906.

69. Rene Bine, November 2, 1906, Rene Bine Papers, California Historical Society.

70. *Daily News*, August 30, 1906.

71. Rene Bine, November 2, 1906.

72. Rene Bine, unpublished letter to the editor, in Rodriguez, *The Earthquake of 1906*, 96–97.

73. Mrs. Johanna Dohrman, letter to Rudolph Spreckels, October 31, 1906, Rene Bine Papers, California Historical Society.

74. Refugee sentiment paraphrased by Rene Bine, Rene Bine Papers, California Historical Society.

75. Rene Bine, re: Mrs. M. Hefferman, Rene Bine Papers, California Historical Society.

76. "Fears Refugees Will Kill Her," *San Francisco Chronicle*, August 5, 1906.

77. Rodriguez, *The Earthquake of 1906*, 49.

78. Refugees and city residents referred to the cottages by many names: refugee shacks, houses or cabins; earthquake cottages or memorials; camp cottages; wooden shanties; and relief houses or cottages. For a local historian's account of the earthquake cottages, see Jane Cryan, "Hope Chest: The True Story of San Francisco's 1906 Earthquake Refugee Shacks" (unpublished manuscript, San Francisco, 1998).

79. Camp admission statements for 1,156 refugees show 76.7 percent single, 12.5 percent married, 10.8 percent unknown. Relief Committee and Associated Charities case records for 961 Ingleside refugees indicate 90 percent single and 10 percent married. Men and women were listed at a 1.6 to 1 ratio. *San Francisco Relief Survey*, 336, 328–329, tables 113 and 119.

80. These refugees were older—92 percent of Ingleside's refugees were over the age of 40 and 62 percent were over the age of 60—and deemed incapable of self-support. At 24 percent, Irish refugees represented the largest single ethnic group. Mary Roberts Coolidge, "The Residuum of Relief," in *San Francisco Relief Survey*, 331–334, table 331.

81. Mary Kelly, *Shame of the Relief* (1908), 11.

82. Coolidge, "The Residuum of Relief," 324.

83. The barracks at the "Speedway Camp" in Golden Gate Park were reserved for "convalescent and enfeebled people." According to Major Greely, "It appears preferable to have *single individuals* and *not families* thus cared for." Major General A. W. Greely to J. A. Gaston, Commander of Permanent Camps, Memorandum, June 12, 1906, Rene Bine Papers, California Historical Society.

84. In the official camp records, seventy refugees were ejected from Ingleside, more than half of the ejections attributed to drunkenness. Coolidge, "The Residuum of Relief," 325.

85. Ibid., 326.

86. Ibid.

87. Ibid., 323.

88. Ibid., 348.

89. Nelly [Eleanor] Joliffe Spreckels, letter to James Phelan, August 4, 1907, James D. Phelan Papers, Bancroft Library.

90. Coolidge, "The Residuum of Relief," 365.

91. Anna Pratt Simpson, "Story of the Associated Charities since the Fire of 1906" (San Francisco: Associated Charities of San Francisco, 1906), 10.

92. James M. Motley, "Housing Rehabilitation," in *San Francisco Relief Survey*, 224, table 66.

93. Cryan, "Hope Chest," 38.

94. "Rules Adopted by the Board of Election Commissioners May 24th, 1906, in Relation to Determination as to Legal Residence of Voters," in *San Francisco Municipal Reports, 1905–1906 and 1906–1907*, 413.

95. George P. Adams, "Department of Elections' Report," June 30, 1906, in *San Francisco Municipal Reports, 1905–1906 and 1906–1907*.

96. "Department of Elections' Report," June 30, 1907, in *San Francisco Municipal Reports, 1905–1906 and 1906–1907*.

97. Captain James Bowen, letter to his mother, June 14, 1906, San Francisco Earthquake and Fire Collection, San Francisco Public Library.

98. For analysis of gender and housing in American history, see Dolores Hayden, *The Grand Domestic Revolution: A History of Feminist Designs for American Homes, Neighborhoods, and Cities* (Cambridge, MA: MIT Press, 1981); Dolores Hayden, *Redesigning the American Dream: Gender, Housing, and Family Life* (New York: W. W. Norton, 2002); and Gwendolyn Wright, *Building the Dream: A Social History of Housing in America* (New York: Pantheon Books, 1981).

99. Chicago Relief and Aid Society, "Special Report," quoted in Karen Sawislak, *Smoldering City: Chicagoans and the Great Fire, 1871–1874* (Chicago: University of Chicago Press, 1995), 94. The restoration of post-disaster homeownership was, as Sawislak concludes, an "essential part of the construction and maintenance of a republican citizenry." Sawislak, *Smoldering City*, 95.

100. Elizabeth Brown Pryor, *Clara Barton: Professional Angel* (Philadelphia: University of Pennsylvania Press, 1987), 260.

101. Cortlandt Whitehead, letter to Clara Barton, December 11, 1889, quoted in ibid., 263.

102. O'Connor, "Organizing the Force," 70.

103. A survey of 680 cottage families found 28 percent of the cottages allotted to widows. *San Francisco Relief Survey*.

104. Ibid., 16.

105. Ibid.

106. Mary E. Hart, letter to James Phelan, October 20, 1907, James D. Phelan Papers, Bancroft Library.

107. Katharine Felton, letter to Mary E. Hart, October 8, 1907, James D. Phelan Papers, Bancroft Library.

108. Of a total of 5,610 cottages built, 5,343 were moved and became the permanent homes of the owners. Motley, "Housing Rehabilitation," 222.

109. Katharine Felton, "Work of the Associated Charities in Connection with the Clearing of the Camps and the Permanent Housing of the Refugees," in *The Associated Charities of San Francisco: Annual Reports, 1904–1910*, 46.

110. Ibid., 45.

111. Simpson, "Story of the Associated Charities," 18.

112. Ibid.

113. Sarah Brastow, letter to James D. Phelan, April 20, 1907, James D. Phelan Papers, Bancroft Library.

114. Sarah Brastow, letter to James D. Phelan, n.d., James D. Phelan Papers, Bancroft Library.

115. The shacks came in three sizes: Type A, 10′ × 14′; Type B, 14′ × 18′; Type C, 15′ × 25′ and 16′ × 18′. Type B was the most common shack, although the larger Type C could be divided into three rooms.

116. "San Francisco Relief and Red Cross Funds Camp Notice," Rene Bine Papers, California Historical Society.

117. Alva Udell, "Refugees and Comrades Pay No Rent to the Red Cross," broadside, San Francisco Virtual Museum Archives.

118. Kelly, Shame of the Relief, 8–9.

119. According to one news account, she "had locks attached and . . . posted notices on each one of the houses to the effect that they were reserved for certain refugees and warning all others from trespassing." "Mrs. Mary Kelly Takes Possession of Cottages," San Francisco Chronicle, November 2, 1906.

120. Kelly, Shame of the Relief, 3, 7, 10–11.

121. "Mary Kelly's Home Is Placed on Hay Wagon," San Francisco Chronicle, November 4, 1906.

122. "Mary Kelly Refuses to Move," San Francisco Call, November 3, 1906.

123. Mary Kelly's eviction notice, Rene Bine Papers, California Historical Society; O'Connor, "Organizing the Force," 80, table 23.

124. "Mary Kelly Refuses to Move."

125. "Mary Kelly's Home Is Placed on Hay Wagon."

126. Kelly, Shame of the Relief, 11.

127. "Eject Woman and House from Square," San Francisco Examiner, November 4, 1906.

128. "Mrs. Kelly's House Is Her Fort," San Francisco Call, November 5, 1906.

129. "Mrs. Kelly Still Holds the Fort," San Francisco Chronicle, November 6, 1906.

130. "Mrs. Kelly's House Is Her Fort."

131. Ibid.

132. Ibid.

133. Shame of the Relief, 11; "Mrs. Kelly's Home Torn to Pieces," San Francisco Call, November 7, 1906.

134. "An Appreciation of Mary Kelly," San Francisco Call, November 7, 1906.

135. "Mayor Signs Ordinance Which Stops Relief Corporation from Collecting Rents from Refugees," San Francisco Examiner, December 23, 1906.

136. "Mrs. Kelly's House Is Her Fort."

137. "Mrs. Kelly Is Registered," San Francisco Chronicle, October 18, 1911.

138. Gordon, "Family Violence"; Gordon, Heroes of Their Own Lives.

139. Faust, Mothers of Invention, 243.

CHAPTER 5

1. Insurance payments had a similar impact after the Great Chicago Fire in 1871. See Karen Sawislak, Smoldering City: Chicagoans and the Great Fire, 1871–1874 (Chicago: University of Chicago Press, 1995).

2. The fire insurance payments ranged from less than $500 to $20,000. In addition to insurance payments, 72 percent of the applicants obtained loans from either banks or relatives and friends. The additional property owned by grant recipients was valued

at an average of $4,000 to $7,500. Philip Fradkin estimates between $220 and $250 in insurance payments. James M. Motley, "Housing Rehabilitation," in Russell Sage Foundation, ed., *San Francisco Relief Survey* (New York: Survey Associates, 1913), 246; Philip L. Fradkin, *The Great Earthquake and Firestorms of 1906: How San Francisco Nearly Destroyed Itself* (Berkeley: University of California Press, 2005), 234–235.

3. Civic and business leaders celebrated when the population reached its pre-disaster count in 1909 with the Portolá Festival in October 1909. See William Issel and Robert W. Cherny, *San Francisco, 1865–1932: Politics, Power, and Urban Development* (Berkeley: University of California Press, 1986), 39.

4. Integrated Public Use Microdata Series (hereafter IPUMS), U.S. Census, 1910.

5. Kevin Rozario, *The Culture of Calamity: Disaster and the Making of Modern America* (Chicago: University of Chicago Press, 2007), 87, 96.

6. Issel and Cherny, *San Francisco*, 78.

7. William H. Wilson, *The City Beautiful Movement* (Baltimore: Johns Hopkins University Press, 1989), 86. See also Peter Geoffrey Hall, *Cities of Tomorrow: An Intellectual History of Urban Planning and Design in the Twentieth Century* (Oxford, UK: Blackwell Publishers, 1996); Giorgio Ciucci and Barbara Luigia La Penta, *The American City: From the Civil War to the New Deal* (London: Granada, 1980).

8. As historian Gayle Gullett explains, "The women achieved a place in the civic arena as people who worked altruistically for the public good." California Outdoor Art League, form letter, October 20, 1902, and California Outdoor Art League, leaflet, August 12, 1902, quoted in Gayle Gullett, *Becoming Citizens: The Emergence and Development of the California Women's Movement, 1880–1911* (Urbana: University of Illinois Press, 2000), 134, 137.

9. According to Burnham, "the beauty of its arrangement and its buildings made a profound impression not merely upon the educated part of the community, but still more perhaps upon the masses." Burnham designed plans for Washington, D.C., in 1901 and Cleveland in 1902 before beginning work in San Francisco in 1904. Daniel H. Burnham, quoted in Judd Kahn, *Imperial San Francisco: Politics and Planning in an American City, 1897–1906* (Lincoln: University of Nebraska Press, 1979), 73. See also Wilson, *The City Beautiful Movement*.

10. For a brief, detailed comparison to Baron Haussmann's rebuilding of Paris, see Kevin Rozario, *The Culture of Calamity*, 89–90, 92–94.

11. Kahn, *Imperial San Francisco*, 87–88. See also Daniel Burnham, *Report on a Plan for San Francisco* (San Francisco: Sunset Press, 1905).

12. Pierre N. Beringer, "The Destruction of San Francisco," *Overland Monthly*, May 1906, 398.

13. "Her Spirit Still Is Undaunted," *Portland Oregonian*, April 24, 1906.

14. James D. Phelan, letter to Thomas M. Caleb, April 30, 1906, James D. Phelan Papers, Bancroft Library, University of California, Berkeley.

15. James D. Phelan, letter to Daniel H. Burnham, May 2, 1906, James D. Phelan Papers, Bancroft Library.

16. James D. Phelan, letter to Clinton Rogers Woodruf, June 19, 1906, James D. Phelan Papers, Bancroft Library.

17. James D. Phelan, "Report in Relation to the Burnham Plan," May 28, 1906, *San Francisco Municipal Reports for the Fiscal Years 1905–1906 and 1906–1907* (San Francisco: Neal Publishing, 1908), 796.

18. Marsden Manson, *Report of Marsden Manson to the Mayor and Committee on Reconstruction* (San Francisco, 1906).

19. James D. Phelan, n.d., James D. Phelan Papers, Bancroft Library.

20. As historian Kevin Rozario concludes, the Burnham plans fell short in large part because of the reformers' contradictory goals. Their commitment to beautification and economic expansion "inevitably undermined their efforts to control the urban

environment." In other words, Burnham's imperial city (their first beautification goal) created an impediment to persistent commercial development (their second economic expansion goal). Rozario, *The Culture of Calamity*, 91.

21. Kahn, *Imperial San Francisco*, 168, 184.

22. Ibid., 189–191.

23. Christine Misner Rosen, *The Limits of Power: Great Fires and the Process of City Growth in America* (Cambridge: Cambridge University Press, 1986), 249–295.

24. Laura Lyon White, letter to city engineer, August 6, 1906, San Francisco Earthquake and Fire Collection, San Francisco Public Library.

25. "Today—and This Day a Year Ago," *San Francisco Call*, April 18, 1907.

26. James D. Phelan, n.d., James D. Phelan Papers, Bancroft Library.

27. The Schmitz conviction was invalidated by the district court of appeals on January 9, 1908, while Ruef served his sentence in San Quentin. See Walton Bean, *Boss Ruef's San Francisco* (Berkeley: University of California Press, 1952).

28. "Labor Leaders on New Board," *San Francisco Chronicle*, July 27, 1907.

29. Edward Robeson Taylor, quoted in Gullett, *Becoming Citizens*, 154.

30. Ibid., 155. Middle-class women had been making a bid for participation in the political realm since the late nineteenth century. The women's suffrage amendment had already been voted down in 1896, losing Mayor Phelan's endorsement as well as the working-class immigrant vote. Phelan opposed suffrage because it violated the divinely ordained social order: "They [women] should not appeal for the ballot to right fancied wrongs; they should appeal to men for even greater consideration." James D. Phelan, "Has Woman a Vocation Outside the Home?" February 12, 1894, cited in Philip J. Ethington, *The Public City: The Political Construction of Urban Life in San Francisco, 1850–1900* (New York: Cambridge University Press, 1994), 385. Historian Michael Kazin argues that "the misgoverning of San Francisco" typified the period between 1908 and 1911. Michael Kazin, *Barons of Labor: The San Francisco Building Trades and Union Power in the Progressive Era* (Urbana: University of Illinois Press, 1987), 177.

31. As one historian concludes, McCarthy failed because of his attempt to "return to the practices of the era before the fire when gambling, prostitution, and other rackets had flourished virtually without hindrance." Oscar Lewis, *San Francisco: Mission to Metropolis* (San Diego: Howell-North Books, 1966), 213.

32. Rolph pledged to end patronage, improve civil service, and expand the municipal ownership of utilities. He also allowed unions to organize by adhering to a policy of noninterference in labor disputes. Issel and Cherny, *San Francisco*, 162. See also Carole Hicke, "The 1911 Campaign of James Rolph Jr., Mayor of All the People" (master's thesis, San Francisco State University, 1978).

33. "Headquarters Mission Relief District," LearnCalifornia.org, http://www.learncalifornia.org/GoDocUserFiles/2660.hq-mission-relief-dist.jpg (accessed May 22, 2009).

34. Issel and Cherny, *San Francisco*, 166.

35. Lewis, *San Francisco*, 214.

36. See Issel and Cherny, *San Francisco*, 166.

37. Quoted in ibid., 172.

38. Citizens' Committee Meeting Minutes, no. 14, April 28, 1906, James D. Phelan Papers, Bancroft Library, 4; Citizens Committee Meeting Minutes, no.13, April 27, 1906, James D. Phelan Papers, Bancroft Library, 3.

39. Citizens' Committee Meeting Minutes, no. 14, 5.

40. Lewis, *San Francisco*, 202.

41. For more on Chicago's fire limit debate, see Sawislak, *Smoldering City*; Rosen, *The Limits of Power*; and Carl Smith, *Urban Disorder and the Shape of Belief: The Great Chicago Fire, the Haymarket Bomb, and the Model Town of Pullman* (Chicago: University of Chicago Press, 1995).

42. *San Francisco Bulletin*, June 7, 1906, quoted in Kahn, *Imperial San Francisco*, 193.

43. Garrett W. McEnerney, "The Title and Document Restoration vs. Frank H. Kerrigan" (San Francisco: Pernau Publishing, 1906), 159.

44. "The Necessary McEnerney Act," *San Francisco Merchants' Association Review*, December 1906, 12.

45. The owner was required to file an affidavit enumerating the person from whom the property was purchased, the pre-disaster condition and use of the property, mortgages against the property, and a list of names of any individuals who might also make a claim to the parcel. After the filing of the affidavit, the courts served summons to anyone known to have a claim on the property and the summons was published weekly for a period of two months in a local newspaper. Angelo J. Rossi, letter to Dean Achison, May 5, 1941, San Francisco Earthquake and Fire Collection, San Francisco Public Library; *San Francisco Municipal Reports for the Fiscal Year 1907–1908* (San Francisco: Neal Publishing, 1909), 189.

46. The city compensated for the property losses by charging $509,220 in back taxes. "Actions to Obtain Decree Quieting Title against City and County of San Francisco in lieu of a City Deed," *San Francisco Municipal Reports, 1907–1908*.

47. Rosen, *The Limits of Power*, 293, 307.

48. The city ultimately prevailed, keeping the disputed nine inches of land. *San Francisco Municipal Reports, 1907–1908*, 189.

49. Insurance was primarily provided by U.S.-based companies but included international companies in England, Germany, Sweden, Scotland, Canada, and Austria. *Report of the Special Committee of the Board of Trustees of the Chamber of Commerce of San Francisco on Insurance Settlements Incident to the San Francisco Fire* (San Francisco: San Francisco Chamber of Commerce, 1906), 14.

50. By May 31, 1906, the major insurance companies agreed on the following terms: first, any building that fell during the earthquake would not be insured; second, policies on buildings destroyed by the authorities subsequent to the conflagration would not be honored "until the facts have been definitely ascertained"; third, in cases where buildings were probably damaged during the earthquake and fire suppression, and where the owners had lost their proof of insurance, such "claims should be settled by a reasonable compromise"; fourth, all insurance coverage for building contents must be adjusted for salvage. Ibid., 16.

51. Many insurance companies settled at 75 percent, with some negotiating settlements as low as 40 percent. The greatest losses for policyholders were among those paying premiums to the German companies, where four companies defaulted on total of $16 million in insurance policies. Albert W. Whitney, "On Insurance Settlements Incident to the 1906 San Francisco Fire" (Pasadena: Center for Research on the Prevention of Natural Disasters, 1973) 45–51.

52. "Situation," Atlas Assurance Company Manager, August 3, 1906, Atlas Insurance Company Records, Bancroft Library, 1.

53. *Report of the Special Committee of the Board of Trustees of the Chamber of Commerce of San Francisco on Insurance Settlements*, 28.

54. Zoeth S. Eldredge, "Letter from the President," National Bank of the Pacific at San Francisco, November 15, 1906, Bancroft Library, 2.

55. Debris was dumped into the bay near North Beach as well as south of the Ferry Building. See Oscar Lewis's account of reconstruction for additional detail. Lewis, *San Francisco*, 200–203.

56. Ibid., 200.

57. Gray Brechin argues that elite interest in San Francisco water rights were similar to the watering of Los Angeles. For an account of the economic and political factors

behind San Francisco water, see Gray Brechin, *Imperial San Francisco: Urban Power, Earthly Ruin* (Berkeley: University of California Press, 1999); *Public Work of San Francisco since 1906: Supplement to Municipal Reports 1908–9* (San Francisco, 1909).

58. During 1909, 1,866,577 square feet of asphalt pavement was added to the city, with asphalt provided by a newly purchased municipally owned asphalt plant. *Public Work of San Francisco since 1906.*

59. Lilas Mugg in Patricia Turner, ed., *1906 Remembered* (San Francisco: Friends of the San Francisco Public Library, 1981), 41.

60. *Organized Labor*, April 21, 28, and May 5, 1906 (Combined edition), San Francisco Virtual Museum Archives.

61. Union membership rose to a record high of 65,000 in 1907, before dropping to 50,000 in 1909 as a result of a nationwide business slump and the tapering off of reconstruction. Kazin, *Barons of Labor*, 124, 178. According to historian Oscar Lewis, these earnings were comparable to those paid during the gold rush. Lewis, *San Francisco*, 201.

62. City Engineer Woodward received letters from men living in small towns and cities in at least fifteen states, with one request mailed from New Zealand. Woodward Papers, San Francisco Earthquake and Fire Collection, San Francisco Public Library, San Francisco.

63. "Executive Commission Meeting Minutes," July 18, 1906, James D. Phelan Papers, Bancroft Library.

64. Walter Harman, in Turner, *1906 Remembered*, 50.

65. Rene Bine, re: Mrs. Mary Murphy, Rene Bine Papers, San Francisco Historical Society.

66. Rene Bine, re: Mrs. Heffernan, Rene Bine Papers, San Francisco Historical Society.

67. Rene Bine, re: Mrs. Schwartz, Rene Bine Papers, San Francisco Historical Society.

68. Because McAllister's two sons sent her rent money whenever they were employed, the Associated Charities contributed only small amounts of aid during a four-year period after the disaster. C. A. Clivio, June 3, 1912, Associated Charities Case No. 714, San Francisco Labor Papers, Bancroft Library, University of California, Berkeley.

69. Kenneth T. Jackson, *Crabgrass Frontier: The Suburbanization of the United States* (New York: Oxford University Press, 1985), 115. See also Robert Fishman, *Bourgeois Utopias: The Rise and Fall of Suburbia* (New York: Basic Books, 1987); Sam Bass Warner, Jr., *Streetcar Suburbs: The Process of Growth in Boston, 1870–1900* (Cambridge, MA: Harvard University Press, 1978); Jon Teaford, *City and Suburb: The Political Fragmentation of Metropolitan America, 1850–1970* (Baltimore: Johns Hopkins University Press, 1979); and Jon Teaford, *The Twentieth-Century American City* (Baltimore: Johns Hopkins University Press, 1986). Jon Teaford offers a new review of American suburbs in *The American Suburb: The Basics* (New York: Routledge, 2008).

70. J. Eugene Haas, Robert W. Kates, and Martyn J. Bowden, eds., *Reconstruction following Disaster* (Cambridge, MA: MIT Press, 1977), 75; Brian J. Godfrey, "Urban Development and Redevelopment in San Francisco," *Geographical Review* 87, no. 3 (July 1997): 309–333.

71. In 1905, 45 percent of the population lived inside the boundaries of the disaster zone. Haas, Kates, and Bowden, *Reconstruction following Disaster*, 73, 95–96.

72. "Examples of Architectural Beauty and Structure," *San Francisco Chronicle*, April 18, 1909.

73. After one-third of the destroyed housing had been replaced during this period, rebuilding continued at a reduced but steady rate until 1911, when the city's

pre-disaster housing capacity was attained. Haas, Kates, and Bowden, *Reconstruction following Disaster*, 73.

74. Ibid., 82, 95–96.

75. "Lafayette Square District Committee," April 30, 1906, Bancroft Library, 3.

76. African Americans were not subject to segregation in the relief camps. Perhaps the low number of black refugees made segregation an unrealistic endeavor for relief officials. The typed camp directory excluded Asian refugees, and according to a handwritten notation on its cover, a separate directory for Asians was "as yet not reduced to typewritten form." "Directory of Camp Lafayette," May 1, 1906, Bancroft Library.

77. This is based on a search of city directories from 1908, 1910, and 1915.

78. Richard Harris, "American Suburbs: A Sketch of a New Interpretation," *Journal of Urban History* 15, no. 1 (1988): 100.

79. After the calamity, the financial district spread into adjacent blocks and residents increasingly represented the professional/white collar workforce. Two additional neighborhoods struck by the calamity, North Beach and the Mission, housed roughly the same number of working-class residents in 1900 and 1910.

80. Brian J. Godfrey, *Neighborhoods in Transition: The Making of San Francisco's Nonconformist Communities* (Berkeley: University of California Press, 1988), 66.

81. Edmund Cavagnaro, quoted in Michael Svanevik and Shirley Burgett, "La Peninsula," *Journal of the San Mateo County Historical Society* 19, no. 2 (1979): 8.

82. Patricia Hatfield, interview with author, October 2003.

83. Harris, "American Suburbs," 100. Michael Ebner also traces how economic factors, such as the relocation of industry outside the city center, encouraged the relocation of workers. Michael H. Ebner, "Re-reading Suburban America: Urban Population Decentralization, 1810–1980," *American Quarterly* 37, no. 3 (1985): 368–381. For an account of working-class suburbanization, see Harris, *Unplanned Suburbs: Toronto's American Tragedy, 1900–1950* (Baltimore: Johns Hopkins University Press, 1996).

84. These changes are statistically significant at $p < 0.01$ and $p < 0.001$, respectively.

85. This change is statistically significant at $p < 0.05$.

86. Cleveland Elementary School, letter to Mayor P. H. McCarthy, September 18, 1910, reprinted in *SFGate*, January 11, 2011.

87. Brian J. Godfrey, "Inner City Neighborhoods in Transition: The Morphogenesis of San Francisco's Ethnic and Nonconformist Communities" (Ph.D. diss., University of California, Berkeley, 1984), 71.

88. Commerce Secretary Victor Metcalf, *Message from the President of the United States, Japanese in the City of San Francisco Cal.*, Senate Document No. 147, December 18, 1907, quoted in Fradkin, *The Great Earthquake*, 299.

89. The resolution required that all Asian students attend the rebuilt Oriental Public School within four days. See Ronald Takaki, *Strangers from a Distant Shore: A History of Asian Americans* (New York: Penguin, 1990); Fradkin, *The Great Earthquake*, 300. For more on post-1906 Chinatown, see Yong Chen, *Chinese San Francisco, 1850–1943: A Trans-Pacific Community* (Stanford, CA: Stanford University Press, 2000); Judy Yung, *Unbound Feet: A Social History of Chinese Women in San Francisco* (Berkeley: University of California Press, 1995).

90. Fradkin, *The Great Earthquake*, 303.

91. Richard Walker, "Industry Builds Out the City: The Suburban Manufacturing in the San Francisco Bay Area, 1850–1940," in *Manufacturing Suburbs: Building Work and Home on the Metropolitan Fringe*, ed. Robert Lewis (Philadelphia: Temple University Press, 2004, 92. Walker challenges the suburbanization periodization set by

Kenneth Jackson and others. See Richard Walker and Robert D. Lewis, "Beyond the Crabgrass Frontier: Industry and the Spread of North American Cities, 1850–1950," *Journal of Historical Geography* 27, no. 1 (2001): 3–19.

92. Godfrey, *Neighborhoods in Transition*, 66.

93. *Chung Sai Yat Po*, n.d., translated and quoted in Erica Y. Z. Pan, *The Impact of the 1906 Earthquake on San Francisco's Chinatown* (New York: Peter Lang, 1995), 90.

94. The immigration officials believed that the number of Chinese claiming birth in San Francisco meant that 500 to 800 male children would have been born for every Chinese woman living in the city before the disaster. McKeown's calculations of native-born citizens traveling to China between 1907 and 1924 show a minimum of six male children for every Chinese woman resident in pre-disaster San Francisco. Adam McKeown, "Ritualization of Regulation: The Enforcement of Chinese Exclusion in the United States and China," *American Historical Review* 108, no. 2 (2003): 377–403, 393. Historian Judy Yung discusses the personal and collective impact of falsifying immigration documentation in Judy Yung, "The Fake and the True: Researching Chinese Women's Immigration History." *Chinese America: Historical Perspectives*, 1998 (1998): 25–50. For more on paper sons, see Erika Lee, *At America's Gates: Chinese Immigration during the Exclusion Era, 1882–1943* (Chapel Hill: University of North Carolina Press, 2003).

95. Hay Ming Lee, quoted in Victor G. Nee and Bret de Bary Nee, *Longtime Californ': A Documentary Study of an American Chinatown* (Stanford, CA: Stanford University Press, 1972), 63.

96. This change is statistically significant at $p < 0.001$.

97. Lee, *At America's Gates*.

98. "Chinese Relocation," *The Pacific* (1906): 2.

99. *Chung Sai Yat Po*, May 3, 1906, translated and quoted in ibid., 91.

100. *Chung Sai Yat Po*, February 8, 1907, translated and quoted in Pan, *The Impact of the 1906 Earthquake*, 93.

101. Pan, *The Impact of the 1906 Earthquake*, 101.

102. L. Eve Armentrout Ma, *Hometown Chinatown: The History of Oakland's Chinese Community* (New York: Garland Publishing, 2000), 69.

103. Shah, *Contagious Divides: Epidemics and Race in San Francisco's Chinatown* (Berkeley: University of California Press, 2001), 152.

104. "The Chinese Question," *San Francisco Newsletter*, August 4, 1906.

105. Shah, *Contagious Divides*, 152–153.

106. "Starts a Movement for an Artistic Chinatown," *San Francisco Merchants' Association Review*, November 1906, 3.

107. Philip P. Choy, "The Architecture of San Francisco Chinatown," *Chinese America: History and Perspectives*, 1990 (1990): 42.

108. Linda McDowell, *Gender, Identity and Place: Understanding Feminist Geographies* (Minneapolis: University of Minnesota Press, 1999), 4.

109. Chamber of Commerce, *Report of the Los Angeles Chamber of Commerce Citizens' Relief Committee* (Los Angeles, 1908), 8–9.

110. "Thousands Seek Refuge in Marin," *San Francisco Bulletin*, April 21, 1906, 3.

111. G. H. Marx, "Citizens of Palo Alto," Proclamation, April 23, 1906, in Linda Dick, *Palo Alto 1906* (Cupertino: California History Center, 1979), 24.

112. In one of the Committee of 50's first discussions, the group estimated that Berkeley could care for 6,000 refugees, Alameda 3,000–4,000, Stockton 1,000, and Fresno 1,500. San Francisco Citizens' Committee Meeting Minutes, No. 6, April 21, 1906, James D. Phelan Papers, Bancroft Library.

113. Phelan's statements were paraphrased in the meeting minutes. San Francisco Citizen's Committee, No. 6, April 21, 1906, James D. Phelan Papers, Bancroft Library, 3.

114. San Francisco Citizen's Committee, No. 11, April 25, 1906, James D. Phelan Papers, Bancroft Library, 4. Prior to the disaster, transbay ferries facilitated the daily commute of "a sizable group living in the East Bay and working in San Francisco." In 1873, for example, 2,655,671 ferry passengers made the trip between Oakland and San Francisco. James E. Vance, *Geography and Urban Evolution in the San Francisco Bay Area* (Berkeley: Institute for Government Studies, 1964), 45.

115. According to Mel Scott, a "San Francisco-Oakland axis in the Bay Area" was established in the 1870s, when Oakland gained the major railroad terminus. Mel Scott, *The San Francisco Bay Area: A Metropolis in Perspective* (Berkeley: University of California Press, 1959), 67.

116. "God Bless Oakland," *San Francisco Call*, reprinted in the *Oakland Enquirer*, April 28, 1906.

117. During the first week after the disaster, free transit from the Southern Pacific Railroad made Oakland the hub of refugee transport. Southern Pacific officials reported that most refugees went by ferry to Oakland, departing San Francisco at a rate of 70 per minute the first day after the disaster. From April 18 through April 26, the Southern Pacific Railroad offered free transport to 300,684 refugees. An undetermined number of these people, however, made daily trips to San Francisco. *San Francisco Relief Survey*, 58–59, table 12.

118. Dr. N. K. Foster, quoted in "Relief Camps Will Be Concentrated," *Oakland Tribune*, April 29, 1906. Major General A. W. Greely, the Presidio commander in charge of San Francisco's relief camps, commanded the relief effort in Oakland. James B. Erwin, "Work of the Military," in Harris Bishop, *Souvenir and Resume of Oakland Relief of Oakland Relief Work to San Francisco Refugees* (Oakland: Finance Committee, circa 1906), 9, 12.

119. Evarts I. Blake, *Greater Oakland* (Oakland: Pacific Publishing, 1911).

120. Oakland had waged a court battle to regain control of its own waterfront from private interests since 1852. *City of Oakland v. Oakland Waterfront Co.*, cited in Beth Bagwell, *Oakland: The Story of a City* (Novato, CA: Presidio Press, 1982), 187, 193.

121. "Sheriff Takes Precautions," *Marin Journal*, April 18, 1906.

122. William W. Morrow, *The Earthquake of April 18, 1906, and the Great Fire in San Francisco on That and Succeeding Days, Personal Experiences* (San Francisco, circa 1906), 13–15. As in San Francisco, women's volunteerism was critical to the town's relief program. The "Ladies of San Rafael" extended their hospitality to refugees by creating their own relief committee and fundraising by publishing their home recipes in the *San Rafael Cook Book 1906*. Some of the women who contributed recipes also donated their time to disaster relief. Mrs. L. A. Lancel, for example, was a member of the Ladies Relief Committee in San Rafael as well as secretary of the new Red Cross chapter that was organized after the disaster. Lancel administered the distribution of clothing and food from the headquarters. Inside the camp, the Sisters of St. Dominics ran an emergency hospital tent to nurse the sick. Ladies of San Rafael, ed., *San Rafael Cook Book 1906* (San Rafael: First Presbyterian Church, 1906); "Relief Work at San Rafael," *San Francisco Chronicle*, April 29, 1906.

123. Jackson defines railroad suburbs as places where 30 percent to 50 percent of heads of households traveled a minimum of five miles to work "and whose families were devoted to the pursuit of culture and recreation in the company of equals." Jackson, *Crabgrass Frontier*, 97, 99.

124. "Speed and Comfort," *San Francisco Newsletter*, July 14, 1906. The article in this newspaper, which frequently ran ads for Hotel Rafael, reported, "The citizen of San Francisco who has elected residence at the Hotel Rafael for the summer has found it so agreeable that the stay will be lengthened far into the fall months."

125. Helen de Young, *Nineteen Nineteen: The Story of the de Young House at 1919 California Street San Francisco* (Unknown binding), 32.

126. Ibid.

127. Eleanor Warner Rawlings, letter to Stuart Rawlings, April 22, 1906, reprinted in "'Mamma's' Earthquake Letter," *Mill Valley Historical Review* (Spring 1991): 2.

128. "Good Work of the Sausalito Board of Health," *Sausalito News*, April 28, 1906; "Saloons in Sausalito Must Remain Closed," notice in *Sausalito News*, April 28, 1906; Phil Frank, "Witness to Disaster," *Moments in Time: Sausalito Historical Society Newsletter* (Spring 2002): 2.

129. *Sausalito News*, April 28, 1906.

130. "Relief Committees Doing Great Work," *Berkeley Reporter*, April 20, 1906.

131. At least 10,250 refugees were registered in Berkeley, 2,000 of which were Chinese and Japanese refugees from San Francisco. "The Work Berkeley Has Done," *Berkeley Daily Gazette*, April 26, 1906.

132. A total of 5,584 refugees were accounted for in 1,137 homes by the second housing card survey. Conservative estimates counted 570 refugees that were originally housed by Berkeley volunteers, bringing the total number of privately housed refugees to 6,154. Records of the total number of refugees in Berkeley did not survive. The *Berkeley Daily Gazette* estimated 8,250 non-Asian refugees in Berkeley on April 26. Calculated from Berkeley Relief Committee Housing Cards, Berkeley Relief Committee Records, Bancroft Library, University of California, Berkeley; "The Work Berkeley Has Done."

133. John Dundas Fletcher, "An Account of the Work of Relief Organized in Berkeley in April and May, 1906, for the Refugees from San Francisco" (unpublished study, University of California, Berkeley, 1909), 36. Records confirming the formation of an Italian Camp do not exist. BRC workers made note of Italian refugees. One BRC investigator described one refugee as "Italian wants blanket but does not want to work." Mrs. Weiss, 2311 Haste, May 11, 1906, Berkeley Relief Committee Records, Bancroft Library.

134. Tents were provided to house three hundred to four hundred Chinese refugees, but on May 3 there were only thirty occupants. On May 22, the Chinese Camp was closed, and the twenty-two remaining refugees were moved to Oakland. Fletcher, "An Account of the Work of Relief," 9.

135. A total of 1,396 households were recorded by the Berkeley Relief Committee, 49 percent (678) listed female occupants, almost all of whom were married. In the second survey, of 1,137 residences, less than 1 percent (41) charged refugees for room and/or board. Calculated by author from the Berkeley Relief Committee Housing Cards, Berkeley Relief Committee Records, Bancroft Library.

136. Mrs. Puter, 1517 Spruce Street, Berkeley Relief Committee Records, Bancroft Library; Mrs. M. E. Delong, 2645 Benvenue Avenue, Berkeley Relief Committee Records, Bancroft Library.

137. The committee printed up information cards on which volunteers could specify the number and gender of refugees that they could accommodate. Relief committee investigators matched refugees to volunteers, sending the refugees with an announcement stating "In response to your generous offer, please accommodate the bearer of this Card." Of the original 259 volunteer housing cards, at least 64 percent of the volunteers were sent refugees. Calculated by author from Berkeley Relief Committee Housing Cards, Berkeley Relief Committee Records, Bancroft Library; "E. J. Peck, 2229 Channing Way," Berkeley Relief Committee Records, Bancroft Library.

138. "Joseph LeConte, 2739 Bancroft Way," Berkeley Relief Committee Records, Bancroft Library.

139. "George Roberts, 2720 Derby," Berkeley Relief Committee Records, Bancroft Library.

140. "Mrs. J. G. Wright, 2001 Francisco," Berkeley Relief Committee Records, Bancroft Library.

141. "Mrs. L. A. McAfee, 2640 Dwight Way," Berkeley Relief Committee Records, Bancroft Library.

142. Calculated by author from the Berkeley Relief Committee Housing Cards, Berkeley Relief Committee Records, Bancroft Library.

143. Berkeley Relief Committee Records, Bancroft Library.

144. Mel Scott, *The San Francisco Bay Area: A Metropolis in Perspective* (Berkeley: University of California Press, 1959), 94. For a brief biography of Francis Smith, see Bagwell, *Oakland*.

145. The Magee Tract went from present-day Martin Luther King to California Street and Addison Street to Dwight Way. Magee Tract Advertisement, Ferrier and Company, cited in Richard Schwartz, *Berkeley 1900: Daily Life at the Turn of the Century* (Berkeley: RSB Books, 2000), 172.

146. Robert Duponey, *Berkeley Reporter*, December 1906, cited in ibid., 157.

147. Kingsley Davis and Eleanor Langlois Davis, *Future Demographic Growth of the San Francisco Bay Area* (Berkeley: Institute of Governmental Studies, 1963), 29, appendix A.

148. *Official Handbook of the Panama-Pacific International Exposition, 1915* (San Francisco: Wahlgreen, 1914), 68.

149. James Rolph, Jr., quoted in "San Francisco Commemorates Her Great Triumph," *San Francisco Chronicle*, April 18, 1915.

150. Scott, *The San Francisco Bay Area*, 157.

151. *San Francisco: Center of the California Vacation Land*, 7.

152. Frank Morton Todd, *The Story of the Exposition* (New York: Knickerbocker Press, 1921), 41.

153. Issel and Cherny, *San Francisco*, 168.

154. Ibid., 168–169.

155. Anna Pratt Simpson, *Problems Women Solved: Being the Story of the Woman's Board of the Panama-Pacific International Exposition* (San Francisco: Woman's Board, 1915), 5.

156. The Woman's Board expanded beyond 1915 Exposition organizational needs and created a statewide California Woman's Auxiliary. Charles C. Moore, letter to Woman's Board, May 22, 1913, in Simpson, *Problems Women Solved*, 14.

157. Simpson, *Problems Women Solved*, 3.

158. Scott, *The San Francisco Bay Area*, 159.

159. The Exposition buildings were commonly referred to as the "Dream City." In the lavish prose of Louis Stellman, the fair was the fulfillment of a dream: "The Flury of the Flame that came with it [earthquake] was near our undoing. We had to build up a city again. In three years we did it—the city the World declared could not be built in then—and then we came back to our Dream." Louis J. Stellmann, *That Was a Dream Worth Building* (San Francisco: H. S. Crocker, 1916).

160. San Francisco Real Estate Board, "Secretary's Report for Quarter Ending December 31, 1910," James D. Phelan Papers, Bancroft Library.

161. Property owners, who were not necessarily cottage dwellers, raised objections. But a temporary restraining order on January 30, 1912, only temporarily blocked the removal of cottages. Building and Grounds Committee, Exposition Company, March 15, 1912, cited in Marie Bolton, "Recovery for Whom? Social Conflict after the

San Francisco Earthquake and Fire, 1906–1915" (Ph.D. diss., University of California, Davis, 1997); Director of Works, Exposition Company, letter to W. Chatfield, March 29, 1912, cited in Bolton, "Recovery for Whom?"

162. "Dwellings Condemned by San Francisco Board of Health, October 1908–December 1915," cited in Bolton, "Recovery for Whom?" 72.

163. Bolton, "Recovery for Whom?" 143–149.

164. Ibid., 134; San Francisco Examiner, January 9, 1914.

165. San Francisco Call and San Francisco Post, January 7, 1914, quoted in Bolton, "Recovery for Whom?" 137.

166. Todd, The Story of the Exposition, 288.

167. Ibid., 68.

168. Ibid.

169. Simpson, Problems Women Solved, 69.

170. Although the California legislature passed the Redlight Abatement Law in 1913, which opened brothels to public nuisance lawsuits, the law had not yet been enforced in San Francisco. See Lewis, San Francisco, 227; and Issel and Cherny, San Francisco, 106–109.

171. Burton Benedict, M. Miriam Dobkin, and Elizabeth Armstrong, A Catalogue from San Francisco's Panama Pacific International Exposition, 1915, ed. Lowie Museum of Anthropology (Berkeley: Regents of the University of California, 1982).

172. For a detailed analysis of the Pioneer Mother statue, see Brenda D. Frink, "Pioneers and Patriots: Race, Gender, and Historical Memory in California, 1875–1915" (Ph.D. diss., Stanford University, 2010).

173. The statue's inscription, penned by University of California president Benjamin Ide Wheeler, read: "Over rude paths beset with hunger and risk she pressed on toward the vision of a better country. To an assemblage of men busied with the perishable rewards of the day she brought the three-fold leaven of enduring society, faith, gentleness, hope with the nurture of children." Benjamin Ide Wheeler, quoted in Simpson, Problems Women Solved, 160.

174. Maybeck suggested that "when the people of California visit the grounds they should think of the fact that the Fair is an expression of future California cities." Bernard R. Maybeck, Palace of Fine Arts and Lagoon (San Francisco: Paul Elder, 1915), 1, 13.

175. Benjamin Ide Wheeler, June 30, 1915, quoted in Simpson, Problems Women Solved, 163.

176. Issel and Cherny, San Francisco, 78.

EPILOGUE

1. Carl Smith, Urban Disorder and the Shape of Belief: The Great Chicago Fire, the Haymarket Bomb, and the Model Town of Pullman (Chicago: University of Chicago Press, 1995), 7.

2. Ernest P. Bicknell, Pioneering with the Red Cross: Recollections of an Old Red Crosser (New York: Macmillan, 1935), 16–17.

3. George C. Pardee, "Governor's Message, June 2, 1906," in Journal of the Senate, Thirty-Sixth Legislature of the State of California (Sacramento: W. W. Shannon, 1906), 11.

4. James Horsburgh, Jr., circular to Stockton Chamber of Commerce, 1906, Stockton Chamber of Commerce, San Francisco Virtual Museum Archives.

5. Gladys Hansen and Emmet Condon, Denial of Disaster: The Untold Story and Photographs of the San Francisco Earthquake and Fire of 1906, ed. David Fowler (San Francisco: Cameron, 1989), 78. A postcard of the South of Market fires burning

toward Market Street had also been doctored so that it did not show much of the earthquake damage. Ibid., 98.

6. "The Progress of the World," *American Monthly Review of Reviews*, June 1906, 644.

7. Bailey Millard, "When Altruria Awoke," *Cosmopolitan*, June 1906.

8. William James, *Memories and Studies* (New York: Longmans, Green, 1911), 223.

9. Frank Putnam, "Loss and Gain at San Francisco," *National Magazine*, June 1906, 304.

10. "San Francisco," *Harper's Weekly*, May 5, 1906, 619.

11. Lawrence J. Vale and Thomas J. Campanella, eds., *The Resilient City: How Modern Cities Recover from Disaster* (Oxford: Oxford University Press, 2005), 350.

12. Historian Mary Johnson argues that "social historians, interested in groups of people who have left few or no written records, cannot afford to neglect nonverbal remains." Mary Johnson, "Women and Their Material Universe: A Bibliographic Essay," *Journal of American Culture* 6, no. 1 (Spring 1983): 32.

13. Laurel Thatcher Ulrich, *The Age of Homespun: Objects and Stories in the Creation of an American Myth* (New York: Alfred A. Knopf, 2001), 133.

14. Disaster remnants are best described by curators Steven Lubar and Kathleen Kendrick's definition of relics as objects that gain interest because of their stories. Steven Lubar and Kathleen M. Kendrick, *Legacies: Collecting America's History at the Smithsonian* (Washington, DC: Smithsonian Institution Press, 2001), 36.

15. Anna Wolfson Samuel, handwritten memories, n.d., San Francisco Earthquake and Fire Collection, California Historical Society, San Francisco.

16. Marion Baldwin Hale, "The 1906 Earthquake and Fire, San Francisco," taped recollections (1975), San Francisco Earthquake and Fire Collection, San Francisco Public Library.

17. Laura P. Williams, "First Oriental Home Built and Work Grows," *California Christian Advocate* 69 (October 21, 1920): 18.

18. Frank, letter to Harriet, n.d., San Francisco Earthquake and Fire Collection, California Historical Society.

19. See E. McClung Fleming's model for artifact interpretation. E. McClung Fleming, "Artifact Study: A Proposed Model," *Winterthur Portfolio* 9 (1974): 153–173.

20. Kathy Peiss, *Cheap Amusements: Working Women and Leisure in Turn-of-the-Century New York* (Philadelphia: Temple University Press, 1986), 17, 20. See also Roy Rosenzweig, *Eight Hours for What We Will: Workers and Leisure in an Industrial City, 1870–1920* (New York: Cambridge University Press, 1983).

21. William Issel and Robert W. Cherny, *San Francisco, 1865–1932: Politics, Power, and Urban Development* (Berkeley: University of California Press, 1986), 61.

22. Lenora Busby Moore married Joseph Henry Moore on March 16, 1906. Joseph Moore was born in San Francisco in 1878.

23. See Jan Shipps, *Mormonism: The Story of a New Religious Tradition* (Urbana: University of Illinois Press, 1987); Jan Shipps, *Sojourner in the Promised Land: Forty Years among the Mormons* (Urbana: University of Illinois Press, 2000).

24. Arthur Downey, *After the Earthquake* (1982), San Francisco Earthquake and Fire Collection, San Francisco Public Library, 25.

Bibliography

PRIMARY SOURCES

Published

The Associated Charities of San Francisco: Annual Reports, 1901–1903. San Francisco, 1905.

The Associated Charities of San Francisco: Annual Reports, 1904–1910. San Francisco: Blair-Murdock, 1911.

The Associated Charities of San Francisco: Annual Reports, 1911–1912. San Francisco: Associated Charities, 1912.

The Associated Charities of San Francisco: Annual Reports, 1912–1913. San Francisco: Associated Charities, 1913.

Backes, Reverend Mother Pia. *Her Days Unfolded.* Translated by Mother Bernadina Michel. San Jose: Benedictine Press, 1953.

Banks, Charles Eugene. *The History of the San Francisco Disaster and Mount Vesuvius Horror.* San Francisco: C. E. Thomas, 1906.

Barker, Malcom E. *Three Fearful Days: San Francisco Memoirs of the 1906 Earthquake and Fire.* San Francisco: Londonborn, 1998.

Bicknell, Ernest P. "In the Thick of Relief Work at San Francisco." *Charities and the Commons* 16, no. 9 (1906): 297.

———. *Pioneering with the Red Cross: Recollections of an Old Red Crosser.* New York: Macmillan, 1935.

Bishop, Harris. *Souvenir and Resume of Oakland Relief Work to San Francisco Refugees.* Oakland: Finance Committee, circa 1906.

Blake, Evarts I. *Greater Oakland.* Oakland: Pacific Publishing, 1911.

Brandt, Lilian, "Rehabilitation Work in San Francisco." *Charities and the Commons* 17, no. 1 (1906): 45

Brown, Helen Hillyer. *The Great San Francisco Fire.* San Francisco: Hillside Press, 1906.

Burnham, Daniel. *Report on a Plan for San Francisco.* San Francisco: Sunset Press, 1905.

Chamber of Commerce. *Report of the Los Angeles Chamber of Commerce Citizens' Relief Committee*. Los Angeles, 1908.

Coleman, Minnie. Letter to her sister, April 24, 1906, reprinted in *Noe Valley Voice*, June 2006.

Davis, Carrie G. "The Latest from Our Chinese Home." *Woman's Home Missions* 24 (April 1907): 63.

Devine, Edward T. *Efficiency and Relief: A Programme of Social Work*. New York: Columbia University Press, 1906.

———. *The Principles of Relief*. London: Macmillan, 1905.

Funston, Frederick. "How the Army Worked to Save San Francisco." *Cosmopolitan* 41, no. 3 (July 1906): 239–248.

Irwin, Will. *The City That Was: A Requiem of Old San Francisco*. New York: Huebosch, 1906.

James, William. *Memories and Studies*. New York: Longmans, Green, 1911.

Johnson, Alexander. *Proceedings of the National Conference of Charities and Correction*. Edited by Alexander Johnson. Philadelphia: Press of Fred J. Heer, 1906.

Kelly, Mary. *Shame of the Relief*. 1908.

Kip, William Ingraham. *The Early Days of My Episcopate*. New York: Thomas Whittaker, 1892.

Ladies of San Rafael, ed. *San Rafael Cook Book 1906*. San Rafael: First Presbyterian Church, 1906.

Lawson, Andrew C. "Preliminary Report of the State Earthquake Investigation Commission." Berkeley: State Earthquake and Investigation Commission, 1906.

Lawson, Andrew C., and Harry Fielding Reid. "The California Earthquake of April 18, 1906: Report of the State Earthquake Investigation Commission." Washington, DC: Carnegie Institution of Washington, 1908.

Linthicum, Richard, and Trumbull White. *Complete Story of the San Francisco Horror*. Chicago: Hubert Russel, 1906.

Livingstone, Alexander. *Complete Story of San Francisco's Terrible Calamity of Earthquake and Fire*. San Francisco: Continental, 1907.

Mahoney, Margaret. *The Earthquake, the Fire, the Relief*. San Francisco, July 28, 1906.

Manson, Marsden. *Report of Marsden Manson to the Mayor and Committee on Reconstruction*. San Francisco, 1906.

Mavrogenes, Nancy A. "Experiencing the '06 Earthquake—with a Female Physician Who Was There." *California Historical Courier* 32, no. 2 (1980): 3–5.

Maybeck, Bernard R. *Palace of Fine Arts and Lagoon*. San Francisco: Paul Elder, 1915.

McEnerney, Garrett W. "The Title and Document Restoration Company vs. Frank H. Kerrigan." San Francisco: Pernau Publishing, 1906.

Morris, Charles. *The San Francisco Calamity by Earthquake and Fire*. Philadelphia: J. C. Winston, 1906.

Morrow, William W. *The Earthquake of April 18, 1906, and the Great Fire in San Francisco on That and Succeeding Days, Personal Experiences*. San Francisco, circa 1906.

Official Handbook of the Panama-Pacific International Exposition, 1915. San Francisco: Wahlgreen, 1914.

The "Old Frisco" Souvenir Book: The Saddest Story Ever Told in Pictures. Oakland: Progressive Novelty, 1906.

Pardee, George C. "Governor's Message, June 2, 1906." In *Journal of the Senate, Thirty-sixth Legislature of the State of California*. Sacramento: W. W. Shannon, 1906.

The Picture Story of the San Francisco Earthquake, Wednesday, April 18, 1906. Los Angeles: George Rice and Sons, 1906.

"Proceedings of the 39th Annual Meeting of the National Board of Fire Underwriters." 1905.

Public Work of San Francisco since 1906: Supplement to Municipal Reports 1908–9. San Francisco, 1909.

Rawlings, Eleanor Warner. Letter to Stuart Rawlings, April 22, 1906, reprinted in "'Mamma's' Earthquake Letter," *Mill Valley Historical Review* (Spring 1991): 2.

Report of the Special Committee of the Board of Trustees of the Chamber of Commerce of San Francisco on Insurance Settlements Incident to the San Francisco Fire. San Francisco: San Francisco Chamber of Commerce, 1906.

Russell Sage Foundation, ed. San *Francisco Relief Survey.* New York: Survey Associates, 1913.

San Francisco: Center of the California Vacation Land. San Francisco: Californians, 1934.

San Francisco City Directory, 1905–1915.

The San Francisco Disaster Photographed: Fifty Glimpses of Havoc by Earthquake and Fire. New York: C. S. Hammond, 1906.

San Francisco Municipal Reports for the Fiscal Years 1905–1906 and 1906–1907. San Francisco: Neal Publishing, 1908.

San Francisco Municipal Reports for the Fiscal Years 1907–1908. San Francisco: Neal Publishing, 1909.

Schussler, Hermann. *The Water Supply of San Francisco, California: Before, during, and after the Earthquake of April 18th, 1906, and the Subsequent Conflagration.* New York: Martin B. Brown Press, 1906.

Searight, Frank. *The Doomed City: A Thrilling Tale.* Chicago: Laird and Lee, 1906.

Simpson, Anna Pratt. *Problems Women Solved: Being the Story of the Woman's Board of the Panama-Pacific International Exposition.* San Francisco: Woman's Board, 1915.

———. *Story of the Associated Charities since the Fire of 1906.* San Francisco: Associated Charities of San Francisco, 1909.

Smith, Mary Roberts. "Relief Work in Its Social Bearings." *Charities and the Commons* 16, no. 9 (1906): 310.

Sohier, William D., and Jacob Furth. "Massachusetts Association for the Relief of California Report." Massachusetts Red Cross, 1906.

Soule, Frank, John H. Gihon, and James Nisbet. *The Annals of San Francisco.* New York: D. Appleton, 1855.

Stellmann, Louis J. *That Was a Dream Worth Building.* San Francisco: H. S. Crocker, 1916.

Todd, Frank Morton. *The Story of the Exposition.* New York: Knickerbocker Press, 1921.

Tyler, Sydney. *San Francisco's Great Disaster: A Full Account of the Recent Terrible Destruction of Life and Property by Earthquake, Fire and Volcano in California and at Vesuvius.* Philadelphia: P. W. Ziegler, 1906.

Views: Ruins of San Francisco, April 18, 1906. Watsonville, CA: Meddaugh and Chapman, 1906.

Wall, Louise Herrick. "Heroic San Francisco." *Century Magazine,* August 1906.

Watkins, Eleanor. "The 1906 San Francisco Earthquake: A Personal Account by Mrs. James T. Watkins." In *Eyewitness to Disaster: Five Women (Each in Her Own Words) Tell Their Stories of the 1906 Earthquake and Fire in San Francisco.* San Francisco: National Society of the Colonial Dames of America in California, 1987.

Wells, Emmeline B. "Earthquake and Fire." *Woman's Exponent* 34 (May 1906): 68.

Whitney, Albert W. "On Insurance Settlements Incident to the 1906 San Francisco Fire." Pasadena: Center for Research on the Prevention of Natural Disasters, 1973.

Williams, Laura P. "First Oriental Home Built and Work Grows." *California Christian Advocate* 69 (October 21, 1920): 18.

Wilson, James. *San Francisco's Horror of Earthquake and Fire: Terrible Devastation and Heart-Rending Scenes*. Philadelphia: Percival Supply, 1906.

Woman's Occidental Board of Foreign Missions, 33rd and 34th Annual Reports. 1905–06, 1906–07.

Wong, Ella Clemens. *Chinatown*. San Francisco, 1915.

Unpublished

Allen, Emma S. "After the Earthquake and Fire." *Women's Home Missionary Society*. New York, n.d. San Francisco Disaster Papers, California State Archives.

Eaves, Lucile. "Industrial Bureau Report." San Francisco Relief and Red Cross Funds, circa 1906.

Fletcher, John Dundas. "An Account of the Work of Relief Organized in Berkeley in April and May, 1906, for the Refugees from San Francisco." University of California, Berkeley, 1909.

Freeman, Frederick N. "Report." Mare Island, CA: U.S. Navy, 1906, no. 8.

Funston, Brigadier-General Frederick. General Orders No. 12, April 22, 1906.

Kennedy, Lawrence J. "The Progress of the Fire in San Francisco April 18th–21st, 1906: As Shown by an Analysis of Original Documents." Master's thesis, University of California–Berkeley, 1906.

Mack, O. E. "A Study in Disaster Preparedness." San Francisco, circa 1906.

San Francisco Fire Department Reports, 1906.

Archival Collections

Allan Pollock Papers, Bancroft Library, University of California, Berkeley.

Atlas Insurance Company Records. Bancroft Library, University of California, Berkeley.

Berkeley Relief Committee Records. Bancroft Library, University of California, Berkeley.

Clara Barton Papers (microfilm). Stanford University Library, Stanford University.

Fred J. Bowlen Papers. Bancroft Library, University of California, Berkeley.

Ivie Papers. Bancroft Library, University of California, Berkeley.

James D. Phelan Papers. Bancroft Library, University of California, Berkeley.

Katherine Hooker Papers. San Francisco Virtual Museum Archives, San Francisco.

Letterman General Hospital Records. National Archives, Burlingame, California.

Oral Histories. History Room, Mill Valley Library, Mill Valley, California.

Oral Histories. Kent Room, Marin County Library, San Rafael, California.

Rene Bine Papers. California Historical Society, San Francisco.

Rosalie Meyer Stern Papers. Judah Magnes Museum, Berkeley.

San Francisco Earthquake and Fire, 1906. Paperless Archives.

San Francisco Earthquake and Fire Collection. California Historical Society, San Francisco.

San Francisco Earthquake and Fire Collection. San Francisco Public Library, San Francisco.

San Francisco Earthquake and Fire Collection. San Francisco Theological Seminary Archives, San Anselmo, California.

San Francisco Earthquake and Fire Collection. San Francisco Virtual Museum, San Francisco.

San Francisco Earthquake and Fire Collection. Stanford Special Collections, Stanford University.

San Francisco Earthquake and Fire Papers. Presentation Archives, San Francisco.
San Francisco Earthquake and Fire Papers. Sisters of Mercy Archives, Burlingame, California.

Newspapers, Magazines, Journals

American Monthly Review of Reviews
Argonaut
Berkeley Daily Gazette
Berkeley Reporter
Century Magazine
Charities and the Commons
Chicago Record Herald
Chung Sai Yat Po
Cosmopolitan
Daily News
Dallas News
Fresno Morning Republican
Gilroy Advocate
Harper's Weekly
Leslie's Weekly
Marin Journal
Mining and Scientific Press
Monitor
National Magazine
Oakland Enquirer
Oakland Examiner
Oakland Herald
Oakland Tribune
Organized Labor
Outlook Magazine
Overland Monthly
The Pacific
Portland Oregonian
San Francisco Bulletin
San Francisco Call
San Francisco Chronicle
San Francisco Examiner
San Francisco Merchants' Association Review
San Francisco Newsletter
Sausalito News
SFGate
Star
Woman's Exponent

SECONDARY SOURCES

Published

Abbott, Carl. *The Metropolitan Frontier: Cities in the Modern American West*. Tucson: University of Arizona Press, 1993.
Agnew, Elizabeth N. *From Charity to Social Work: Mary E. Richmond and the Creation of an American Profession*. Urbana: University of Illinois Press, 2004.

Bagwell, Beth. *Oakland: The Story of a City.* Novato, CA: Presidio Press, 1982.

Baker, Paula. "The Domestication of Politics: Women and American Political Society, 1780–1920." *American Historical Review* 89 (1984): 620–647.

Bancroft, Hubert Howe. *History of California.* Vol. 6, *1848–1859.* San Francisco: History Company, 1888.

Barth, Gunther. *Instant Cities: Urbanization and the Rise of San Francisco and Denver.* New York: Oxford University Press, 1975.

Bean, Walton. *Boss Ruef's San Francisco.* Berkeley: University of California Press, 1952.

Benedict, Burton, M. Miriam Dobkin, and Elizabeth Armstrong. *A Catalogue from San Francisco's Panama Pacific International Exposition, 1915.* Edited by Lowie Museum of Anthropology. Berkeley: Regents of the University of California, 1982.

Berglund, Barbara. *Making San Francisco American: Cultural Frontiers in the Urban West, 1846–1906.* Lawrence: University Press of Kansas, 2007.

Biel, Steven, ed. *American Disasters.* New York: New York University Press, 2001.

Blumin, Stuart M. *The Emergence of the Middle Class: Social Experience in the American City, 1760–1900.* New York: Cambridge University Press, 1989.

Boardman, Mabel T. *Under the Red Cross Flag at Home and Abroad.* Philadelphia: J. B. Lippincott, 1915.

Bonadio, Felice A. *A. P. Giannini: Banker of America.* Berkeley: University of California Press, 1994.

Boyer, Paul. *Urban Masses and Moral Order in America, 1820–1920.* Cambridge, MA: Harvard University Press, 1978.

Brechin, Gray. *Imperial San Francisco: Urban Power, Earthly Ruin.* Berkeley: University of California Press, 1999.

Bremner, Robert H. *From the Depths: The Discovery of Poverty in the United States.* New York: New York University Press, 1956.

Bronson, William. *The Earth Shook, the Sky Burned.* New York: Doubleday, 1959.

Burton, David. *Clara Barton: In the Service of Humanity.* Westport, CT: Greenwood Press, 1995.

Burton, Jean. *Katharine Felton and Her Social Work in San Francisco.* Stanford, CA: James Ladd Delkin, 1947.

Carson, Mina. *Settlement Folk: Social Thought and the American Settlement Movement, 1885–1930.* Chicago: University of Chicago Press, 1990.

Chan, Sucheng, ed. *Entry Denied: Exclusion and the Chinese Community in America, 1882–1943.* Philadelphia: Temple University Press, 1991.

Chen, Shehong. *Being Chinese, Becoming Chinese American.* Urbana: University of Illinois Press, 2002.

Chen, Yong. *Chinese San Francisco, 1850–1943: A Trans-Pacific Community.* Stanford, CA: Stanford University Press, 2000.

Chow, Willard T. *The Reemergence of an Inner City: The Pivot of Chinese Settlement in the East Bay Region of the San Francisco Bay Area.* San Francisco: R&E Research Associates, 1977.

Choy, Philip P. "The Architecture of San Francisco Chinatown." *Chinese America: History and Perspectives, 1990* (1990): 37–65.

Dauber, Michele Landis "San Francisco Chinatown's Historic Development." In *The Chinese American Experience: Papers from the Second National Conference on Chinese American Studies,* edited by Genny Lim, 126–130. San Francisco: The Chinese Historical Society of America and the Chinese Culture Foundation of San Francisco, 1984.

Cinel, Dino. *From Italy to San Francisco.* Stanford, CA: Stanford University Press, 1982.

Crocker, Ruth Hutchinson. *Social Work and Social Order: The Settlement Movement in Two Industrial Cities, 1889–1930.* Urbana: University of Illinois Press, 1991.

Crunden, Robert M. *Ministers of Reform: The Progressives' Achievement in American Civilization, 1889–1920.* New York: Basic Books, 1982.

Ciucci, Giorgio, and Barbara Luigia La Penta. *The American City: From the Civil War to the New Deal.* London: Granada, 1980.

Dauber, Michele Landis. "The Sympathetic State." *Law and History Review* 23, no. 2 (Summer 2005): 387–442.

Davis, Kingsley, and Eleanor Langlois. *Future Demographic Growth of the San Francisco Bay Area.* Berkeley: Institute of Governmental Studies, 1963.

Davis, Mike. *Ecology of Fear: Los Angeles and the Imagination of Disaster.* New York: Metropolitan Books, 1998.

de Young, Helen. *Nineteen Nineteen: The Story of the de Young House at 1919 California Street San Francisco.* Unknown binding.

Deutsch, Sarah. *Women and the City: Gender, Space, and Power in Boston, 1870–1940.* Oxford: Oxford University Press, 2000.

Dick, Linda. *Palo Alto 1906.* DeAnza College, Cupertino: California History Center, 1979.

Diner, Steven J. *A Very Different Age: Americans of the Progressive Era.* New York: Hill and Wang, 1998.

Dolan, Jay P. "Catholicism and American Culture: Strategies for Survival." In *American Religious History,* edited by Amanda Porterfield, 117–136. Oxford: Blackwell Publishers, 2002.

Dondero, Raymond Stevenson. *The Italian Settlement of San Francisco.* San Francisco: R&E Research Associates, 1974.

Dulles, Foster Reah. *The American Red Cross: A History.* New York: Harper and Brothers, 1950.

Ebner, Michael H. "Re-reading Suburban America: Urban Population Decentralization, 1810–1980." *American Quarterly* 37, no. 3 (1985): 368–381.

Ethington, Philip J. *The Public City: The Political Construction of Urban Life in San Francisco, 1850–1900.* New York: Cambridge University Press, 1994.

Everist, Robyn. "Women Stretching Outwards: Feminism and the Club Woman Movement in the United States at the Turn of the Twentieth Century." *Lilith* 2 (1985): 30–41.

Ewen, Elizabeth. *Immigrant Women in the Land of Dollars: Life and Culture on the Lower East Side, 1890–1925.* New York: Monthly Review Press, 1985.

Faust, Drew Gilpin. *Mothers of Invention: Women of the Slaveholding South in the American Civil War.* New York: Vintage Books, 1996.

Filene, Peter G. "An Obituary for 'The Progressive Movement.'" *American Quarterly* 22 (1970): 22–34.

Fishman, Robert. *Bourgeois Utopias: The Rise and Fall of Suburbia.* New York: Basic Books, 1987.

Fitzpatrick, Ellen. *Endless Crusade: Women Social Scientists and Progressive Reform.* New York: Oxford University Press, 1990.

Flanagan, Maureen A. *America Reformed: Progressives and Progressivism, 1890s–1920s.* New York: Oxford University Press, 2007.

———. *Seeing with Their Hearts: Chicago Women and the Vision of the Good City, 1871–1933.* Princeton, NJ: Princeton University Press, 2002.

Fleming, E. McClung. "Artifact Study: A Proposed Model." *Winterthur Portfolio* 9 (1974): 153–173.

Foley, Neil. *The White Scourge: Mexicans, Blacks, and Poor Whites in Texas Cotton Culture.* Berkeley: University of California Press, 1998.

Fradkin, Philip L. *The Great Earthquake and Firestorms of 1906: How San Francisco Nearly Destroyed Itself.* Berkeley: University of California Press, 2005.

Frank, Phil. "Witness to Disaster." *Moments in Time: Sausalito Historical Society Newsletter* (Spring 2002): 2

Fredrickson, George M. *The Inner Civil War: Northern Intellectuals and the Crisis of the Union.* Urbana: University of Illinois Press, 1965.

Gere, Anne Ruggles. *Intimate Practices: Literacy and Cultural Work in U.S. Women's Clubs, 1880–1920.* Urbana: University of Illinois Press, 1997.

Ginzberg, Lori. *Women and the Work of Benevolence: Morality, Politics, and Class in the Nineteenth-Century United States.* New Haven, CT: Yale University Press, 1990.

Godfrey, Brian J. *Neighborhoods in Transition: The Making of San Francisco's Nonconformist Communities.* Berkeley: University of California Press, 1988.

———. "Urban Development and Redevelopment in San Francisco." *Geographical Review* 87, no. 3 (July 1997): 309–333.

Goodwin, Joanne L. *Gender and the Politics of Welfare Reform: Mothers' Pensions in Chicago, 1911–1929.* Chicago: University of Chicago Press, 1997.

Gordon, Linda. "Family Violence, Feminism, and Social Control." In *Women, the State, and Welfare,* edited by Linda Gordon, 178–198. Madison: University of Wisconsin Press, 1990.

———. *Heroes of Their Own Lives: The Politics and History of Family Violence.* London: Virago, 1989.

———. *Pitied but Not Entitled: Single Mothers and the History of Welfare, 1890–1935.* Cambridge, MA: Harvard University Press, 1994.

———. "Putting Children First: Women, Maternalism, and Welfare in the Early Twentieth Century." In *U.S. History as Women's History: New Feminist Essays,* edited by Alice Kessler-Harris, Linda K. Kerber, and Kathryn Kish Sklar, 63–86. Chapel Hill: University of North Carolina Press, 1995.

Griswold, Robert L. "Anglo Women and Domestic Ideology in the American West in the Nineteenth and Early Twentieth Centuries." In *Western Women: Their Land, Their Lives,* edited by Lillian Schlissel, Vicki L. Ruiz, and Janice Monk, 15–34. Albuquerque: University of New Mexico Press, 1988.

Guglielmo, Thomas A. *White on Arrival: Italians, Race, Color, and Power in Chicago, 1890–1945.* New York: Oxford University Press, 2003.

Gullett, Gayle. *Becoming Citizens: The Emergence and Development of the California Women's Movement, 1880–1911.* Urbana: University of Illinois Press, 2000.

Gutierrez, Ramon A., and Richard J. Orsi, eds. *Contested Eden: California before the Gold Rush.* Berkeley: University of California Press, 1998.

Haas, J. Eugene, Robert W. Kates, and Martyn J. Bowden, eds. *Reconstruction following Disaster.* Cambridge, MA: MIT Press, 1977.

Habermas, Jurgen. *The Structural Transformation of the Public Sphere: An Inquiry into a Category of Bourgeois Society.* Edited by Thomas Berger and Frederick Lawrence. Cambridge, MA: MIT Press, 1989.

Hall, Peter Geoffrey. *Cities of Tomorrow: An Intellectual History of Urban Planning and Design in the Twentieth Century.* Oxford, UK: Blackwell Publishers, 1996.

Hansen, Gladys. "Who Perished?" San Francisco: San Francisco Archives, 1980.

Hansen, Gladys, and Emmet Condon. *Denial of Disaster: The Untold Story and Photographs of the San Francisco Earthquake and Fire of 1906.* Edited by David Fowler. San Francisco: Cameron, 1989.

Harris, Richard. "American Suburbs: A Sketch of a New Interpretation." *Journal of Urban History* 15, no. 1 (1988): 98–103.

————. *Unplanned Suburbs: Toronto's American Tragedy, 1900–1950.* Baltimore: Johns Hopkins University Press, 1996.

Hayden, Dolores. *The Grand Domestic Revolution: A History of Feminist Designs for American Homes, Neighborhoods, and Cities.* Cambridge, MA: MIT Press, 1981.

————. *Redesigning the American Dream: Gender, Housing, and Family Life.* New York: W. W. Norton, 2002.

Heig, James, and Shirley Mitchell, eds. *Both Sides of the Track: A Collection of Oral Histories from Belvedere and Tiburon.* San Francisco: Scottwall Associates, 1985.

Henderson, Sandra L. "The *Civitas* of Women's Political Culture: The Twentieth Century Club of Berkeley, 1904–1929." In *California Women and Politics: From the Gold Rush to the Great Depression,* edited by Robert W. Cherny, Mary Ann Irwin, and Ann Marie Wilson. Lincoln: University of Nebraska Press, 2011.

Hittell, John S. *A History of the City of San Francisco and Incidentally of the State of California.* San Francisco: A. L. Bancroft, 1878.

Howard, Christopher. "'Sowing the Seeds of 'Welfare': The Transformation of Mothers' Pensions, 1900–1940." *Journal of Policy History* 4 (1992): 188–227.

Irwin, Mary Ann. "'The Air Is Becoming Full of War': Jewish San Francisco and World War I." *Pacific Historical Review* 74, no. 3 (August 2005): 331–365.

————. "'Going About and Doing Good': The Politics of Benevolence, Welfare, and Gender in San Francisco, 1850–1880." *Pacific Historical Review* 68, no. 3 (August 1999): 365–396.

Issel, William, and Robert W. Cherny. *San Francisco, 1865–1932: Politics, Power, and Urban Development.* Berkeley: University of California Press, 1986.

Jackson, Kenneth T. *Crabgrass Frontier: The Suburbanization of the United States.* New York: Oxford University Press, 1985.

Jacobson, Matthew Frye. *Whiteness of a Different Color: European Immigrants and the Alchemy of Race.* Cambridge, MA: Harvard University Press, 1998.

Johnson, Mary. "Women and Their Material Universe: A Bibliographic Essay." *Journal of American Culture* 6, no. 1 (Spring 1983): 32–51.

Jolluck, Katherine R. *Exile and Identity: Polish Women in the Soviet Union during World War II.* Pittsburgh, PA: University of Pittsburgh Press, 2002.

Jorae, Wendy Rouse. *The Children of Chinatown: Growing Up Chinese American in San Francisco, 1850–1920.* Chapel Hill: University of North Carolina Press, 2009.

Kahn, Judd. *Imperial San Francisco: Politics and Planning in an American City, 1897–1906.* Lincoln: University of Nebraska Press, 1979.

Kates, Robert W. "Natural Hazard in Human Ecological Perspective: Hypotheses and Models." *Economic Geography* 47, no. 3 (July 1971): 438–451.

Kates, Robert W., and David Pijawka. "From Rubble to Monument: The Pace of Reconstruction." In *Reconstruction Following Disaster,* edited by J. Eugene Haas, Robert W. Kates, and Martyn J. Bowden, 1–4. Cambridge, MA: MIT Press, 1977.

Katz, Michael. *Poverty and Policy in American History.* New York: Academic Press, 1983.

Kazin, Michael. *Barons of Labor: The San Francisco Building Trades and Union Power in the Progressive Era.* Urbana: University of Illinois Press, 1987.

Kennedy, John Castillo. *The Great Earthquake and Fire: San Francisco, 1906.* New York: Morrow, 1963.

Krainz, Thomas A. *Delivering Aid: Implementing Progressive Era Welfare in the American West.* Albuquerque: University of New Mexico Press, 2005.

Ladd-Taylor, Molly. *Mother-Work: Women, Child Welfare, and the State, 1890–1930.* Urbana: University of Illinois Press, 1994.

Lau, Estelle T. *Paper Families: Identity, Immigration Administration, and Chinese Exclusion.* Durham, NC: Duke University Press, 2006.

Lee, Erika. *At America's Gates: Chinese Immigration during the Exclusion Era, 1882–1943.* Chapel Hill: University of North Carolina Press, 2003.

Lewis, Oscar. *San Francisco: Mission to Metropolis.* San Diego: Howell-North Books, 1966.

Lipow, Arthur. *Authoritarian Socialism in America: Edward Bellamy and the Nationalist Movement.* Berkeley: University of California Press, 1982.

Lissak, Rivka Shpak. *Pluralism and Progressives: Hull House and the New Immigrants, 1890–1919.* Chicago: University of Chicago Press, 1989.

Lockwood, Charles. *Suddenly San Francisco: The Early Years of an Instant City.* San Francisco: California Living, 1978.

Loo, Chalsa M. *Chinatown: Most Time, Hard Time.* New York: Praeger, 1991.

Lubar, Steven, and Kathleen M. Kendrick. *Legacies: Collecting America's History at the Smithsonian.* Washington, DC: Smithsonian Institution Press, 2001.

Ma, L. Eve Armentrout. "Chinese in Marin County, 1850–1950: A Century of Growth and Decline." *Chinese America: History and Perspectives, 1991* (1991).

———. *Hometown Chinatown: The History of Oakland's Chinese Community.* New York: Garland Publishing, 2000.

Margolin, Malcolm. *The Ohlone Way: Indian Life in the San Francisco–Monterey Bay Area.* Berkeley: Heyday Books, 1978.

Martin, Mildred Crowl. *Chinatown's Angry Angel: The Story of Donaldina Cameron.* Palo Alto, CA: Pacific Books, 1986.

Matsumoto, Valerie J. "What Was the Impact of Internment on Japanese American Families and Communities?" In *What Did the Internment of Japanese Americans Mean?* edited by Alice Yang Murray, 121–150. Boston: Bedford/St. Martin's, 2000.

Mazumdar, Sucheta. "Through Western Eyes: Discovering Chinese Women in America." In *A New Significance: Re-envisioning the History of the American West,* edited by Clyde Milner, 158–162. New York: Oxford University Press, 1996.

McDowell, Linda. *Gender, Identity, and Place: Understanding Feminist Geographies.* Minneapolis: University of Minnesota Press, 1999.

McKeown, Adam. "Ritualization of Regulation: The Enforcement of Chinese Exclusion in the United States and China." *American Historical Review* 108, no. 2 (2003): 377–403.

Mink, Gwendolyn. *Old Labor and New Immigrants in American Political Development: Union, Party, and State, 1875–1920.* Ithaca, NY: Cornell University Press, 1986.

———. *The Wages of Motherhood: Inequality in the Welfare State, 1917–1942.* Ithaca, NY: Cornell University Press, 1995.

Muncy, Robyn. *Creating a Female Dominion in American Reform, 1890–1935.* New York: Oxford Univeristy Press, 1991.

Narell, Irena. *Our City: The Jews of San Francisco.* San Diego: Howell-North Books, 1981.

Nash, Gerald D. *A. P. Giannini and the Bank of America.* Norman: University of Oklahoma Press, 1992.

Nee, Victor G., and Brett de Bary Nee. *Longtime Californ': A Documentary Study of an American Chinatown.* Stanford, CA: Stanford University Press, 1972.

Neville, Amelia Ransome. *The Fantastic City.* Cambridge, MA: Riverside Press, 1932.

Olmsted, Roger R., and Nancy L. Olmsted. *San Francisco Waterfront: Report on Historical Cultural Resources for the North Shore and Channel Outfalls Consolidation Projects.* San Francisco: San Francisco Wastewater Management Program, 1977.

Pan, Erica Y. Z. *The Impact of the 1906 Earthquake on San Francisco's Chinatown.* New York: Peter Lang, 1995.

Pascoe, Peggy. *Relations of Rescue: The Search for Female Moral Authority in the American West, 1874–1939.* New York: Oxford University Press, 1990.

Peiss, Kathy. *Cheap Amusements: Working Women and Leisure in Turn-of-the-Century New York.* Philadelphia: Temple University Press, 1986.

Pittenger, Mark. *American Socialists and Evolutionary Thought, 1870–1920.* Madison: University of Wisconsin Press, 1993

Platt, Rutherford H. *Disasters and Democracy: The Politics of Extreme Natural Events.* Washington, DC: Island Press, 1999.

Pryor, Elizabeth Brown. *Clara Barton: Professional Angel.* Philadelphia: University of Pennsylvania Press, 1987.

Quarantelli, E. L., ed. *Disasters: Theory and Research.* London: Sage Publications, 1978.

———. *What Is a Disaster? Perspectives on the Question.* London: Routledge, 1998.

Rodgers, Daniel T. *Atlantic Crossings: Social Politics in a Progressive Age.* Cambridge, MA: Harvard University Press, 1998.

———. "In Search of Progressivism." *Reviews in American History* 10, no. 4 (December 1982): 113–132.

Rodriguez, Marie Louise Bine. *The Earthquake of 1906.* San Francisco: Privately printed, 1951.

Roediger, David. *The Wages of Whiteness: Race and the Making of the American Working Class.* London: Verso, 1991.

Rogers, Daniel. *Asian America: Chinese and Japanese in the United States since 1850.* Seattle: University of Washington Press, 1988.

Rosen, Christine Misner. *The Limits of Power: Great Fires and the Process of City Growth in America.* Cambridge: Cambridge University Press, 1986.

Rosen, Ruth. *The Lost Sisterhood: Prostitution in America, 1900–1918.* Baltimore: Johns Hopkins University Press, 1982.

Rosenzweig, Roy. *Eight Hours for What We Will: Workers and Leisure in an Industrial City, 1870–1920.* New York: Cambridge University Press, 1983.

Rothman, Sheila M. *Living in the Shadow of Death: Tuberculosis and the Social Experience of Illness in American History.* Baltimore: Johns Hopkins University Press, 1994.

Rozario, Kevin. *The Culture of Calamity: Disaster and the Making of Modern America.* Chicago: University of Chicago Press, 2007.

Ryan, Mary P. *Cradle of the Middle Class: The Family in Oneida County, New York, 1790–1865.* New York: Cambridge University Press, 1981.

———. "The Public and the Private Good: Across the Great Divide in Women's History." *Journal of Women's History* 15, no. 2 (Summer 2003): 10–27.

Salyer, Lucy. *Laws Harsh as Tigers: Chinese Immigrants and the Shaping of Modern Immigration Laws, 1891–1905.* Chapel Hill: University of North Carolina Press, 1995.

Saul, Eric, and Don DeNevi. *The Great San Francisco Earthquake and Fire, 1906.* Millbrae, CA: Celestial Arts, 1981.

Sawislak, Karen. *Smoldering City: Chicagoans and the Great Fire, 1871–1874.* Chicago: University of Chicago Press, 1995.

Schwartz, Richard. *Berkeley 1900: Daily Life at the Turn of the Century.* Berkeley: RSB Books, 2000.

Scott, Joan Wallach. *Only Paradoxes to Offer: French Feminists and the Rights of Man.* Cambridge, MA: Harvard University Press, 1996.

Scott, Mel. *The San Francisco Bay Area: A Metropolis in Perspective.* Berkeley: University of California Press, 1959.

Self, Robert O. *American Babylon: Race and the Struggle for Postwar Oakland.* Princeton, NJ: Princeton University Press, 2003.

Shah, Nayan. *Contagious Divides: Epidemics and Race in San Francisco's Chinatown.* Berkeley: University of California Press, 2001.

Shipps, Jan. *Mormonism: The Story of a New Religious Tradition.* Urbana: University of Illinois Press, 1987.

————. *Sojourner in the Promised Land: Forty Years among the Mormons.* Urbana: University of Illinois Press, 2000.

Sklar, Kathryn Kish. *Hull House in the 1890s: A Community of Women Reformers.* Chicago: University of Chicago Press, 2005.

Skocpol, Theda. *Protecting Mothers and Soldiers: The Political Origins of Social Policy in the United States.* Cambridge, MA: Harvard University Press, 1992.

Smith, Carl. *Urban Disorder and the Shape of Belief: The Great Chicago Fire, the Haymarket Bomb, and the Model Town of Pullman.* Chicago: University of Chicago Press, 1995.

Solnit, Rebecca. *A Paradise Built in Hell: The Extraordinary Communities that Arise in Disaster.* New York: Viking, 2009.

Steinberg, Ted. "Smoke and Mirrors: The San Francisco Earthquake and Seismic Denial." In *American Disasters*, edited by Steven Biel, 103–128. New York: New York University Press, 2001.

Svanevik, Michael, and Shirley Burgett. "La Peninsula." *Journal of the San Mateo County Historical Society* 19, no. 2 (1979).

Takaki, Ronald. *Strangers from a Distant Shore: A History of Asian Americans.* New York: Penguin, 1990.

Teaford, Jon. *The American Suburb: The Basics.* New York: Routledge, 2008.

————. *City and Suburb: The Political Fragmentation of Metropolitan America, 1850–1970.* Baltimore: Johns Hopkins University Press, 1979.

————. *The Twentieth-Century American City.* Baltimore: Johns Hopkins University Press, 1986.

Thomas, Gordon, and Max Morgan Witts. *The San Francisco Earthquake.* New York: Stein and Day, 1971.

Trattner, Walter I. *From Poor Law to Welfare State: A History of Social Welfare in America.* New York: Free Press, 1974.

Turner, Elizabeth Hayes. *Women, Culture, and Community: Religion and Reform in Galveston, 1800–1920.* New York: Oxford University Press, 1997.

Turner, Patricia, ed. *1906 Remembered.* San Francisco: Friends of the San Francisco Public Library, 1981.

Ulrich, Laurel Thatcher. *The Age of Homespun: Objects and Stories in the Creation of an American Myth.* New York: Alfred A. Knopf, 2001.

Vale, Lawrence J., and Thomas J. Campanella, eds. *The Resilient City: How Modern Cities Recover from Disaster.* Oxford: Oxford University Press, 2005.

Vance, James E. *Geography and Urban Evolution in the San Francisco Bay Area.* Berkeley: Institute for Government Studies, 1964.

Wade, Richard C. *The Urban Frontier: The Rise of Western Cities, 1790–1830.* Cambridge, MA: Harvard University Press, 1959.

Walker, Richard. "Industry Builds Out the City: The Suburban Manufacturing in the San Francisco Bay Area, 1850–1940." In *Manufacturing Suburbs: Building Work and Home on the Metropolitan Fringe*, edited by Robert Lewis, 92–123. Philadelphia: Temple University Press, 2004.

Walker, Richard, and Robert D. Lewis, "Beyond the Crabgrass Frontier: Industry and the Spread of North American Cities, 1850–1950." *Journal of Historical Geography* 27, no. 1 (2001): 3–19.

Walsh, James P. "Peter Yorke and Progressivism in California, 1908." *Eire-Ireland* 10 (1975): 73–81.

Warner, Sam Bass, Jr. *Streetcar Suburbs: The Process of Growth in Boston, 1870–1900*. Cambridge, MA: Harvard University Press, 1978.

Wermiel, Sara. *The Fireproof Building: Technology and Public Safety in the Nineteenth-Century American City*. Baltimore: Johns Hopkins University Press, 2000.

White, Richard. *"It's Your Misfortune and None of My Own": A New History of the American West*. Norman: University of Oklahoma Press, 1991.

Wiebe, Robert H. *The Search for Order, 1877–1920*. New York: Hill and Wang, 1967.

Wilson, Carol Green. *Chinatown Quest: One Hundred Years of Donaldina Cameron House*. San Francisco: California Historical Society, 1974.

Wilson, William H. *The City Beautiful Movement*. Baltimore: Johns Hopkins University Press, 1989.

Winchester, Simon. *A Crack in the Edge of the World: America and the Great California Earthquake of 1906*. New York: HarperCollins, 2005.

Wong, Laura. "Vallejo's Chinese Community, 1860–1960." *Chinese America: Historical Perspectives, 1988* (1988): 153–168.

Wright, Gwendolyn. *Building the Dream: A Social History of Housing in America*. New York: Pantheon Books, 1981.

Yu, Connie Young. "Chinatown, 1906: The End and the Beginning." *Chinese Chamber of Commerce souvenir booklet*. 1968.

Yung, Judy. "The Fake and the True: Researching Chinese Women's Immigration History." *Chinese America: Historical Perspectives, 1998* (1998): 25–50.

———. *Unbound Feet: A Social History of Chinese Women in San Francisco*. Berkeley: University of California Press, 1995.

———. *Unbound Voices: A Documentary History of Chinese Women in San Francisco*. Berkeley: University of California Press, 1999.

Unpublished

Bolton, Marie. "Recovery for Whom? Social Conflict after the San Francisco Earthquake and Fire, 1906–1915." Ph.D. diss., University of California, Davis, 1997.

Cryan, Jane. "Hope Chest: The True Story of San Francisco's 1906 Earthquake Refugee Shacks." San Francisco: Unpublished manuscript, 1998.

Douty, Christopher Morris. "The Economics of Localized Disasters: An Empirical Analysis of the 1906 Earthquake and Fire in San Francisco." Ph.D. diss., Stanford University, 1969.

Dow, Gerald. "Bay Fill in San Francisco." Master's thesis, California State University, 1973.

Frink, Brenda D. "Pioneers and Patriots: Race, Gender, and Historical Memory in California, 1875–1915." Ph.D. diss., Stanford University, 2010.

Godfrey, Brian J. "Inner-City Neighborhoods in Transition: The Morphogenesis of San Francisco's Ethnic and Nonconformist Communities." Ph.D. diss., University of California, Berkeley, 1984.

Goodrich-Boyd, Lisa Anne. "Charity Redefined: Katherine [sic] Felton and the Associated Charities of San Francisco." Master's thesis, San Francisco State University, 1995.

Hicke, Carole. "The 1911 Campaign of James Rolph Jr., Mayor of All the People." Master's thesis, San Francisco State University, 1978.

Irwin, Mary Ann. "Servant to the Poor: The St. Vincent de Paul Society of San Francisco, 1860–2010." Draft internal document dated January 2010, in possession of author.

Prince, Samuel Henry. "Catastrophe and Social Change, Based on a Sociological Study of the Halifax Disaster." Ph.D. diss., Columbia University, 1920.

Rozario, Kevin L. "Nature's Evil Dreams: Disaster and America, 1871–1906." Ph.D. diss., Yale University, 1996.

Index

Andrea Rees Davies is an Assistant Professor in the Department of History at California State University, Northridge.